Praise for *The No Club*

"[T]he rewards that flow from collaborativeness are uneven. *The No Club* . . . examines the disproportionate amount of 'non-promotable work' done by women—tasks like covering absences, organizing logistics, and mentoring. Collaboration is a much less attractive proposition if helping others means spending less time on the sort of work that gets recognized when it is time to hand out actual promotions."

—*The Economist*

"To progress in their careers, employees typically need to check three boxes: Does it advance the goals of the organization? Is it visible? And does it require specialized skills, or can anyone do it? The rest is 'non-promotable work.' And unsurprisingly, women do more of it."

—*Fortune*

"[T]aking one for the team could be holding all women back. A new book argues that 'non-promotable work'—the kind that is important to organizational functioning, but unlikely to be rewarded or even recognized—is the invisible hurdle to gender equality in the workplace."

—*The Guardian*

"Four female academics have identified the non-promotable tasks that have obstructed their, and their peers', career paths."

—*Financial Times*

"When women perform less promotable work than their colleagues do, they have fewer opportunities to demonstrate their skills and their value to the organization's mission. The result is that they advance more slowly than their male coworkers."

—*Forbes*

"With hard data, personal anecdotes from women of all stripes, and innovative advice from the authors' consulting Fortune 500 companies, this book will forever change the conversation about how we advance women's careers and achieve equity."

—Next Big Idea Club

"Say yes to your dreams and the long-term potential of your organization. How? By learning how to say no. *The No Club* is a long overdue manifesto on gender equality in the workplace, a practical playbook with tips you can put into action immediately, and the story of four women whose collective wisdom on how to sustain personal success is simply priceless."

—Angela Duckworth, *New York Times* bestselling author of *Grit*

"In many organizations, women are in the minority but end up doing the majority of the thankless jobs. This important book helps women learn when and how to say no, and should be a wake-up call to management: give every man a yellow pad and tell them to learn to take notes. Better yet, change the way that work is allocated and rewarded."

—Richard Thaler, recipient of the Nobel Prize in Economics and *New York Times* bestselling coauthor of *Nudge*

"Unfair treatment of women in the workplace has been well-reported, but there's a lack of available literature on what women are actually supposed to *do* about it. *The No Club* is the answer we've been waiting for—these experts and researchers explain what to look for, how to advocate for yourself, and how to empower others to do the same. This is an achievable and overdue call to action for the system to change."

—Emily Chang, bestselling author of *Brotopia: Breaking Up the Boys' Club of Silicon Valley*

"This is a critical read for women who inevitably find themselves balancing their personal goals with endless dead-end tasks in the workplace. This book not only gives women validation to say no to tedious work, but clearly lays out how caving to these pressures only serves to derail their full potential."

—Ana Kasparian, executive producer and host of
The Young Turks

"I am in a No Club inspired by the authors of this amazing book! Now, all of us can go behind the scenes of their journey, which will leave you feeling seen and guided. *The No Club* is packed with examples, advice, and research. I'll be recommending it as essential reading to colleagues, students, and friends."

—Dolly Chugh, author of *The Person You Mean to Be* and
professor at the NYU Stern School of Business

"A guide for achieving balance and equity in the workplace. . . . [Readers] will learn valuable tips for changing the status quo, including how to craft an effective *no* and avoid the traps that lead to *yes*. Sound guidance for sparking change in organizations."

—*Kirkus Reviews*

"Outstanding . . . the advice proffered here will last a work-time."

—*Booklist*

The
No Club

Putting a Stop to Women's Dead-End Work

**LINDA BABCOCK, BRENDA PEYSER,
LISE VESTERLUND, and LAURIE WEINGART**

SIMON & SCHUSTER PAPERBACKS

NEW YORK   AMSTERDAM/ANTWERP   LONDON
TORONTO   SYDNEY   NEW DELHI

For MJ Tocci

Simon & Schuster Paperbacks
An Imprint of Simon & Schuster, LLC
1230 Avenue of the Americas
New York, NY 10020

First Simon & Schuster trade paperback edition March 2025

SIMON & SCHUSTER PAPERBACKS and colophon are registered trademarks of Simon & Schuster, LLC

For information about special discounts for bulk purchases, please contact Simon & Schuster Special Sales at 1-866-506-1949 or business@simonandschuster.com.

The Simon & Schuster Speakers Bureau can bring authors to your live event. For more information or to book an event, contact the Simon & Schuster Speakers Bureau at 1-866-248-3049 or visit our website at www.simonspeakers.com.

Interior design by Carly Loman

Manufactured in the United States of America

10 9 8 7 6 5 4 3 2 1

Library of Congress Cataloging-in-Publication Data is available.

ISBN 978-1-9821-5233-8
ISBN 978-1-9821-5234-5 (pbk)
ISBN 978-1-9821-5235-2 (ebook)

CONTENTS

Foreword

Almost fifteen years ago, we uncovered a driver of persistent gender disparities in the workforce: Women perform different tasks than men do. Men receive more assignments that are visible and count more toward their performance evaluations. It may not seem like a big deal—the assignments women are often given might seem like the right fit for them. But the gender disparity across men's and women's workloads increases quickly, harming women *and* their organizations in the short and long term. The less time women spend on the work that leverages their valuable skill sets, the less they directly contribute to the bottom line, the more their companies suffer. That makes this a crucial organizational issue.

We knew that everyone was worse off, so we wrote this book, *The No Club*, to make clear all the tasks that women do behind the scenes without glory or simple recognition—and importantly, without the potential to be promoted from doing them—and to tell women and their colleagues how to manage this problem. In your hands is a book to help both women—who are just as smart, capable, experienced, and strategic as their male colleagues—to advance in their careers and organizational leaders meet their own strategic goals by balancing the portfolios of work that they assign.

Since *The No Club* was first published, we have done hundreds of interviews, podcasts, keynotes, articles, and speeches to spread the word about how organizations can change the dynamic that so negatively affects women and their workplaces. Whether in the United States or abroad, at every single presentation, women have shared their experiences, sought us out afterward, and thanked us with standing ovations. We even got a hallelujah or two because finally, *finally*, someone was naming their problem.

Organizations have brought us in for advice, many times asking us to talk with their employees and leadership. Digging in and investing in answering these calls, we have been eager to see improvements. But the landscape has changed since we originally published this book. The principles of diversity, equity, and inclusion have come under attack; some organizations have slowed down, or even stopped, the efforts they had been making to advance women, people of color, and the LGBTQIA+ community. We learned (for the millionth time) that change is hard and that organizations are a lot like tankers, set on a course and slow to turn.

But the women? They were *on* it. They shared their experiences of being asked: "Can you stay late and proof my report? You are so good at that!" "Would you train the summer interns?" "Can you pick up bagels for the morning meeting?" Fed up with feeding the men, these women have taken matters into their own hands, implemented our ideas, started book clubs and No Clubs, formed mentoring and advisory groups, and stood up for themselves and others. Women have been banding together to get the work assignments they deserve. If these do not come about formally, then the women do it informally. They know they cannot wait.

Like clockwork, International Women's Day and Equal Pay Day roll around, with the usual headlines: "Women Earn 82 Cents to the

Dollar of Men," "The Gender Gap in Burnout Is Rising," "For Every 100 Men Promoted to Entry-Level Manager Only 87 Women Are Promoted," etc. These articles anger us and make us worry for the young women we love and future generations. But we need not wait another year for the familiar statistics—we can take action now.

And that leads us to the advice we can impart today. Keep this issue at the forefront every day because it's time to change those headlines. We advise you to do what women have always done: Roll up your sleeves. Take charge of the things you can. Use the guidelines and suggestions we provide; they're easy to understand and implement—and they cost almost nothing. Find other women to rally together. We believe that organizations *will* address this problem, but we recognize that it will happen more slowly than we had anticipated. Do not lose hope, it's time for work to work for women too.

Follow our activities (www.thenoclub.com) or write to us for help (thenoclubmail@gmail.com) because we're here for you and your colleagues, friends, sisters, daughters, granddaughters, and all women. Now is your time. Let's meet this moment together.

September 2024

CHAPTER 1

The No Club

Five women sat around the table at a local restaurant with two bottles of wine. We wondered who would be the first to admit her life was out of control. We didn't know one another well, but we all had one thing in common—we were drowning in our jobs and were suffering both personally and professionally.

Brenda filled our glasses as Linda dove in: "I asked you all here because I need help and I think you might too. I am completely overwhelmed with work. I've lost control of my time. I can't keep up with everything, and more stuff just keeps coming at me. Every time someone asks me to do something, I want to say no, but I feel like I can't. I'm a mess. Is it just me?" The rest of us simultaneously answered, "No!" We looked at one another and let that sink in. This became the first of many meetings of The No Club.

It all had started two weeks earlier, the day Linda realized that she just couldn't keep up with her work load. Here's how she remembers it:

I finally had it. My calendar was filled with back-to-back meetings that left me almost no time for research. I'm a professor of economics at Carnegie Mellon University, so research is not only a key part of my job, it is the primary factor in my performance evaluation. That means the amount of time I spend on research really matters, so it is critical that I schedule "non-teaching" days to focus on my research.

On one of my non-teaching days, the morning started with a rush as I ran to and from meetings. I noticed my across-the-hall colleague, George, sitting at his desk every time I passed by. He didn't move all day. I couldn't understand how he managed to spend so much time in his office, and when he joked about how much running around I did, I asked what his schedule for the day was like. He showed me his calendar, and as I compared it to mine, I was shocked.

	LINDA'S DAY	GEORGE'S DAY
8:30–10:30	Institutional review board meeting	**Research**
10:30–12:00	Curriculum committee meeting	**Research**
12:00–1:30	Student presentation	Student presentation
1:30–2:00	Interview with reporter	**Research**
2:00–3:00	Executive education meeting	**Research**
3:00–4:00	**Research**	**Research**
4:00–5:00	Prepare talk for women's group	**Research**
5:00–6:00	Faculty meeting	Faculty meeting

Out of the entire day, I had one hour devoted to research, while George had seven. He had only two non-research commitments, where I had seven! How was his schedule so focused on research—a critical part of both of our jobs—when mine wasn't? I looked at all the things on my calendar and realized that I had agreed to every single one of them. How did this happen? I needed an intervention, so I reached out to four of my friends for help.

February 12, 2010 1:15 PM

Hi Brenda, Lise, Laurie, and MJ:

This email is to invite you to the inaugural meeting of the
"I Just Can't Say No Club." I've decided to start this club
so that a group of smart women can have a few drinks and
talk about the difficulties we all have in saying no to things
that we ought to. This is one of the hardest things I face and
I think we can all help each other out a lot on this. Since I
know that none of you can say no to my invitation, please
fill out the form at the following link that will let me know
what days you can come to the inaugural meeting. I thought
we'd meet at 5 p.m., say at the Union Grill, but I'm always
willing to start drinking early.

I think this will be really helpful and at the very least, all
you cool women will get to meet each other.

Thanks!
Linda

Then I got nervous: I was the only one who knew everyone, and
I was having second thoughts about whether this could work. I had
chosen each woman for a reason: Brenda and I were close, having
worked together for years. An associate dean in the public policy
school at Carnegie Mellon (CMU), Brenda was always the first person to offer to help, which was great for everyone but her. I noticed
she was doing a lot of work that no one else would do, and she
wasn't getting credit for it. I had also asked Lise, a fellow economics
professor at the University of Pittsburgh, because we bonded on a

plane ride home from a gender conference at Harvard. During that flight, I was surprised to learn how much stress she had managing her workload, since she is a prolific scholar and seemed to have it all together. Laurie, a professor in Carnegie Mellon's business school, and I shared an interest in negotiation research, and we'd taught a course together. Laurie was another person who seemed to have everything under control—but I suspected that she might not. MJ and I had met doing a project with the Women and Girls Foundation. She was a major contributor to women's organizations in our region, and people always wanted her expertise for free. Because she ran her own consulting business, she relied on opportunities for visibility, but was spread too thin. Everyone agreed to join.

Brenda was excited. When she told her husband about the club, he laughed. He said, "Perfect group for you. Do you know that any time anyone asks you anything, you say 'happy to' before they even put the question mark on the end of the sentence?" She hadn't realized that she did this and was surprised, because she thought of herself as decisive and, frankly, no pushover. She had spent decades in executive-level positions in the private sector and higher education. She had consulted with Fortune 100 companies, founded Carnegie Mellon's campus in Australia (the first foreign university in the country), and overseen the creation and growth of a number of master's programs. With all that experience, you'd think she'd be able to prioritize and manage her workload, but she was overwhelmed with work, and her plate never got emptier. An early riser by nature, she was getting up even earlier, sending emails at four thirty a.m., just to keep from getting even further backlogged. She figured she had nothing to lose by joining the club, and for the next week, paid attention to how she responded to requests. Her husband was right; she said yes immediately and often.

Lise didn't respond to the email for several days because she was too busy. She was teaching a full load, recruiting new faculty for her own department and for the public policy school, and supervising projects for eight PhD students. Having agreed to serve on the editorial boards of four different academic journals, she was, to put it mildly, struggling. Plus, with a three-year research grant from the National Science Foundation, her pile of work was towering. She spent her days playing whack-a-mole to free up her calendar and sleepless nights compiling to-do lists. She had been juggling too many things for too long. While the club seemed like the right group for her, she wasn't sure she had the time—and because of that, she knew she needed to join. She emailed Linda letting her know she'd be there.

Laurie was pretty sure she didn't have a problem saying no. She knew she was doing a lot, but thought her workload was fine. She was organized and capable, managing her time reasonably well. She had a busy research agenda, writing papers and book chapters, while advising doctoral students and teaching three MBA courses. She was also serving as president of a new professional association and leading the design and delivery of a leadership training center for the MBA program, but she felt she could handle it. She kept a detailed set of work, family, and personal calendars to keep track of everything, and if it wasn't in her calendar, it didn't get done. She acknowledged that she was stretched thin and wasn't sure whether that was by choice or happenstance. She didn't think she needed the help, but since she and Linda were friends, and this would be an opportunity to meet new people, she figured what the hell, why not.

MJ was an attorney who spent the early part of her career as a prosecutor in San Francisco, named one of California's most effective prosecutors by *California Lawyer* magazine. She and her family moved east, where she founded Fulcrum Advisors to teach lawyers how to try cases effectively and worked with law firms and corporations to recruit, retain, and promote talented women. MJ was involved with dozens of women's and community organizations, and she had a reputation for getting things done, which meant she received endless requests for her expertise. She rarely said no because she felt that the stakes were high with the work she was doing. She was very good at calling out BS anytime she saw it—and she saw it plenty with us—but like the rest of us, she decided to join the club because she realized she needed to be called out herself. Most often, this was for agreeing to give yet another talk (for free) to a women's group. MJ jumped into Linda's invite with gusto. "I'm in! I never turn anyone down and it's all too much. An hour ago, I said maybe to someone when I should have said no. Our meeting isn't soon enough for me!"

During the dreariest time in Pittsburgh, winter, in 2010, we kicked off our inaugural I Just Can't Say No Club meeting at a cozy restaurant where we could get a meal and $10 bottles of wine (really!). We went around the table sharing, or actually, confessing. We each described the things we had agreed to when we were asked (this turned out to be a lengthy list for all of us), and then contrasted that with what we had said no to (these were very short lists). We asked one another for advice on how to say no, since we found it so hard to do. Wanting to get a better handle on our workload, we knew the extra support from the group would help, so we agreed to meet every few weeks. We left the meeting feeling unburdened and exhilarated. None of us realized what a transformative experience this would become for each of us. This first meeting laid the groundwork for us to grow personally and was the tiny spark that lit our significant research agenda, led us to mentor women and consult with companies—and then, finally, to write this book and share what we learned to help other women address their struggles too.

Our meetings were a high point for us. Well, sort of. We were serious about holding ourselves accountable for taking on too much work, so as we went around the table, each admitting our latest bad choice, we were anxious and embarrassed and, at times, shed tears. Divulging that you had made the same mistake four times in a row was difficult. Worse was when everyone else at the table, except for you, saw what you had done. We first took comfort in the fact that four other women were similarly overwhelmed and were relieved to have each other to try to figure it out. Then we started to question why we found ourselves in this position—and realized that many others did, too; perhaps even you.

We came to every club meeting ready to bare our souls and support one another. We were fully invested in one another's success. MJ stood out in this regard. She was our heart, the truth teller in the group. She had a way of arching one eyebrow that stopped you midsentence, and you knew right away that you had taken on too much. But we were in for some terrible news. Shortly after we started the club, MJ was diagnosed with ovarian cancer. She spent four years undergoing treatment; we cheered at every sign of progress and marveled at her grace and fancy new hairdos. Through her treatment, MJ continued to come to club meetings and contribute to our burgeoning research agenda. She kept up with her professional work, while fully invested in the club. She told us how much our work meant to her and how the club held a piece of her heart. We were devastated to lose her on February 15, 2014. We mourned together, wondering what the club would be like without her. We felt incomplete and unfinished without her smile that lit up the room and her personality that felt as big as the world. For months, we stumbled even more than we had previously. It took time to re-establish ourselves. While we grieved the loss of our friend, we also wanted to do right by her. MJ's legacy of helping women succeed in the workplace gave our club a greater purpose. In working through our own struggles, we understood why other women were struggling as well, and we began to see how to improve that. Doing right by MJ meant that we had to carry on, for women more broadly and for ourselves. We were still a work in progress, and picturing MJ's arched eyebrow as we continued to say yes and overcommit kept us moving forward. We began to think of her as a guardian angel, albeit a sardonic one, who still would call us out for bad decisions.

One such moment came when an academic journal offered Lise an editorial position. Professors are expected to accept these types of invitations to pay it back to the profession. Being an editor adds many hours of work per week, on top of your regular job, and offers limited compensation or support. Lise already was serving on several other editorial boards, and the new editorship would take even more time away from her research. At a club meeting, Lise shared how torn she was, offering many reasons why she should take the position. The rest of us could see she was already overloaded, so *another* editorial position would make her big pile even higher. We were adamant that she had to say no, especially since she already had the visibility and work of several other editorial boards. So what did she do? She said yes, and as expected, the decision haunted her. More than a year went by as she carved out evenings and weekends to review manuscripts, delaying her research, and she struggled to keep up with her teaching and departmental obligations. It was obvious to us all, including her, that she had taken on too much. But how could she reverse the decision? Wouldn't that be even worse than having said no in the first place? A club meeting made her see the light: While it might be terrifying to resign, saving her sanity was more important. She resigned, and we toasted her at the next club meeting.

Our progress was slow, but we were learning. We realized that we said yes to requests from others far too often. Rather than being strategic about where to focus our attention, we were running around trying to fulfill other people's needs and expectations. We each made a list of the work we were drowning in. Much of it didn't seem critical to our jobs—like serving on a committee to select the company's new online calendar system, identifying a new travel vendor, providing feedback on new risk mitigation procedures. We dubbed these "crappy tasks" and were surprised by how often we were asked to do this type of work, and how quick we were to take it on.

Elizabeth Blackburn, former president of the Salk Institute, observed: "Often these situations which go on in a woman's career—workplace situations—they don't seem big. But I heard someone say a marvelous thing in this context: 'A ton of feathers still weighs a ton.'" The number of yesses—small as each was—had the cumulative effect of becoming a very heavy weight for us to carry. We felt overwhelmed and buried by all of these seemingly unimportant tasks, convinced that we were "just getting by" on some things and doing a bad job on others. While we were sprinting and often working very long hours, we were not keeping up with the work that mattered for our careers.

With time, we realized that what we considered crappy tasks weren't necessarily crappy. What was a slog to us was quite important to our organizations. For example, putting together the class schedule for the entire school fell to Brenda for years, even though technically assigned to both her and a male colleague. Arranging each semester's schedule well matters, and it's complicated to pull off because there are lots of moving parts. Required courses can't all be at the same time, otherwise students can't take them; a seminar class needs a room where tables and chairs can be moved around; faculty want to teach all their classes on the same days so they can set the other days aside for research. So scheduling is important to students and faculty and to the smooth functioning of the university, but no one really knows what goes into it, and no one cares—unless it goes badly. It took Brenda a great deal of time to ensure it didn't go badly, but it had no bearing on her career advancement. The task was critical to the organization, but wasn't going to earn her praise, a raise, or a promotion. It was invisible unless she messed it up.

We started to call these crappy tasks *non-promotable* because while they were important to our organizations, they took time away from the work that was core to our jobs and mattered for our advancement. In some cases, like Brenda's, the task was invisible. Other times they didn't require any unique skills or capabilities; someone—anyone—just needed to take them on. You might recognize non-promotable tasks (NPTs) in your own job: maybe you prepare a presentation deck, organize the charity fundraiser, screen the summer interns, take on the time-consuming but low-revenue client, or simply help others with their work.

We noticed that many of our coworkers didn't seem to be bogged down with these types of dead-end assignments, and often looked like they were getting a free ride. We wanted what they had—more time for promotable tasks. We didn't really understand the root of the problem (blame the wine), but we thought that if we just stopped saying yes, our lives would improve.

As it turns out, the club was a game changer in developing our individual ability to say no. We were so pleased with our progress that we renamed ourselves The No Club to reflect our growth. Together we learned to identify NPTs, and we honed strategies to say "no." When any one of us waffled, the others pointed out the problem in concrete terms, gave advice on an approach, and helped instill the confidence to say no. We offered scripts for responses to requests, practiced role-playing, and prepared for possible pushback. With one another's help, we started to develop our "no" muscles—and we got better at saying it—which carved out room for more promotable work. Pleased that we'd gotten so good at saying no, we were disappointed to discover that when we said no, the task was most often reassigned to another woman.

Saying no wasn't the solution—the problem of non-promotable work was bigger than that. Wanting to learn more, we looked for research on this topic. We wanted to understand who was doing non-promotable tasks and why, but finding only limited literature, we started our own initiative, sketching out questions and hypotheses. We undertook studies at the University of Pittsburgh Experimental Economics Laboratory (PEEL), interviewed women across industries and jobs, conducted surveys, and worked closely with organizations to gather data and understand their experience with the problem.

In our own and others' work, we found substantive and overwhelming evidence that women more than men are tasked with non-promotable work. Less saddled with these tasks, men have the freedom to concentrate on work that helps them advance, while women's careers are stalled or stymied. In exploring why this might be, our pioneering research uncovered two drivers. First, we ask women more often than we ask men to do such tasks. Second, when we ask, women are more likely to agree than men are. Importantly, we discovered that the key explanation for these drivers lies in the collective expectation that women, more than men, will do the un-rewarded and non-promotable work. This finding not only pointed to effective solutions, but also made clear that women cannot tackle this problem on their own. It is an organizational problem. And it is in the interest of organizations to address it.

Our book shows that non-promotable work has a negative effect on women's careers and lives, but also a detrimental impact on the productivity and profitability of their organizations. Fixing the dis-tribution of non-promotable assignments is in the interest of both employees and organizations, and we show how this can be solved in a coordinated fashion—bottom up and top down, with women initiating the charge and their organizations taking ownership of the change.

As we talked about our research on NPTs, we began hearing from other women who shared stories of their struggles and feelings of helplessness. So many stories. We've included some in these pages to show how non-promotable tasks affected them and to help you reflect on how it may be hurting you. These women represent dif-ferent industries, jobs, experience levels, races, and socioeconomic backgrounds. In order to tell their stories without potential reprisal, we've changed their names and sometimes identifying details (like their industry or job title). In our stories, we identify a woman's race only when she told us that it affected her experience. All of these very personal examples helped us understand the impact of NPTs, and we hope they're helpful to you too.

Being trusted with these women's stories is humbling, and telling them through this book has been a labor of love. We want to share our collective stories and research to move the needle on gender equity. Women's excessive load of non-promotable work is the an-chor that has been holding them back, and we will share with you the straightforward solutions for freeing them of this work. It took us ten years to understand the challenges surrounding the distribution of non-promotable work and find solutions. Through our research and work with organizations, we learned a lot about what works and what doesn't, and we will share the effective and easily implemented solutions with you. But we want to be explicit that none of our solutions suggest that women should fix themselves because:

Women aren't the problem.
Organizational practices are.

So this is *not* a fix-the-women book. Instead, we focus on how individual women and their allies, working with their organizations, can systematically address the problem and help both women and their organizations reach their potential.

This book is also the story of our journey of personal exploration, where we learned about NPTs and how to handle them in our own careers, and, more importantly, how we set about addressing changes that organizations can make to help all women. We recognize that we are a group of women who have worked hard to achieve success in our roles. But we're also women who have been lucky to have gone to good schools and grown up in supportive communities, and who have jobs that provide a stable and comfortable life, as tenured professors or high-level university leaders, all white women not facing systemic racism or classism at the same time. We believe that our challenges with non-promotable work apply to all women, while also recognizing that they are much more severe for women with less privilege than we have.

Our book is focused on gender, but it would be a mistake to take a monolithic approach to the topic. Women differ in myriad ways, and we discuss how specific subsets of women experience NPTs differently when we have research that supports that distinction. The research on NPTs is still in its infancy, and so there is scant data that provides a nuanced understanding of how other aspects of identity, such as race and class, intersect with gender regarding NPTs. We attempt to supplement this deficit through the many stories we heard from a diverse set of women.

Now is the time to provide women with relief from carrying a too-heavy load of non-promotable work. We suspect you're tired and burned out just like we were. We can help. Stick with us through these pages and we'll guide you through assessing what type of work matters in your organization, understanding your own NPTs, and developing tactics to change what's not working for you. We'll also help you become a catalyst for change within your own organization so you can help solve the problem for both yourself and other women. Working together, we can redistribute work and take critical and overdue steps to put a stop to women's dead-end work and finally achieve gender equity in the workplace.

CHAPTER 2

What Are Non-Promotable Tasks?

A third-year associate at a prestigious regional law firm, Francesca loved her job, especially the client work. She was thrilled when her boss gave her a lot of positive feedback and asked her to assist in the summer associate interview process. She felt flattered that he trusted her judgment with managing the pipeline into the firm—soliciting and reviewing résumés, providing input on who to interview and scheduling those interviews, and summarizing the feedback from the interviewers. She assumed this opportunity could only help in the promotion process.

What Francesca didn't realize was how time-consuming the summer associate program would be. For the next three years, her recruitment efforts kept her billable hours on the low side, but she excelled at both recruiting associates and her client work, and felt confident that she was on track for promotion. It wasn't until her sixth-year review that she understood she was in trouble. While she got a bump in salary, her feedback was mixed, and her boss explained that her path to equity partnership would be tricky. Her work was solid, but she was behind target in billable hours, and so they weren't cashing in on her legal expertise.

The law firm appreciated Francesca's efforts in screening summer associates, but this task was of lesser consequence than her client work. Even though her boss had asked her to help with hiring, it didn't count as much as other work did. That was when she understood that *all tasks are not equal*, even those you are asked to do and that need to be done. What mattered most to Francesca's organization was client-facing work and billable hours—that was the ticket to success. While hiring summer associates contributed to the firm, it was not tied directly to the criteria for promotion—bringing in revenue or expanding the client base—and it was secondary to the firm's overall objectives.

Although the four of us are more senior than Francesca, we still resonate with her plight. Over the last decade, we've given talks about our club and our associated research to all kinds of audiences—employees in companies, women's professional associations, organizational leaders, academic colleagues, and numerous conferences. At these events, women like Francesca often share their stories with us, and we can't help but see ourselves in them. We, too, were spending a lot of time on tasks important to our organization but not to our careers. In the early days of our club meetings, we talked a lot about this work, but the more we talked, the more questions we had. What were the characteristics of the tasks that seemed to drag us down? Could we identify them? If they mattered to our organizations, then why weren't they rewarded? What were the consequences of doing the work, and why were *we* the ones doing so much of it? Throughout this book, we will address these questions, but first let's identify and better understand this unrewarded work.

Non-Promotable Tasks

We created a name for this type of work: *non-promotable tasks*.

> A *non-promotable task* matters to your organization
> but will not help you advance your career.

We use the word "advance" quite broadly to encompass a multitude of outcomes, like earning a promotion, improving your performance evaluation, getting plum assignments, increasing your compensation, and enhancing your marketability for other jobs.

Non-promotable tasks exist in all types of jobs, not just office jobs. Take Sally, who is a bartender at Rudy's Bar & Grill. Serving drinks and treating customers well generates revenue for Rudy's and tips for Sally; those are promotable tasks for a bartender. When a new bartender is hired, Rudy assigns an experienced employee to train the new person to ensure that everyone knows what they're doing from the start. Bartenders work together in a tight space and need to coordinate to promptly serve customers, avoid collisions behind the bar, and be consistent in crafting signature cocktails. Being asked to onboard a new hire is a vote of confidence, but at the same time, you don't serve as many customers when you train someone, so you make fewer tips per hour. Sally is always asked to train new employees, and when she does, she loses part of that shift's income. For Sally, training others is a non-promotable task. Rudy's Bar & Grill benefits because it has a well-trained bartender, but Sally doesn't—she makes less money. And even though Rudy appreciates Sally's efforts, this task is overlooked when he assesses employees' performance, and is treated as less important because it isn't directly linked to sales. Like Francesca's, Sally's promotable work is sacrificed for the non-promotable.

It's clear that organizations recognize that some tasks are important but unrewarded. In a 2021 report, McKinsey & Company, in partnership with Lean In, conducted an extensive survey of 423 organizations and 65,000 employees about issues related to women in the workplace. Eighty-seven percent of companies reported that employees' work to support their co-workers' well-being was critical to the functioning of the organization, yet only 25 percent of companies reported that such work was formally recognized in performance evaluations. The same is true for diversity, equity, and inclusion work, where 70 percent of companies reported that this work was critical to the organization yet only 24 percent of companies reported that such work was formally recognized.

While we talk of work being promotable and non-promotable, in truth, most tasks carry some element of promotability, but the degree varies. Imagine them on a continuum:

Low Promotability   High Promotability

The more promotable a task, the more likely it is to advance your career in terms of pay, performance evaluations, assignments, promotions, and status. This positive impact can occur now or in the future.

The *Currency* of Your Organization Determines the Promotability of Your Tasks

Before you can determine a task's promotability, you need to know what your organization cares about most, which is its currency. All organizations focus keenly on accomplishing their objectives, and a task that closely aligns to an organization's goals has high currency. Conversely, a task that is less important to the organization's goals will have low currency. What does that mean, exactly? The objectives of for-profit companies are easy to see: the pursuit of profits, market share, and growth, and the activities most directly tied to these objectives have the highest value to the company. For a consulting firm, it is bringing in high-revenue clients; for a pharmaceutical company, developing the latest breakthrough drug; for a retail store, increasing customer traffic and improving sales; for a restaurant, quickly turning over tables. You get the idea.

Nonprofit organizations typically have objectives that are less quantifiable, but still well-defined, and reflected in the organization's mission statement, like this one from our zoo in Pittsburgh:

The Pittsburgh Zoo & PPG Aquarium strives to foster positive, lifelong connections between animals and people. Whether through our exhibits, educational programs, or our many conservation projects, our goal is to make certain the Earth remains a suitable home for all life by our discovery of the interconnectedness of the natural world.

We can infer that the zoo most values tasks that educate an increasing number of visitors about the natural world and conserve endangered and threatened species, along with ones that raise money to support the organization. That's their currency.

At the end of this chapter, we will walk you through a series of steps to identify your organization's currency. You'll look at what your organization measures, what it shares as important news, and what it celebrates, so you can understand what it values. Once you identify your organization's currency, you can evaluate which of your tasks are promotable and which are non-promotable.

How Do You Know If a Task Is Promotable?

If you are a police detective, you know exactly what is promotable: solving crimes. A hospital nurse's promotable tasks center on patient care. For an architect, it's designing buildings and attracting clients. Tasks that are highly promotable for you will depend on your job, skills, and level of experience, as well as your organization's objectives. Moreover, what moves you forward today might not next year, because what is promotable changes as you develop new skills, advance, and take on new duties.

You need to understand which of your tasks are promotable now. How? You could look to your job description, but most job descriptions are just a broad blueprint of the work typically done in your position and do not provide the level of detail you need to determine the promotability of the tasks you do. You could ask your boss, but they might not be aware of every task you undertake or be willing to discuss what is more promotable. You could look at your performance evaluation form for clues, but that is likely lacking as well—it often outlines the expectations of *how* work will be performed, but may not go into detail of *what* work should be performed. You need to understand which tasks matter to your success, and, just as importantly, which don't. Since no document defines what is and isn't promotable, you'll need to find out yourself. To help you do that, let's look at the task characteristics we have identified that differentiate promotable tasks from non-promotable ones.

Promotable Tasks Are Instrumental to Increasing the Organization's Currency

No matter what your job is, some of your tasks align more closely with and have greater impact on your organization's currency. Tina is a real estate agent who works for a commercial and residential real estate company. The best use of Tina's time is to make contacts and sell retail space and homes, because it is more central to her company's business than, say, the task of archiving property photos for the website. Tina can have an even bigger impact on her company's success if she is able to sell new mall space to Target. Bringing in that level of revenue from a prestigious client matters a lot to her employer. For Tina, the sale of a home is promotable, and a commercial sale to a name-brand client is highly promotable, whereas archiving photos is low in promotability.

Promotable Tasks Are Visible to Others

The more visible a task, the more likely it is to be promotable because other people can directly see your efforts or the impact of your efforts. The nature of the task itself can make it more visible. If you work for an auto dealership, selling an extended warranty for a new car is promotable because your name is on the sales contract. In a manufacturing firm, if you develop a new product line that has the potential to boost revenue, then the tracked sales data make your efforts visible and the work promotable.

How work is performed also influences its visibility. If you give a presentation at your company, it will be more promotable if your boss is in the audience than if she never learns about it. Working remotely erodes our knowledge of who is doing what, and with the pandemic-induced surge in such work, tasks that were visible and easily attributed to you in the office may no longer be.

Promotable Tasks Often Require Specialized Skills That Can Differentiate You from Others

Sometimes, employees are hired because they fill a skills gap in the organization. If you are that employee, then completing tasks that require your unique talents is the best use of your time for the organization—and for you. Think of a surgeon who is highly adept at removing cancerous cells from the throat. She would not be as valuable to her hospital if she spent her days performing tonsillectomies, a more common procedure that many other surgeons can do. Even though tonsillectomies are promotable, cancer surgery is more promotable.

Tasks that Prepare You for Future Promotable Work Are Indirectly Promotable

The three characteristics above directly influence the promotability of a task. Other tasks can *indirectly* influence it; those that allow you to develop your skills have the potential to enhance your future success. Think of them as investments, with a payoff down the road. At a technology company we worked with, programmers reviewed others' code, and while this task was not immediately promotable, it allowed them to learn alternative approaches to programming. By improving their programming skills, they were on the path to advance to more promotable work.

Tasks that Improve Your Access to Future Promotable Work Are Indirectly Promotable

Some tasks introduce you to important people in your organization or deepen your relationships with them—these tasks can be indirectly promotable. Laurie was asked to serve on a university committee to review and recommend academic practices to enhance students' success. The topic mattered to everyone on campus and was a key initiative of the provost but was not directly promotable for a faculty member. Laurie led multiple public meetings where she presented the committee's recommendations, responded to questions, and helped steer the sometimes-heated discussion that ensued, and made a strong case for change. The provost hadn't worked with her before and was impressed with her abilities. He later became president of the university and asked her to serve as interim provost. Her non-promotable committee work gave her access to a new and important relationship, which in turn provided her new opportunities.

While this experience advanced Laurie's career, we want to caution that an outcome like hers is actually pretty rare. For every time an "opportunity" benefited Laurie's career, there were handfuls of times that they went unrewarded. There can be future value in taking on tasks that provide you with high-level visibility and showcase your skills; you just need to choose them carefully. (More on this in Chapter 8.)

Now that you have a better sense of the characteristics of tasks high in promotability, let's look at the flip side: non-promotable tasks that matter to your organization but will not advance your career.

How Do You Identify a Non-Promotable Task?

Non-promotable tasks (NPTs) do not help you succeed and, while your organization benefits, doing too many will put you at a disadvantage. Harvard Business School professor Rosabeth Moss Kanter coined a term that is a close cousin to NPTs—*office housework*— which includes tasks such as getting coffee, planning parties, and taking notes. While office housework tasks are indeed NPTs, they are but a small portion of what non-promotable work encompasses. NPTs have the opposite characteristics of promotable tasks and will have some, though perhaps not all, of the characteristics listed below.

Non-Promotable Tasks Are Not Instrumental to Increasing the Organization's Currency

While performing NPTs matters and may be part of your core responsibilities, your efforts will have less of an impact on the organization's mission and currency. We keep minutes of meetings so we can track decisions and activities; however, doing so is not instrumental for improving organizational currency. If you are the person taking notes, then you are not able to participate as fully in the meeting, nor are you getting noticed for your expertise, so the task has limited benefits for you. If you spend even more time writing a beautiful summary, you might get a nice thank-you, but that's about it. Think of Francesca's work to recruit summer associates at her law firm; this was not closely tied to bringing in revenue and thus was non-promotable.

Non-Promotable Tasks Are Often Not Visible

When work is done behind the scenes and no one knows what you did, you cannot get credit for doing it. Suppose you teach second grade in a large school district. Teachers across the district come to you for advice for teaching reading creatively and effectively. They become better teachers because of you, which is promotable for them, but not you. Your principal has no idea that you spend time doing this because other teachers reach out to you directly. Since this task isn't visible to your supervisor, it is non-promotable for you.

***Non-Promotable Tasks May Not Require Specialized Skills. Many
People Can Do Them (Not Just You)***

NPTs are often tasks that many people can do. Even after formal
training has been completed, new employees may still have questions about anything from workplace norms to how to get reim-
bursed for a business expense. Almost anyone in your workplace
can answer these questions; it doesn't take any special skill or expertise. The person who helps the new employee helps the organization (and the new person) succeed, but it takes time away from
their own promotable work.

The Promotability of Tasks Can Wane Over Time

Sometimes, something that starts as promotable becomes a task
that isn't later on. That's what happened to Carina, a tax accountant
at a boutique firm. A few years ago, some significant and complex
changes in tax law affected small businesses, the firm's primary cli-
entele. Carina wrote up an analysis of the changes and her recommendations, which she shared with the other accountants in her
firm. She made the complexities understandable for her colleagues,
and Eduardo, the firm's owner, wasted no time in praising her work.
He then asked her to write a monthly internal newsletter to share
her insights with the firm. Carina knew she was a good accountant,
and she was honored that Eduardo had chosen her to communicate
new legal changes. She thought he was recognizing her knowledge
and skills. So, once a month she wrote a newsletter to update her
colleagues and explain some of the more obscure tax issues. It saved
time for her colleagues, but it was a lot of work for her. What made
it even more trying was that Carina's colleagues began asking her
for help with their clients because they saw her as the expert. Carina

was spending a minimum of ten hours a week on the newsletter and other people's work—adding a full 25 percent of a normal workweek to her plate. To make room for this extra work, she had to cut back on the time she was spending with clients. Before she knew it, her colleagues' salary increases were exceeding hers.

What started as a good idea soon spiraled out of control. The initial write-up created a lot of visibility for Carina, but once Eduardo made it part of her job, the additional work the newsletter created soon outweighed its benefit and ended up harming her productivity. We've seen this over and over—doing a task one time can initially create visibility, but doing it on a regular basis provides no additional benefit and incurs an ongoing cost.

In our interviews and through our surveys, we've collected hundreds of stories from women of all ages and races and across a multitude of industries and occupations. From this work, we've compiled our "top ten" most common NPTs. It's possible you do only some of these tasks. It's possible that you do them all (though we really hope not). Whether these are non-promotable for you depends on your job. When the task is a core function of your job, it is probably promotable (e.g., editing and proofreading are promotable if you are an editor; recruiting, onboarding, training, and mentoring are promotable if you are in HR).

The No Club's Top Ten NPTs

1. Helping others do their work and filling in when people are absent
2. Organizing and coordinating (but not managing) the work of others
3. Editing, proofreading, and compiling, especially the work of others

4. Logistical planning and special events
5. Governance work, such as safety committees, ethics committees, diversity committees, climate committees, and review committees
6. Recruiting
7. Resolving conflict among coworkers
8. Helping coworkers with their personal problems
9. Onboarding, training, and mentoring
10. Office housework such as getting coffee and cleaning

These tasks are likely quite familiar as many of them are lauded as positive organizational citizenship behaviors. While these tasks are good for the organization, they are bad for the good citizen whose workday is overloaded with them.

NPTs Are a Problem Hiding in Plain Sight

Once we discovered NPTs, we couldn't unsee them. They were everywhere. We started talking about NPTs all the time, at lunch with coworkers, out with friends, at home. We got different reactions from the people we spoke with. Some commiserated with our overload of NPTs and eagerly told us their own stories. Other people, usually men, looked at us quizzically, asked why we'd "allowed" ourselves to get in that situation, and told us to "just stop" doing the dead-end work. Through it all, our female friends and colleagues were much more likely to commiserate and share their own stories than our male friends and colleagues. Why was that? Did this issue affect women more than men? We launched our research initiative to find out, and the next chapter dives into what we learned.

Before moving on, you need to figure out which of your tasks are promotable and which are not. To help you do that, we've developed exercises from our own experience in diagnosing our own tasks and working with other women. We think you'll find them eye-opening. They were for us. In the early days of our club, we really hadn't thought about these questions. In some cases, we didn't even know the answer (e.g., "Is serving on the ethics committee instrumental to the organization's currency?"). Once you've completed the exercises, take some time to review the results and think about the balance of your promotable and non-promotable work. You'll see that the exercises in this chapter are a bit of a lift, but they serve as the critical foundation for shorter ones in the rest of the book. If they seem too daunting to complete right now, then keep reading and come back to them later—do what works best for you. After the exercises below, we provide an example of how Maria, a database analyst, assessed her portfolio of promotable and non-promotable work, which you can refer to for guidance as you complete yours.

EXERCISE 1: UNDERSTANDING YOUR MIX OF PROMOTABLE AND NON-PROMOTABLE WORK

These exercises might take some effort, but as with any good training program, the results will be worth it. They helped us understand why we didn't have enough time in our day to do the work that mattered most to our careers. We want that same awareness for you.

EXERCISE 1.1: What Is Your Organization's Currency?

Step 1. What does your organization say it values in written documents? Look for information in its mission statement, strategic plan, annual reports to shareholders or other constituents, and any marketing or other materials your organization publishes and disseminates externally (in print or online).

Step 2. What does your organization measure? Review the documents you collected above. What are key performance indicators (KPIs): Sales? Profits? Patents? Patients? Customer satisfaction? Donations? Awareness? We measure what matters. Look at the type of data your organization tracks to calibrate success.

Step 3. What do your organization's press releases, website, or newsletters share as important news? These communications provide clues to the organization's values.

Step 4. What work gets noticed the most? What makes your boss or colleagues excited or anxious? What accomplishments are most commonly mentioned in meetings, company-wide emails, and casual conversations? Who gets a pat on the back and why? If your organization is large, focus just on your division or department.

Step 5. Look at your lists in steps 1–4. What are the common themes? They encapsulate what matters most to your organization, its currency.

EXERCISE 1.2: What Do You Do at Work?

Step 1. Start a list of all the tasks you perform. Write down everything you can think of. The tasks do *not* need to be a formal part of your job to count. Don't judge them, just list them.

Step 2. It's likely you won't be able to remember all the tasks you've done, so look at documents to help jog your memory: calendar entries over the past month, email and text correspondence, your job description and recent performance evaluations. Use these sources to add tasks that aren't on your original list.

Step 3. Combine steps 1 and 2 into the "task" column in the table below, putting similar tasks under a suitable category name. Then list each individual task (sub-tasks) under the category label (you'll need them later).

Tasks (*Exercise 1.2*)	Hours/week (*Exercise 1.3*)	Promotability (*Exercises 1.1 and 1.4*)
Task Category A - task 1 - task 2		
Task Category B - task 1 - task 2		
Task Category C - task 1 - task 2		

EXERCISE 1.3: How Much Time Do You Spend on Your Tasks?

Step 1. Estimate the time you spend on each of the sub-tasks in a typical week (make your best guess). For tasks you don't perform on a weekly basis, estimate the amount of time you spend on them in a typical month, then divide by 4 to get a rough weekly estimate.

Step 2. To help you with these estimates, keep a detailed calendar for a full week. Record everything you do for your job (whether at or away from your workplace) and how much time you spend on each activity. Using an online calendar, and entering start and stop times, can help with this step.

Step 3. Add your time estimates to the "hours/week" column in the table.

EXERCISE 1.4: How Promotable Are Your Tasks?

Now it is time to classify your tasks on the promotability continuum.

Step 1. For each task, ask yourself:
   a. Is the task directly connected to my organization's currency? Use your analysis from Exercise 1.1 to determine how each of your tasks aligns with the currency of the organization.
   b. Is my performance on the task visible to others?
   c. Does the task require specialized skills?
   d. Does the task let me develop useful skills and/or relationships that could lead to promotable tasks in the future?

   Assign each task a value of high, moderate, or low for each of the dimensions (a–d) above. Then look at all your ratings and come up with an overall assessment of the promotability of each task category—high, moderate, or low. Enter them into the "promotability" column in your table. We all have tasks that run the gamut of promotability, so you should see both lows and highs.

Step 2. Seek out additional perspectives on the promotability of your tasks (because you might be wrong or just might not know). Ask your mentor or a colleague who has your back, or if you feel comfortable doing so, set up a meeting with your supervisor to discuss these questions or wait until your performance evaluation. Then update your table in light of the information that you gather on what is promotable for you. These three questions will help frame your discussions:

- Are there certain tasks that I should spend more or less time on?
- What does the organization value most from someone in my position and those above me?
- Are there tasks that the organization pays particular attention to at the time of promotion?

Case Study: Maria's Assessment of Her Work Portfolio

Maria is a database analyst at a large international company in the fashion industry. In the early days of her job, she was excited to be doing highly technical work: solving complex database system problems, writing algorithms to mine data, and proposing ideas for how to use the information her company collected. Her analyses informed business decisions such as which product lines to continue and which to phase out, whether a particular store location should be closed, and which regions would be prime targets for new retail stores. Maria could answer any question her manager put to her, and this was exactly the kind of work she loved. When we met her, five years into her job, she was less happy than when she started. Swamped with his own work and tight on staff, her boss had gradually assigned Maria more and more administrative work. Early tasks that had been interesting and challenging were gone, now replaced by others that required less intellectual rigor and more time coordinating the work of her peers. As a result, she was becoming less and less satisfied with her job. We suspected that her unhappiness had to do with non-promotable work, and so we used our exercises to see if that was the case.

Maria's first step was to understand her organization's currency, following the instructions in Exercise 1.1.

Step 1: **What Maria's organization says it values:** Market share, new business, well-organized internal processes, reputation, efficient supply chain, profits

Step 2. **What Maria's organization measures:** Sales, market share, new sales contracts, customer satisfaction, conversion rate of advertising to sales, procurement costs, positive media mentions, customer loyalty, cost of production, profit margin, operating expenses

Step 3: **What Maria's organization shares as important news:** Sales figures, new strategic hires, profit margin, organizational awards, new product lines and collections, new store openings, cost savings initiatives

Step 4. **What Maria's department celebrates:** Creative ways to solve database systems problems, meeting or beating an aggressive project deadline, generating new insights from data, successful presentations to top management

*Step 5. **Summary of Maria's organization's currency:***
Customer attraction and retention
Market share and growth
Profitability
Innovation

Next, using Exercise 1.2, Maria generated her list of tasks to understand what she actually does at work, shown in the table that follows. Her list included items from her job description (build systems, work on new projects), along with others that were not (take minutes, help people with their work, complete work that others left unfinished). Even though she knew she was spending a lot of time on administrative work, she was surprised when she compared those hours to the number she spent on building systems and writing algorithms. The hours were the same!

Next, Maria worked hard to evaluate the promotability of her tasks. Here's how she assessed each of the tasks she identified:

- **Build systems and write algorithms**
  These tasks help her company understand customer purchasing decisions, advertising effectiveness, and the efficiency of procurement and distribution processes, which all have a direct effect on attracting customers and increasing profit margins. These tasks are **visible**, they require **specialized skills**, and they are closely tied to her **organization's currency**. The more she learns **new skills** in doing this work, the more she can grow within the organization, which is indirectly promotable. Overall, these tasks are high in promotability.

- **Organize social events**
  No one notices that she arranges these events—these tasks are **invisible**. Social events have no relationship to what her organi-

Maria's Assessment of Her Work Portfolio

MARIA'S TASKS (Exercise 1.2)	Hours/week (Exercise 1.3)	Promotability (Exercises 1.1 and 1.4)
Build systems and write algorithms - Write and execute queries - Prepare summary reports of findings and recommendations	12	Overall: H H H
Organize social events - Birthday parties, baby showers - Holiday party - Charity golf outing	1.5	Overall: L L L L
Help others with their work - Complete work on projects that other team members said they didn't have time to do - Remind people of deadlines and help them with their work	8	Overall: L L L
Coordinate and compile others' work - Project management for large database projects: develop project plans, take minutes at project meetings, coordinate work of others - Prepare for team's monthly meeting with chief analytics officer: put together materials on the team's analysis and findings for presentation by another group member. Explain materials to presenter.	9	Overall: M M L
Administrative work - Summarize entries from departmental time-tracking system and prepare report on employees' time by project or activity - Organize weekly staff meeting for entire team (about fifty people). Create agenda, produce slide deck, and arrange logistics. - Manage administrative assistants and junior project managers - Take minutes in staff meetings and distribute	12	Overall: L L L L L
Generate ideas and strategies - Generate ideas and create strategies for new projects to increase company revenue	2	Overall: H H
Committee work - Department representative on company-wide safety and integrity committees	1	Overall: L L

zation values and **no visible impact on its success.** They **don't require specialized skills**; anyone can do them. She **doesn't learn any new skills** when doing them. The charity golf outing comes closest to being promotable because it gives her visibility with high-level executives from her company and others, but that hasn't seemed to make a difference in her career. Low in promotability.

- *Help others with their work*
  While this helps others contribute to organizational currency, it doesn't really help Maria. Her supervisor is unaware that she is the go-to person for so many people in her department. It's **invisible** work. Low in promotability.

- *Coordinate and compile others' work*
  Some tasks in managing database projects are **visible** and require **specialized skills,** such as developing project plans and coordinating workflow, and the outcomes of these projects contribute to **organizational currency.** However, other tasks, such as taking minutes at project meetings and reminding people of their deadlines, are routine, and **don't help develop new skills.** Medium promotability. Preparing for the team's monthly meeting is grunt work, and she's not the one making the presentation. It **doesn't help her develop new skills and isn't visible.** Low promotability.

- *Administrative work*
  These are pretty low-level tasks—**anyone could do them,** and they are **invisible.** They don't contribute directly to the organization's business goals. Low in promotability.

- *Generate ideas and strategies*

  These tasks get noticed because they **affect the bottom line**. Maria can help improve the effectiveness of advertising (to attract new customers), influence the direction the next season's collection will take, or uncover cost efficiencies. These are **directly related to organizational currency**, and they use **specialized skills**. High in promotability.

- *Committee work*

  At first, these committees helped Maria meet new people, which gave her **connections** with higher management. They were indirectly promotable, but now, everyone knows her so there's no new benefit to her career. The work **doesn't require any special skills**. It is important to be on one committee, but she doesn't see the need for two or more. Low in promotability.

CHAPTER 3

Women Are Burdened with Non-Promotable Tasks

When Laurie walked into the first meeting of an important committee she had been asked to serve on, she was surprised to find almost all women in the room. Why were so few men working on what was said to be a priority for the university, especially since 80 percent of senior faculty at Carnegie Mellon were male? She scanned the committee membership list, thinking that perhaps some of the men couldn't make it that day, but none were absent.

Meanwhile, Brenda had a male colleague with whom she had some tasks in common. Remember her story from Chapter 1 about putting together the schedule of classes? Although they shared this job, she carried the bulk of it. When they first started working together, something would always come up for him, and Brenda would have to rush to do his part at the last moment. This made Brenda's life miserable, so she gave up waiting, did the entire task herself, and ran the final schedule by him for his input. In truth, Brenda knew that he expected she would do the schedule and not seeing any viable alternative, she did. When she presented the final version for his review, he was always fine with it and took little time to review it; he had other things to attend to. Brenda was carrying his share of the non-promotable work.

At our club meetings, when any one of us talked about such an experience, the rest of us nodded with recognition, we all had similar stories. Like Laurie, we all had been on committees filled with women. And like Brenda, many of our male colleagues seemed to avoid a lot of the dead-end work. Was this happening only to us or was this a broader phenomenon?

We didn't know, but we thought we should find out. So we looked to see what the research said about gender differences in who does non-promotable work. We found relevant studies in the fields of sociology, organizational behavior, education, political science, economics, law, psychology, and women's studies. The research included numerous surveys of employees from a wide range of jobs, as well as some in-depth case studies of particular occupations and companies. While none referred to low-profile and non-challenging work as *non-promotable*, that's what it boiled down to. The existing research formed a solid foundation from which to build our research agenda. Through experiments, surveys, interviews, and organizational data on how employees spend their time, we examined whether women carry a larger load of NPTs and, importantly, discovered why that might be so.

Every study we conducted and/or reviewed showed what we suspected: women do significantly more non-promotable work than men do. It doesn't matter what type of organization or job title— across the board, the gender divide persists. We'll show you the wide range of data documenting this phenomenon and use stories many women have shared with us to illustrate the evidence.

Before we get started, one important note on our use of "gender" in this book as a binary construct. The vast majority of research on gender in the workplace over the past few decades has examined gender using two categories, male and female. As a result, we are limited to discussing gender and NPTs in terms of men and women. We realize that this narrow approach will limit the applicability of our work, and look forward to future research that examines NPT dynamics using a more inclusive view of gender.

Let's begin where our research originated, with faculty at universities, and then we'll proceed to many other professions, where we also find that women are carrying an excessive load of non-promotable work.

Women Faculty Perform the Bulk of Non-Promotable Tasks

In the last chapter, we described how it takes time and effort to discern what is promotable or not in an organization, even after you determine its currency. That's not the case for most tenure-track faculty members, whose jobs have two main currencies in a research-based university: educating students and conducting research that advances the arts, humanities, and sciences. Promotable and non-promotable tasks are clear-cut, and advancement is based on research and teaching. Anything else faculty do is called *service*, and because service fulfills important needs of the university, everyone is expected to help out by taking on tasks like special projects, governance committees, or advising students. Service has all the hallmarks of non-promotable work: it takes time away from promotable work (research and teaching duties) while being largely invisible, often routine, less instrumental to the university's currency, and rarely developing one's skills.

We knew that service work was non-promotable, and a survey of our faculty colleagues verified that they knew it too. Working with

Maria Recalde, one of our PhD students, who is now an economics professor at the University of Melbourne, we presented faculty with four tasks and asked them to rank how an assistant professor should best spend fifty additional hours over a semester to increase the likelihood of promotion. Tasks included working on a research paper, presenting research talks at conferences, participating in an undergraduate curriculum revision committee, and serving on the faculty senate. Of those surveyed, 90 percent ranked spending time on a research paper and conferences as more important for promotion than serving on the curriculum committee or faculty senate. Both men and women could define and agree upon the tasks that would both help (the promotable tasks) and not help (the non-promotable tasks) them move forward.

But significant gender disparities exist in who actually takes on service work. Multiple studies—one that surveyed over five thousand faculty members across US universities, one that did an in-depth study of over three hundred faculty members at the University of Massachusetts at Amherst, and another that surveyed fourteen hundred political science faculty members at US universities—all concluded that female faculty spend more time than male faculty on the type of work we characterize as non-promotable. As an example, at one large public university, women's overrepresentation on faculty senate corresponded to them carrying a load that was almost twice that of men. While serving on the faculty senate sounds like a critical assignment, our faculty survey suggests that it is essentially a non-promotable task.

Research focused on academia also shows that time spent on non-promotable work differs by race. One study found that faculty of color spend three more hours per week on non-promotable service work than do white faculty. This finding is confirmed by numerous other studies showing that the problem of NPTs is worse for people of color, with Black and Latinx faculty spending more time on service activities relative to white faculty. The evidence points to a stark fact: while NPTs are a problem for women in general, they are an even bigger problem for women of color. Service work helps universities, but doesn't help faculty careers. Burdening women, especially women of color, with these dead-end tasks leaves them less time for their research and provides a major roadblock to advancement.

A large research university in California proudly shared a major milestone with us: 50 percent of the members of all university committees were women. What they didn't consider was that women account for less than 25 percent of the faculty, and that made the women's workload much heavier than the men's. Imagine that there are one hundred faculty, seventy-five male and twenty-five female, and one hundred committee assignments. To have women on half of all the assignments, we would have fifty committee assignments for women and fifty for men, but because there are only twenty-five women (and seventy-five men), each of the women would serve on two committees, while each of the men only would serve on two-thirds of a committee, on average. "Equal representation" does not mean equality—in our example, women would do three times as much as the men, without receiving any reward for this extra service work: no additional compensation, time off teaching, or other recognition. Women were "taxed" for their underrepresentation on the faculty.

The effect of performing non-promotable work takes a toll not only on women's time, but also on how other colleagues perceive their status. Several years ago, Linda was at the inaugural conference of a major professional association in her field. At the opening session, two men shared their vision and motivation for creating the conference. Amidst self-congratulatory comments and applause for their efforts, they invited another faculty member—a woman—to the stage who was also prominent in the field and the third cofounder of the conference. They said, ". . . and here's Nicole, who actually did all the work putting the conference together, and she will tell you about the logistics for the day." Everyone laughed, that uncomfortable laugh of recognition that says, *Well, sure, the women* always *do the work*. Linda was the only one who didn't laugh. She was too busy screaming inside. Why? Because the men were being recognized as the "vision guys," and the woman was just the invisible drudge working behind the scenes. Even though she had the same role as the men in cofounding the conference, Nicole only got credit for the logistics. Later on, when Linda asked her about the introduction, Nicole said she hardly noticed it. Her reaction is all too common; women are so accustomed to being relegated to subordinate roles that it doesn't even register to them or anyone else.

Are women in other occupations and industries doing more non-promotable work than men are? (Hint: you already know the answer.)

Women in Government Agencies Do More Non-Promotable Work than Men

A recent study examined how Transportation Security Administration (TSA) employees spend their time at work and found that male and female TSA workers spend their time differently. All TSA workers handle a set of routine tasks that are scripted and mission central: they check travel documents, scan bags, "herd" passengers, and pat down travelers who set off the scanner alarms. TSA employees all rated pat-downs as the most unpleasant task because they involve standing (which is physically taxing) and having disagreeable personal interactions with passengers, who often berate the agents for the screening. The procedure is fairly invasive and uncomfortable, and TSA employees state that they become emotionally exhausted from doing pat-down work.

The study took place at a large urban airport covering 1,223 TSA employees (71 percent of whom were entry level and not supervisors or managers) and included 55 in-depth interviews. Although managers tried to rotate employees across all tasks, female employees did more pat-downs than their male counterparts. Forty percent of flyers are women, but only 33 percent of TSA employees are, and female TSA workers must pat down female travelers (agents can only pat down travelers of their own sex). Because female TSA agents had to do more pat downs, they handled other tasks less often. With a backlog of female travelers always waiting for pat-downs, female TSA agents also had fewer breaks than the men—and more difficult interactions with stressed-out passengers.

What was the impact? Conflict broke out between the male and female agents, since the men knew they had it easier, and the women knew it too. The women were resentful that their jobs were more unpleasant than the men's and, because they were often stuck with one particular task, they didn't get exposed to a wider set of job duties. They had lower prospects to advance because they had less experience performing the full range of duties, which was necessary for promotion to the next level. Not surprisingly, the women quit at higher rates than the men did. The study suggests that when women do more non-promotable work than their male counterparts, their morale suffers and their prospects for promotion are diminished because they don't get to demonstrate their skills on the full range of promotable tasks.

One of our former students, Dorothea, noticed this gender disparity in her job at a large federal government agency. She and her team train enforcement officials on the agency's regulations. Her team is small—with only two men and seven women—but the scope of their work is large, as they create, offer, and evaluate the agency's training programs. Each training session has a presenter and a scribe, and both jobs matter. The scribe must note all the content that the presenter delivers, issues that arise during the training, and how well the participants perform. Typically, the men present, even though there are only two on the team, and the women are the scribes. While all the women have more training and experience in program evaluation (assessing the success of the training program) than the men, their boss rarely relies on their expertise and always seeks feedback from the men first. Dorothea and her female colleagues talk about how their male colleagues not only get the more visible tasks, but how they also make sure the boss notices them so they get credit. The women, on the other hand, say they focus on the work itself, do what needs to be done, and do a good job at it, but they don't need to shine. "The men," Dorothea said, "take up more room."

Dorothea's story also demonstrates how both gender and race can play a role in the visibility and recognition of work. Dorothea is the only Black member of her team. She's been successful in this job and all her past roles, but feels she has had to work much harder for opportunities and recognition. In her experience, organizations readily recognize the contributions of white men, while women, and in particular women of color, have to work much harder to get the same recognition.

For women in academia and government agencies, we see the effects of gender and race on NPTs. Is the private sector any better?

Female Consultants in the Private Sector Are Not Immune to Non-Promotable Work

We wanted to know whether women who have autonomy in their jobs also carry a heavier load of non-promotable tasks than their male colleagues do, so we looked at a large, well-respected professional services firm. The firm provides consulting services to clients, and it keeps meticulous track of employees' time for billing purposes. A coding system records the time spent by type of task—such as specific client projects, mentoring others, and community service. Using these codes, we worked with the firm's executives to categorize tasks on the promotability continuum, from very promotable to non-promotable. We analyzed several years of data, reviewing annual hours worked on tasks that the firm identified as high in promotability and low in promotability. The analysis revealed the following patterns:

- Whether senior or junior, the median woman spent about two hundred more hours per year than the median man on non-promotable work. *That's approximately a month of extra dead-end work!*
- The median junior woman spent about two hundred and fifty fewer hours per year than the median junior man on promotable work, perhaps to make room for the NPTs they had to do. *That's a month's less time on career-impacting work than the man spent!*
- The median senior woman spent the same amount of time on promotable tasks as the median senior man. She just worked more total hours to make room for her excessive load of non-

promotable work. This is likely why the senior women were still with the firm. *They understood that they had to work extra hours to succeed.*

The currency of consulting firms is billable time—that's what brings in revenue. If you want a raise, bonus, or promotion, then your best path is to spend most of your time on client work. In this case, the junior men have a real advantage because their focus is heavily on billable client time, and the junior women's time is much less so. The junior women's promotable hours are being chipped away by non-promotable work, and this is likely to hurt or stall their chances for advancement.

Skeptics might suggest that the differences in how time is spent are due to one group, the men, being better at promotable tasks. Fair enough. We looked at a group of junior and senior men and women whom the firm viewed as being equally good at doing promotable work. Here's the result: while women and men had equally high levels of performance and numbers of billable hours, the women *still* did hundreds more hours per year of non-promotable work than the men did. This group of women figured out what they needed to do to succeed. To run as fast as the men did, they had to log just as many billable hours *and* still find time to handle the additional NPTs. That extra time had to come from somewhere—and it came from working more total hours.

Women Do More Non-Promotable Work Across Industries and Professions

If you feel you still need to be convinced, you can find evidence of a gender divide in who performs non-promotable tasks in many other occupations and across industries. Comparing male and female elementary school teachers reveals that females do more classroom work, while males spend more time on managerial work, thus enhancing the men's prospects for promotion. Female investment bankers work more often with clients in low-revenue-generating areas such as public finance, whereas men work more often with clients in higher-revenue areas such as the technology industry, which is most important to the firm and is more promotable. The Center for WorkLife Law at University of California Hastings conducted two recent national studies of lawyers and engineers, focusing on workplace practices. Their study of over twenty-five hundred lawyers found that women were twenty percentage points more likely than men to report doing more administrative tasks than their colleagues and sixteen percentage points more likely than men to report doing more office housework. One of the female study participants remarked: "Despite superior education credentials and being a lateral transfer from a far more prestigious firm, I was given an appropriate title but slotted into the subservient support role (i.e., expected to take notes, get coffee, hang men's jackets, etc)." While other studies found that women of color often carry a larger load of non-promotable work than white women do, this study did not find such a difference. The level of administrative work and the likelihood of doing office housework was about the same for white women and women of color.

The Center for WorkLife Law's study of over three thousand engineers found similar differences in employees' beliefs about their load of promotable and non-promotable tasks. They asked respondents about their experiences in the workplace regarding work assignments, and the results are presented in the graph below.

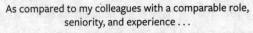

As compared to my colleagues with a comparable role, seniority, and experience . . .

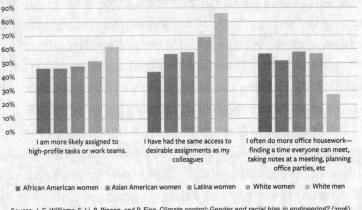

Source: J. C. Williams, S. Li, R. Rincon, and P. Finn, *Climate control: Gender and racial bias in engineering?* (2016)

Compared to women of all races, white male engineers reported that they had more access to promotable tasks and performed less office housework than other engineers. Also notable, race played a role in engineers' access to desirable assignments. While white men have the greatest access, women of color, especially Black women, reported having the least access to those coveted promotable tasks. One of the female engineers in their study described her workplace environment this way: "Just last year they hired a new female [engineer], and one of the managers was telling me how happy they were about hiring her because she really clean[s] up after the guys and keeps the lab tidy."

There is also evidence of gender differences in a study of supermarket clerks. Male clerks were assigned tasks that were interesting and varied, which familiarized them with many parts of the store, and provided the potential for promotion. Female clerks were stuck in the checkout line. In the words of one male supermarket employee: "You are supposed to learn the facets of the store as you progress, but that depends on whether you are a guy or a girl . . . I was really lucky because I got out of the checkstand. It's fun to check for a while, but it gets real monotonous, so not having to check is a privilege. All the girls have to do is check. The guys are always out of the checkstand. It's kind of funny." Another male clerk's manager taught him this rhyme: "If you squat to pee, you check before me."

Do Organizations See the Problem of NPTs?

The many examples above demonstrate that no matter who you are or where you work, women do more non-promotable work than men. Are organizations aware of this gender divide? We explored this question by talking with women and their organizations' leadership in different industries: health care, manufacturing, technology, consumer products, pharmaceuticals, education, law, consulting, and financial services, among others. We attended specialized conferences that brought together human resources and diversity and inclusion leaders from the world's largest companies. They were intrigued with what we found and how it shined a new light on their workplace dynamics. They wanted to understand what processes led to women doing the bulk of this work. We all knew the *what*—that there is a striking gender difference in who performs non-promotable tasks, a difference that is often magnified for women of color—but none of us knew the *why*.

Why are women doing more non-promotable work? Because they like these tasks? Because they want to do them? Because they care more about getting them done? Because they can't say no? Or perhaps they are better at this work than men are? No one had looked into this before in any depth. We decided we needed to do that research, and we designed and conducted laboratory studies to help us understand the answers to those questions. Our findings, which we share with you in the next chapters, gave us a whole lot more to think about.

EXERCISE 2: IS THERE A GENDER DIVIDE IN THE DISTRIBUTION OF PROMOTABLE AND NON-PROMOTABLE WORK IN YOUR ORGANIZATION?

It is time to revisit your list of promotable and non-promotable tasks from Chapter 2 (Exercise 1.4) to assess whether there is a gender divide in the types of work that people in your organization do.

Think about who does the tasks you do. Only you? Mostly women (W)? Mostly men (M)? Both equally (B)? Add the answers to your table. If you have a hard time assessing whether there is a gender divide in who does these tasks, consider discussing this with your coworkers. To keep things informal, you could broach this over lunch or coffee, or at drinks after work. Perhaps show them your list of tasks and ask if they do any of them on a regular basis.

Here are Maria's answers based on the case study from Chapter 2:

Maria's Tasks	Hours/week	Promota-bility	Who does? (W/M/B)
Build systems and write algorithms - Write and execute queries - Prepare summary reports of findings and recommendations	12	Overall: H H H	 B B
Organize social events - Birthday parties, baby showers - Holiday party - Charity golf outing	1.5	Overall: L L L L	 W W W
Help others with their work - Complete work on projects that other team members said they didn't have time to do - Remind people of deadlines and help them with their work	8	Overall: L L L	 W B

Task	#	Rating	
Coordinate and compile others' work - Project management for large database projects: develop project plans, take minutes at project meetings, coordinate work of others - Prepare for team's monthly meeting with chief analytics officer: develop materials on the team's analysis and findings for presentation by another group member. Explain materials to presenter.	9	Overall: M M L	B
Administrative work - Summarize entries from departmental time-tracking system and prepare report on employees' time by project or activity - Organize weekly staff meeting for entire team (about fifty people). Create agenda, produce slide deck, and arrange logistics. - Manage administrative assistants and junior project managers - Take minutes in staff meeting and distribute	12	Overall: L L L L L	W W W W W
Generate ideas and strategies - Generate ideas and create strategies for new projects to increase company revenue	2	Overall: H H	B
Committee work - Department representative on company-wide safety and integrity committees	1	Overall: L L	B

Maria's results reinforce that even when both women and men perform tasks that are promotable, women do the non-promotable tasks more than men do.

CHAPTER 4

Why Do Women Say Yes?

At one of our first club meetings, Linda was struggling with a decision. She had been asked to serve on the university review board that upholds research ethics and regulatory protocols in all studies involving human participants. The board is essential because an ethics or procedural violation puts the university's research program and funding at risk. Linda was worried that if she declined, people would think she wasn't a team player. On the other hand, she knew it would be a time-consuming, non-promotable task. Recognizing that, she still felt as though she had to say yes—the work was important, and she could make a meaningful contribution. To top it off, the set of qualified candidates was limited, and the head of the review board was having trouble finding someone; Linda knew they were counting on her to accept.

When Linda ultimately agreed to serve, she found that the board was an even bigger commitment than she had suspected, but she came to terms with her decision because the work was so important. One day, she and her colleague George were chatting, and she asked if he had ever served on the review board. "No, never. No one has ever asked me. And if they did, *I would say no.*"

Linda was stunned. George had been at the university for thirty years—and he, like she, did research that required ethics review—how had no one asked him to serve? And why would he be so quick to say no to something so critical to their university and to their work as faculty? Then it all made sense: for him, there were no consequences for declining, and he would say no because it would take time away from what interested him, what he would be rewarded for, and what he had been primarily hired to do. His priorities were apparent. Knowing he would decline, why would anyone bother asking?

This story illustrates the dual mechanisms responsible for the gender divide in non-promotable tasks. First, women are more likely than men are *to say yes* to requests for NPTs. Second, women are more likely than men are *to be asked* to do NPTs. The economists among us refer to the first as the *supply* of non-promotable work and the second as *demand*. We deal with the first of these issues, supply, in this chapter, where women are more likely than men to agree to non-promotable tasks, whether in response to a call for volunteers or to a direct request. We will share the evidence for this claim and describe what causes the difference. In the next chapter, we discuss the demand, where women are asked to do more non-promotable work than men are and why. Our research, which we present in these chapters, is the first to identify why women are overloaded with non-promotable work. Understanding these drivers is key to how we address this inequity—and to identifying effective solutions to the problem.

Women, More Than Men, Say Yes to NPTs

In one of our early studies, we surveyed human resource professionals to understand the work they each took on. The Pittsburgh Human Resources Association emailed their members asking for participation in our study. We were surprised (but surely, we should not have been) that women were almost twice as likely as men to volunteer to participate. The irony was not lost on us. Our request was essentially an NPT, and the women were more willing to help than the men were.

Craig, who works at a large state university, needed to find faculty members to serve on a number of faculty senate committees. While the senate plays a central role in university governance, faculty have latitude to decline requests to serve. Committee work like this is valued but unrewarded, and most everyone hopes that someone else will do it, which is a sure sign of an NPT. Craig emailed all 3,271 faculty members, asking each to volunteer for one of the university's senate committees. Now, if a task were promotable, you know that many people would say yes. In this case, only 3.7 percent of the faculty agreed to serve, so the vast majority knew that the committee work was a dead-end assignment that would not advance their careers. Craig shared with us the data on each person's gender and their response, and we found a substantial gender gap in who volunteered. While only 2.6 percent of male faculty members agreed to serve, a much greater percentage of female faculty—7 percent—agreed. This resulted in women being overrepresented on senate committees. Junior (yet to be tenured) women faculty, whose careers depend on publishing and who should be the most reluctant to take on non-promotable work, accounted for 60 percent of junior faculty on senate committees, although they constituted only 38 percent of junior faculty. This made their service load two and a half times that of their male junior colleagues. Similar results were seen for the faculty overall, where women made up 38 percent of the faculty senate committee members but constituted only 25 percent of the faculty.

What could explain this greater propensity for women to say yes to non-promotable work? Perhaps the three most common reasons we heard, including from a Nobel Prize–winning economist, were that women, more than men, like performing these tasks, care about them, and are good at them.

Honestly, we thought these explanations were weak. They came mostly from men, and sounded like a convenient excuse for not doing their share of NPTs. To us, it didn't seem likely that women—who had worked hard to earn their PhDs, and could be juggling both a new academic career and a young family—would want to spend their late afternoon in a senate meeting because they liked it, cared about it, or were good at it. Nonetheless, we wanted to explore if gender differences in volunteering could simply result from these three factors.

What Explains Women's Higher Propensity to Say Yes to NPTs?

In collaboration with Professor Maria Recalde, from the University of Melbourne, we conducted an experiment to determine whether women are more willing to perform non-promotable tasks and to test why that might be.

Our experiment replicated a setting where members of a group are asked to take on a non-promotable task, which was inspired by a frequent experience of Lise's. Faculty promotions at the University of Pittsburgh are decided by senior faculty who review materials for each candidate and then make a recommendation for promotion (or not) to the dean. One meeting is devoted to each candidate, and the dean kicks off each meeting by requesting a volunteer to serve as the chair. While the title sounds prestigious, the job is not. The chair's tasks are to lead the meeting, take notes, and write a report of the committee's deliberations and recommendation—important because the candidate's future employment is at stake, but time-consuming. Lise found the progression of each meeting very predictable. The dean would ask for a volunteer, then, without fail, every faculty member would announce that—big surprise—they were too busy. No one wanted the job, and yet everyone knew that the committee needed to find a chair, and indeed, they always did.

You likely recognize this situation from your own work life. Perhaps you are in a meeting and your manager wants to staff a new project. The project isn't challenging or prestigious; in fact, it's laborious and won't have much impact on your performance evaluation. As your manager describes the project and asks for a volunteer, you and your colleagues become silent and uneasy, everyone hoping that someone else will raise a hand. The wait becomes increasingly uncomfortable. Then, finally, someone speaks up: "Okay, I'll do it."

We designed our lab experiment to capture the decision of volunteering at meetings like these. Our question was whether women were more likely to agree to an undesirable task, when the task was neither enjoyable nor one that any one person was more skilled at doing. We ran our study with undergraduate students at the Pittsburgh Experimental Economics Laboratory (PEEL), at the University of Pittsburgh. We recruited male and female students to the lab, between fifteen to twenty-one at a time, each seated at their own computer. Participants were told that no communication was allowed, and that all decisions were anonymous and had to be made using the computer. In each of ten decision rounds, the computer randomly put participants into new groups of three. Participants knew that they were in a group with other participants in the room, but were unaware of exactly who they were with in any particular round. Without any form of communication, the group's mission was to secure a volunteer for a task, a task that each group member preferred another member do. The group had two minutes to get a volunteer in their group to click a button on the computer screen. There could be no more than one volunteer in each group, and the round ended when someone clicked the button or when two minutes were up. If no one volunteered, each group member received $1 for their time. If someone volunteered, everyone was better off, but the volunteer was less "better off" than the rest of the group—while the volunteer received $1.25, the two other group members each received $2!

In this three-person game of chicken, the worst outcome would be for no one to volunteer because then each person would earn only $1, and the best outcome would be for someone other than you to volunteer so you would get $2. It's certain that each person will spend part of the two minutes hoping someone else will volunteer. As the end of the round gets closer, you might grow convinced that no one is going to volunteer and consider volunteering yourself to receive $1.25 rather than $1. In our experiments, the volunteer usually emerged within seconds of the two-minute deadline, and most groups succeeded in finding one. Only 16 percent of groups failed to have someone click the button before the two minutes were up.

Are you wondering who volunteered more often—men or women? A group composed of three people would be successful and equitable if each member volunteered one-third of the time. Across the ten decision rounds, that works out to a bit more than three times per person. This is exactly the rate at which we saw women volunteer, but not men. Women volunteered on average 3.4 times, while men volunteered only 2.3 times. Women were 48 percent more likely to volunteer than men were! That is a striking difference. We also wondered who contributed the least, so we looked at the percent of people who volunteered once or never: almost half (48 percent) of the men, as compared to a quarter (28 percent) of the women. Who contributed most? A third of the women (33 percent) volunteered five or more times, with men being far less likely to fall in this category (11 percent).

Looking at the data provides a powerful picture. To help visualize this, the graph below shows the proportion of women (black line) and men (gray line) who volunteered in each round. In the first round, 40 percent of women in the group volunteered, but only 24 percent of men did, and from there, you can see that in each round women were more likely to volunteer than men were. Many men started by saying no, and despite seeing others say yes, they kept saying no for the duration of the experiment.

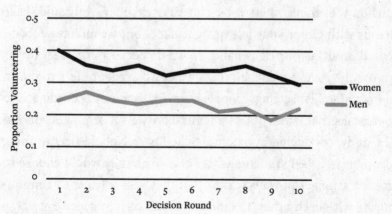

Volunteering in Mixed-Gender Groups

We Expect Women to Say Yes (So They Do)

Why did women volunteer more than men? Some of our fellow researchers conjectured that women volunteered for faculty senate because they were better at it. We can discard that explanation for our experiment; women and men were equally good at clicking the button. Others suggested that women "enjoyed" the work more than men did—and here it seems bizarre to argue that women "enjoyed" pushing a button more than men did, so we can rule out that explanation as well. What about other factors? Our colleagues offered many possible ideas for the difference when we explained our study to them. Perhaps the women were just nicer and more altruistic than the men were and thought it more important that a volunteer was found. Maybe the women were more risk averse and got more nervous while waiting for others to click. These explanations all seemed possible, but we had another thought: What if the women volunteered more because *others expected them to*?

Economists call our experiment a *coordination game*, where individuals benefit from coordinating their behavior and respond based on how they think others will behave. For example, you could shake hands with either your left or right hand, but we all have coordinated on using our right hand, so we do because it is best for us to use the right hand when that's what we expect others to do. In more unfamiliar settings, people have been shown to coordinate on outcomes that stand out as a natural answer. A seminal economics study, conducted by Thomas Schelling, a Nobel Prize–winning economist, asked students where and when they would choose to meet a stranger in New York City if they were unable to communicate with each other. Deciding on their own to coordinate on a noticeable landmark and time, the students' most common answer was at noon at Grand Central Terminal. In our experiment, participants were coordinating their behavior to find a volunteer, and we thought that they were more likely to coordinate on a woman volunteering, because stereotypical expectations would make that outcome seem more "natural" than its alternatives. Here is how to apply this thinking: if we pair one woman with two men and everyone expects the woman to volunteer, then the woman always will volunteer and the men never will. The woman knows the men are waiting for her, and she will be better off if she volunteers and earns $1.25 instead of $1.

That was our hypothesis—that the women would volunteer more because others expected them to—but we wanted to verify that this was driving the difference (rather than, for example, differences in altruism), so we re-ran the study in which the groups of three were *only* women or *only* men. This time, the sessions were all men or all women who sat at the computers in our laboratory. They played the same ten-round game from the first experiment where participants were randomly assigned to groups of three, and each group had two minutes to secure a volunteer to click the button.

Were our peers right that something about the women caused them to click? If altruism or risk aversion caused people to volunteer—and if women had more of these traits than men did— then the all-female groups would succeed more often in securing a volunteer than would the all-male groups.

But that's not what happened. Instead, the all-male and all-female groups had essentially the same rates of success in finding a volunteer. With volunteer rates of 81 percent for the all-female groups and 80 percent for the all-male groups, the rates were not only equal, but they mirrored that of the mixed-gender groups. As seen in the figure below, over the course of 10 rounds, women volunteered 2.71 times and men volunteered 2.67 times (dashed black and gray lines, respectively). It's not that men don't know how to click a button—they just don't do it when the women are around.

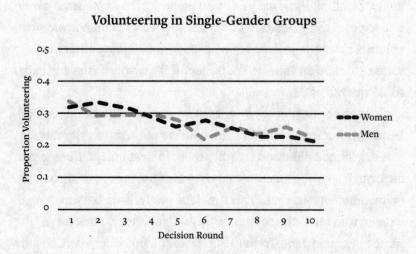

When men move from a mixed-gender group to a single-gender group, they volunteer more. When women move from a mixed-gender group to a single-gender group, they volunteer less. Why?

One of our friends told us a story that demonstrates what is going on. He likes to hunt, and when he does, he spends the weekend with a group of men at a hunting lodge. At the end of the day, they make a meal and all the men cook and clean up. But when our friend goes to dinner parties with heterosexual couples, the men never clean up after dinner—the women do. In a mixed-gender group, we—men and women alike—*expect* women to do the undesirable tasks. We have been taught and internalized the mandate that women take one for the team. That seems to be what happens when men and women are together, whether at a dinner party, at work, or in our laboratory experiment. Men are perfectly capable of doing undesirable tasks, like pushing a button or doing the dishes, and they know that when women are not around they need to step up and do it, so they do. When men are not around, women know that other women will help do the task, and so they can take a step back and secure the same level of group success without personally having to volunteer as much. It isn't that women prefer to do these tasks; otherwise the all-female groups would volunteer more than the all-male groups. Nor is it the case that women believe they are better at these tasks. It is the *expectation* that women will step up to the plate.

Rachel's story illustrates this further. Rachel has been the director of digital marketing for seven years at a company that makes natural products for the food and personal care industries. At one of the weekly marketing meetings of the management group, the senior vice president raised his last agenda item, which was the annual fundraising campaign for the local community food bank. The firm participated each year, as did almost every other employer in the region. The CEO always asked the marketing department to manage the process because he felt that this was an important visibility opportunity for the firm—it mattered to their standing in the community. The senior VP kicked off the process by asking for a volunteer to lead the effort. Rachel, who had run the campaign last year, felt she did not need to do it again. Indira and Miyumi, who also ran it in recent years, felt the same way. With plenty of others to volunteer, they assumed it was someone else's turn. All the other prospective volunteers were men. Rachel, Indira, and Miyumi sat silently—and so did everyone else. The silence lasted for an eternity. The senior VP did not speak, he just waited. It was so uncomfortable that finally, Peter spoke up. "You know the saying, if it ain't broke, don't fix it? Rachel did such a great job last year that she should take it on again." The SVP thanked him, turned to Rachel, and said, "Well?" With all eyes on her, she said yes.

This situation is just like our lab experiment where everyone waited for someone else to volunteer, but with an added element: Peter's comment focused everyone's attention on Rachel as the volunteer. She became the one everyone *expected* to volunteer. By nominating her, Peter pushed the outcome in a certain direction, and Rachel saw no way out. Everyone knew she would say yes because she was expected to, and with no one else stepping up, it was in her best interest to do so. She knew that saying no would drag the situation out, could make her unpopular with the rest of the group, and likely would result in one of her female colleagues volunteering. It was better for her to do the task than to have her colleagues think she wasn't a team player. Men don't face that same expectation and can more easily avoid these tasks because they know the pressure is on women to say yes.

Do we *all* expect women to do more NPTs? We told a new set of participants about our mixed-gender experiment and asked them to guess who volunteered more. Consistent with what we found, they expected women to volunteer more than men. In Rachel's case, the expectation that women volunteer more readily didn't rule out other possible solutions. The SVP could have ignored Peter's suggestion and instead asked him to take on the fundraiser, but leaving it with Rachel was likely an easier choice.

A psychology study explored whether decisions to help or not help in work settings have different impacts on evaluations and recommendations of men and women. In one experiment, the researchers explored beliefs about who should perform particular tasks at work, and asked participants which tasks were "optional" for men and for women. No surprise, the answer depended on the gender of the employee. Here are the tasks participants perceived as more optional for men than for women:

- Putting in extra time to help coworkers with work-related problems
- Resolving conflicts between coworkers
- Helping new employees settle into the job

If these sound familiar, it is because you saw them listed as non-promotable tasks in Chapter 2—time-consuming and unrewarded. What is "optional" for men is often required for women. As in our experiment, the expectation that women will do the task makes everyone else hold off, and the expectation that no one else will do it makes women step up. This, in turn, reinforces the belief that women will help—because we do! Then, because of these expectations, when we don't take on the task, we pay a price.

If women decline and don't fulfill others' expectations, we may be subject to retaliation. Work assignments, collaborations, performance evaluations, reputation, and compensation can be negatively affected by the perception that you aren't a team player. Everyone has internalized these ideas and expectations of how women should behave—including us. So often, women feel guilty when we consider saying no. We think it is our own voice compelling us to feel guilty for not saying yes, and our own voice telling us to be offended when a woman says no. But it's not us! It is the collective expectation that women will take on the non-promotable work.

Women Feel Guilty When They Say No—Because We Expect Them to Say Yes

Laurie was often the one picking up the pieces at work. When a colleague left the university and a graduate student was left without an advisor, Laurie helped the student get to the finish line and complete her dissertation. Another student, who was not making progress toward his PhD, was going to be dropped. Laurie volunteered to deliver the bad news. When a conflict between two faculty members interfered with their work, Laurie tried to move them toward a resolution. None of this was part of her job, but she did it anyway. People were grateful—someone needed to do it, and seeing the organization as a team whose members needed to support one another, Laurie felt good about herself for helping. She realized that people saw her as the fixer, and, as a result, she began to think of herself that way. Everybody expected her to say yes, and now she did too. She had internalized everyone else's expectations that the tasks were hers to do and felt guilty when she considered declining a request for help.

With one of our former students, Amanda Weirup, now a professor at Babson College, we surveyed employees to identify the emotions they felt when they said no to an NPT. Women were more likely than men to say they felt anxious and guilty. Further research backs this up. Linda, Amanda, and Taya Cohen, a professor at CMU, conducted studies in which they described to participants four scenarios where a person needed help: proofreading a report, attending a meeting for a colleague, running a work-related errand for a colleague, and helping to plan an office party. When participants were asked if they would help the coworker, women were more likely to say yes than men. They also found that women felt greater guilt for saying no than men, and this partially explained why women volunteered more than men.

Not only do women feel guilty when they decline non-promotable work, but those feelings are easily exploited. We came across this when we learned of Jasmine's story, which shows how feelings of guilt can push you to take on more work than you should. Jasmine is employed at a nonpartisan commission that works closely with Congress to provide information and education on its areas of expertise to senators through briefings, conferences, and position papers. Jasmine had been selected as a Congressional Black Caucus Fellow. The job at the commission matched her skills and interests and was well aligned with her career goals. As a fellow, her role encompassed highly promotable work (preparing briefings and meeting with members) as well as NPTs (onboarding interns, writing up meeting notes, and registering people at events).

Jasmine had successfully pitched a briefing topic to a member of Congress, which was no small feat, and had been hard at work preparing for the event. The session focused on renewable energy, her area of expertise, and would take place over two days in Minneapolis. She invited members of Congress as well as legislators from the upper Midwest. Two weeks before the event, the congressional member canceled, which meant the session no longer had a sponsor, a requirement for such briefings. Jasmine had already made plane reservations, reserved hotels and meeting rooms, and set up an add-on event at a nearby university. Now her briefing slot was up for grabs, and one of her white male colleagues, Cole, got it; he was able to secure a congressional sponsor on a different energy topic. All her hard work had amounted to nothing. Cole would get the spotlight.

Jasmine handed Cole all of the work she had done—the reservations, the lists of guests, all the administrative details that had taken a good deal of her time. The event was sadly in her rearview mirror, but a new opportunity sprang up: she was invited to join an overseas delegation on a trip to Copenhagen, and her boss approved. The first day in Copenhagen, while she was participating in a meeting, Cole called and berated her for "leaving him high and dry" to plan and organize his event alone. He accused her of trying to sabotage his briefing and said it was on her if it failed. Jasmine was shocked—and torn. She was unhappy about her own briefing being canceled, and while well aware that Cole was playing on her emotions, she felt responsible and guilty for not helping him make his meeting a success. So what did she do? When she and her delegation returned home from Copenhagen two days later, she picked up his work: prepared *his* briefing book, stayed up until two a.m. to collate *his* materials, and carried extra briefing books on the plane ride to *his* event in Minneapolis. She did a lot of the grunt work that should have been his job, work that she would have done on her own if her event hadn't been canceled (and work that would have been his to figure out on his own had he landed the spot originally), and she did it without complaint. She thinks that he played on her guilt because she was a woman, but worst of all, she thinks that if she weren't Black, he might not have done it at all. She knows she shouldn't have let him make her feel guilty, and she knows that she shouldn't have done his work for him, but she didn't know what else to do.

Women Experience Backlash When They Say No—Because We Expect Them to Say Yes

As we can see, saying yes places a costly burden on women, but saying no can also come at a cost. Beyond feeling guilty if they say no, women also risk upsetting the requester. In our survey of employees, we asked women and men why they would agree to do an NPT. Women were more likely than men to say yes so they could avoid negative consequences.

Why? Psychological research examines norms and the consequences of violating them. Many norms apply equally to both men and women. For example, at the movies, we expect everyone to stop talking when the film starts. That is a norm—a standard of acceptable social behavior. If people continue to talk, other audience members hush them, no matter who they are. Not all norms, however, apply equally to men and women—research shows us that *more* norms apply to women than to men and that we respond more strongly to women deviating from those norms. Research shows that women are constrained by a *tight culture*. That is, there are strong norms and many restrictions on how women ought to behave. Think of it like walking a tightrope; there is a narrow band of acceptable behavior, and veering from that can be dangerous. Men, on the other hand, operate within a *loose culture*—they have a lot of latitude in what they can choose to do. For them, it's like a highway, where they have to stay off the shoulders, but can move easily between multiple driving lanes. Men have greater freedom to make decisions based on what they want, not on what others expect them to do.

"Helping others" is a norm that applies more to women than to men, and thus women have less latitude than men to turn down a request for help. There are countless explanations for why we expect women to be helpers and whether these are founded on nurture or nature, the daily images we see reinforce these expectations. Sometimes, they are so blatant that they'd be laughable if they weren't so depressing. A world-renowned women's hospital celebrated International Women's Day by circulating to all its predominantly female doctors, surgeons, and researchers the following "inspirational" quote to make them feel "empowered": "W—Wonderful wife, O—Outstanding friend, M—Marvelous daughter, A—Adorable sister, and N—Nurturing mother." Not only would a celebration of the employees' intelligence, expertise, accomplishments, and leadership have been far more appropriate in a workplace setting, but it would have helped diminish the image of women as merely nurturing helpers. A friend of ours is an avid fan of the Avengers series and loves Scarlett Johansson's portrayal of the Black Widow, a particularly efficient and strong female superhero, who can hold her own in combat against their enemies. But he cringed when he saw a pivotal scene in *Avengers: Endgame* where the "Earth's Mightiest Heroes" were in a brainstorming session with one last chance to save the universe. The superheroes throw out a multitude of ideas to save humanity and, even though they have access to artificial intelligence and every technology imaginable, the Black Widow, the only female superhero in the meeting, takes notes on a yellow legal pad! What's worse? Brenda had watched the movie and didn't even notice the scene. We're so used to seeing women as the helper, and it's reinforced so often that it just goes right by us, even those of us who think we are paying close attention.

Exploring helping behavior at work, one study demonstrated the negative consequences of defying the norm of women as helpers. Participants read a story about an employee who was asked to help a colleague. The story had several possible endings: in the first, the employee agreed to help; in the second, the employee declined to help; and in the third, it wasn't stated whether the employee helped. Participants read only one version of the story and evaluated the likelihood they would hire the employee. When the employee was female, the evaluations were the same whether she helped or if participants didn't know whether she helped. But the evaluations were significantly lower if she didn't help. The takeaway? Women were not rewarded when they helped, but when they didn't help, they were penalized. The pattern was very different for men. When the employee was male, the evaluations were the same whether he didn't help or whether participants didn't know if he helped. They were significantly higher, however, if the man helped. When men didn't help, they weren't penalized, and when they did help, they were rewarded—the opposite of what happened to women!

Why do we respond so differently to men and women who do and do not help? You guessed it—our expectations are different. We have internalized the expectation (or mandate) that women will say yes and are offended when they don't. This greater potential for backlash further pressures women to say yes. What is the "penalty" imposed on women for declining? We've all heard it. "She's difficult." "She's not a team player." "What a bitch." The reason we don't reward a woman for helping is because she's "happy to." In truth, she may not be happy to, but she knows that to avoid backlash, she needs to say yes with a smile on her face. So she does.

Intriguingly, the responses to decisions to help and not to help are aligned with our survey of the emotions employees felt when they said no to an NPT. Those who were expected to do the work, the women, were more likely than men to feel guilty and worry about the consequences, while those who were not expected to do the work, the men, were more likely than women to consider the rewards that would result from helping.

Women are not alone in experiencing a tight culture. Studies of engineers and lawyers, from the Center for WorkLife Law at UC Hastings, show that women, and men of color, were less likely than white men to say they can behave assertively or that they can show anger without pushback. These differences in norms and expectations likely contribute to differences in work assignments where women and men of color are more likely than white men to report feeling pressured to take on tasks such as finding a time everyone can meet, taking notes, or planning office parties.

Interviews with Black Harvard Business School graduates who had since advanced to upper management similarly revealed their awareness that certain behaviors came at a price. They took precautions not to misstep, were aware of penalties for appearing ambitious, feared triggering the "angry Black woman" stereotype, and expended effort to continually moderate and temper their responses. Some of these graduates characterized the scrutiny they were subjected to as a tax that white majority employees didn't have to pay. These interviews also point to differences in work assignments: one leader reported being treated like the nanny and having to clean up after the male executives' hasty decisions.

Our laboratory experiments were designed to shed light on gender, and since we were drawing from a predominantly white student population, unfortunately we are unable to make statements on whether people of color would also be subjected to the expectation of volunteering more, and so would volunteer more. This work is still at its infancy, and it is the obvious next question to explore. However, other research points to people of color facing similar expectations and a narrow band of acceptable behavior, and often carrying a larger load of NPTs. One study found that each week, faculty of color spend an average of three hours more on service than white faculty, leaving them less time for research and less time for teaching. Other scholars have suggested that the expectation for people of color to take on NPTs and their resultant larger service commitment is problematic, as these activities rarely are considered in evaluating performance.

We have seen that women more than men will take on non-promotable work, and it isn't because they are more willing or eager to do this work, but because we expect them to. And, disturbingly, women of color face expectations for both their gender and their race, resulting in an even narrower band of expected behavior for NPTs.

Women agree more often to NPTs, and this, the *supply* side of the issue, is one piece of the puzzle. In the next chapter, we'll look into the other mechanism at play, the demand side.

CHAPTER 5

Why Do Women Get Asked?

One evening, Lise came to a club meeting with a confession. When her boss asked her to find volunteers to serve on several committees, she quickly found six people who all agreed, and after submitting the list to her boss, she realized that she had asked only women. It was ironic that she, of all people, would ask women and not men. She felt terrible for placing yet another burden on her female colleagues, and at our club meeting, she wondered, "How could I ask my female colleagues to take on these dead-end tasks? I am a horrible person." We said, "No, you're not. You're just like everybody else." That was our hunch, so we decided to investigate whether that was true and why that might be.

Whom Do We Ask to Do Non-Promotable Work?

We just explored the supply side of non-promotable tasks in Chapter 4 and saw that women are more likely to say yes than men because they are expected to do so. Now we turn our attention to demand—are women more likely than men to be asked to do non-promotable work? We found very little research on how people allocate work tasks and virtually none on how non-promotable tasks are assigned. That lack of evidence spurred us to do more research, and ours is, perhaps, the only systematic study on the assignment of non-promotable work. We focused directly on the *demand* question, and what we learned will not surprise you: women are asked more than men. By that, we mean that we—all of us—ask women more than men to perform non-promotable tasks.

We went back to the lab and modified our experiment in which a volunteer took on the undesirable task of clicking a button. This time, we added a fourth member, a "manager," to the group, whose job was to ask someone to volunteer. We wanted to know whom they asked—did they end up asking women or men more often or was it equal?

In the new experiment, we still had three group members who had two minutes to find a volunteer to click the button. Before the two minutes started, we instructed the manager to ask one of the members to "volunteer" to click the button. Everyone saw photos of each member in their group and knew whom the manager asked to volunteer. Although the manager could not click the button, every other group member could (not only the person who was asked), and the round ended when someone clicked or when the two minutes were up. Every group member, including the person who was asked to volunteer, hoped that someone else would jump in and click before the round ended.

We conducted a number of experimental sessions with twenty students in each. The sessions were gender balanced and most of the students were first-year undergraduates and white. They each sat at a computer terminal in our lab at the University of Pittsburgh, and all their interactions happened via the computer, with photos of all members of the group displayed on their monitors. In each of ten rounds, the computer randomly formed new groups of four and chose one person to be the manager. As before, the goal was for someone to click the button by the end of two minutes, and the rewards were the same as in our earlier studies: group members who were not assigned to be the manager got $1 if no one clicked, $2 if someone else clicked, and $1.25 if they clicked. The manager earned $1 if no one clicked and $2 if someone clicked—so it was in the manager's interest to ask the right person for the job, that is, the person who would volunteer to click the button.

Suppose you were in this study and you were the manager. If these were your group members, who would you have asked to click the button?

If you were equally likely to ask any group member, then you would ask each person one-third (33 percent) of the time, but our "managers" didn't. In groups with one woman and two men, the woman was asked 40 percent of the time and the men were each asked 30 percent of the time. Why did managers prefer the woman? Maybe she stood out because she was the only woman. To test this idea, we looked at groups that included two women and one man. Of the three people below, who would you ask?

If the same dynamic were at play as in the prior example, then we would ask the man 40 percent of the time, just as we asked the woman when she was the group's only female. What we found instead was that women were *still* asked 40 percent of the time. The group's two women were *each* asked 40 percent of the time, so the man was asked even less frequently than before—getting only 20 percent of the requests.

Remember, this ask is for a volunteer to perform an undesirable task and get a lower relative payoff, to "take one for the team." Who did you ask? A woman? If you're like the students in our study, you are on average 44 percent more likely to ask a woman than a man. Interestingly, both the men *and* women managers asked women more than men. Lise was not alone. Even our college undergraduates, with relatively little exposure to workplace norms, asked women more than men. Because women are expected to say yes when asked, that just seemed like the best bet for getting a volunteer.

Our friend Meihui shared a story of an online meeting she was in with eight physicians, the other seven of whom were men. One of them started the meeting with, "Hey, Meihui, want to be our scribe and consolidate stuff to share back to everyone?" What struck us about this request was how "natural" it was for her male colleague to take charge, and give Meihui a burdensome administrative task, despite all eight being equals. It seemed completely normal to everyone on the call except our friend, who, familiar with our research, saw this as an obvious example of an extra burden on women.

While our study speaks plainly to women being asked more than men, the data cannot speak to other characteristics such as race, ethnicity, class, and age. However, given the evidence that people of color may face backlash for behaving assertively, there are strong expectations that they will agree to do NPTs. For that reason, people may be more likely to ask them to do this work.

Why Do We Ask Women to Do Non-Promotable Work?

We've identified several reasons why people ask women to do NPTs more often than they ask men. Sometimes, we engage in conscious deliberation before deciding to ask a woman. Other times, factors influence our decisions without our awareness. We typically chalk these subconscious decisions up to hunches or intuition where we make a decision based on a gut feeling. You may feel bad that you would have asked the women to click the button in the experiment above, but your decision to choose the woman was likely a subconscious one. We have identified five reasons why we ask women to do non-promotable work. Let's look at them more closely.

Reason #1: We Ask People We Expect Will Say Yes
Why?
- It is faster: It takes so much less time to ask someone who will agree, just a quick "happy to." Problem solved!
- It is easier: There's no begging or having to persuade someone.
- It is less stressful: You don't have to worry about your request

being rejected. Research shows that it is painful to ask and get "no" for an answer, so we want to avoid being rejected.

Lise chose women for the committee assignments because they would agree, which made her life easier. She wanted to get the job done, so she inadvertently gave the men a pass because she didn't have time to deal with potential pushback.

We saw in the last chapter that women volunteer more because we expect them to. Our study also provides evidence that when people are *asked* to do an undesirable task, we expect women to say yes. Our results confirm that expectation—when the manager asked a woman to click the button (and get the lower relative payoff), she said yes 75 percent of the time, whereas when the manager asked a man, he agreed only 50 percent of the time. This higher rate of acceptance by women is all the more surprising because they were asked more often than men were. You could imagine that women would grow tired of the repeated requests and become less likely to accept, but we see no evidence of this. Instead, women kept saying yes, so it made sense to keep asking them.

Reason #2: When We Think about Who Is "a Good Fit" for Non-Promotable Work, Women "Come to Mind" More Easily

Close your eyes and picture a carpenter. If you are like most people, you pictured a man. Because the vast majority of carpenters—96.8 percent—are men, then almost every time we see a carpenter, we see a man. Over time, our brain develops an association between "carpenter" and "man," and it very quickly processes the two as a pair. It takes us much longer to process the image of carpenter and woman. The speed of association makes us think that "carpenter" and "man" is a good match, but "carpenter" and "woman" is not.

This is called *gender congruence*, which captures how good a fit there is between a situation (or job) and a person of a particular gender. Men are more gender congruent with carpenters than women, so we think that men are better suited to being carpenters than women are. This may not be conscious ("I don't think women should be carpenters"), but is likely more "intuitive" ("It's weird to think of women as carpenters, but I'm not sure why").

Gender congruence also affects how we assign tasks at work. If you have a non-promotable task to assign, you think of asking a woman first, even if your workplace consists mostly of men, because she *seems* like a good fit for the task. There are several reasons why you might see NPTs as congruent with women. First, women are frequently seen in these tasks, so like men and carpenters, women and NPTs go together. Second, women taking on NPTs is consistent with the behavior we expect of women. Even in today's world, we expect women to be communal, meaning they are supportive of others and helpful, while men are expected to be agentic—assertive, independent, and self-oriented. Women's gender role likely affects NPT requests. Suppose a new employee needs help—even after training, he still has questions. To whom does he go? Because helping is more consistent with the female gender role, he asks a woman, and that same gender role puts pressure on women to help. Third, stereotypes of women's abilities and status are congruent with characteristics of NPTs. NPTs tend to involve basic skills and can be done by many employees, while PTs often require specialized skills. Stereotyped perceptions of women being less skilled than men make them seem better suited for tasks—like NPTs—that only require basic skills. NPT assignments tend to have low status because they are less connected to the organization's currency and often happen behind the scenes. Stereotyped perceptions of women having less status than men make them seem better suited for tasks—like NPTs—that have little status.

A study Linda conducted with Stanford professor Frank Flynn and Harvard Business School professor Julian Zlatev shows how ingrained this congruence is in us all. Through an online portal, they recruited people with full-time work experience to rate six hypothetical tasks on how *promotable* they are. Participants ranked them—from most promotable to least—as:

1. Helping the company president write a speech
2. Serving on a hiring committee
3. Attending a conference to network
4. Making logistical arrangements for a conference
5. Planning someone's retirement party
6. Ordering office supplies

They then recruited a different set of participants, who also had full-time work experience. The researchers described the six tasks above and provided brief information on each of six employees (i.e., their name, how long they had been with the company, their educational background, and an assessment of their job performance). For each employee, participants rated how likely they were to assign each task to that employee using a scale from 1 to 7. The descriptions of the employees were rotated so that half the time the employee's description was associated with a male name and the other half, a female name. The names were stereotypical male and female names that only served to indicate gender. As expected, the participants were much more inclined to allocate the three least promotable tasks to the women. Why? The participants didn't know much about the hypothetical employees, but their names provided cues to gender. Participants matched the name with how it fit the task—and the NPTs were more congruent with women than they were with men.

Remember the female supermarket clerks, who were more likely to be assigned to the checkout line day after day? Here's how they ended up being stuck with that task. Each day, the managers would look at the total number of clerks working that day and number them 1 through the total number of clerks. If they had ten clerks, they would be numbered 1 through 10. The number determined who would work on checkout; if they needed five clerks on checkout, they would use clerks 1–5 and let 6–10 work in other parts of the store. If the store got busy and they needed an additional clerk to check out customers, they would ask clerk number 6. The researchers found that managers consistently gave women low numbers so they would be at checkout all day, but that they assigned the men higher numbers and hence other duties.

One clerk asked her manager about this gendered task segregation and summarized the response this way: "They don't give you a reason. It's like a parent who says 'because.'" What's actually driving their rankings? We suspect that gender congruence is at play. These managers are likely assigning tasks intuitively without a good explanation for why, automatically defaulting to their gut feeling that women fit these roles. Checkout clerks are expected to be pleasant and helpful to customers—roles that are often associated with women.

Reason #3: Women Are Victims of Their Own "Success"

Suppose a woman is asked to do an NPT; she says yes and she does a good job. Now it becomes her job as she develops a reputation for being good at it and becomes the go-to person for this (undesirable) task. This was the case for Simone, a former student of ours.

Five years after completing her master's degree, Simone was hired at a major US government agency, where she reported directly to the Cabinet secretary and worked on projects that highlighted her skills. A long-serving and well-loved administrative assistant was retiring, and the secretary asked Simone to plan a going-away party for her. Simone knew this would eat into her major projects, but she felt that she had to agree. She planned the party, which was a great success and for which the secretary gave her many kudos. Following the event, she had a lot of catching up to do on her other projects, and she had to spend nights and weekends to accomplish them. Then someone else was retiring, and Simone was asked to coordinate that party as well. You know where this is going, right? She became the de facto party planner, which affected both how much time she had for promotable work and how others began to perceive her. She was no longer being tapped on the shoulder for the projects that mattered for her advancement, like major reports to Congress and research for the secretary's testimony. She knew that she needed to find a way to get involved in those projects so she could get visibility for her *professional* abilities. She volunteered for every big project that fit her skills. She worked crazy hours and ignored her personal life. At her performance evaluation, she was told that she was taking on too much and lacked focus. She went home and cried. She felt that she was being punished for the work her boss had given her. Her "lack of focus" was not that at all. She was *very* focused, which was why she volunteered for the other important projects. Party planning stole time from her professional duties, and her supervisor, failing to see the real problem, interpreted that as scattered. Simone's colleagues—who started when she did—were being promoted to visible and important roles as she was falling behind in her career.

Reason #4: *Cultural Taxation*

Sometimes we get requests to perform particular tasks at work because of our demographic characteristics—for example, our gender, cultural background, or race. This does not always lead to inequity, but it can when a group is underrepresented in a workplace. As the only Black female epidemiologist on staff, Camille was asked regularly to serve on committees to bring her "unique perspective" to the table. She understood that she was being asked, in part, because of her gender and race, not just because she was smart and capable. Workplace governance groups, like committees on ethics and diversity, are often composed of members who "represent" the demographics or topic area. The idea isn't bad per se—you want multiple perspectives on a problem, especially from those who experience it. The problem for underrepresented minorities is that the work is rarely promotable and they are often overtasked with such work. Professor Amado Padilla at Stanford termed this phenomenon *cultural taxation.*

Many studies on work allocation in academia confirm that the problem of NPTs is worse for people of color, with Black and Latinx faculty spending more time on service activities relative to white faculty. Qualitative interview research suggests that institutions sometimes put pressure on faculty of color to participate in NPTs. In one study, a survey respondent describes it this way: "When you are one of three or four Latinos and being a woman, almost every committee wants you to be on it. It gives you opportunities, at the same time, I think, you are expected to do a lot of things not expected of other faculty." As shown in Chapter 3, a related phenomenon occurs when there is a higher proportion of women on committees than their relative proportion in the organization. While the intention isn't bad—"let's make sure that women's voices are heard"—it is likely to place a burden, a tax, on women for their underrepresentation.

After a contentious recruitment and tenure process, professor and Pulitzer Prize–winning journalist Nikole Hannah-Jones declined an offer from University of North Carolina for a position at Howard University, a historically Black university (HBCU). In a public letter, she responded to concerns over how her decision would impact UNC's diversity and inclusion efforts by eloquently noting that "It is not my job to heal this university, to force the reforms necessary to ensure the Board of Trustees reflects the actual population of the school and the state, or to ensure that the university leadership lives up to the promises it made to reckon with its legacy of racism and injustice. For too long, powerful people have expected the people they have mistreated and marginalized to sacrifice themselves to make things whole. The burden of working for racial justice is laid on the very people bearing the brunt of the injustice, and not the powerful people who maintain it. I say to you: I refuse."

Reason #5: Benevolent Sexism

Benevolent sexism doesn't imply that sexism benefits women, but refers instead to a person's benevolent intentions. When people engage in it, their goal is to help women, but the actions taken end up harming them. Recall the professional services firm from Chapter 3, where we analyzed annual hours for their employees and found that junior women spent many more hours than men on NPTs. As we talked with the firm's leadership, they shared some enlightening information: they had assigned women to special projects and intra-organizational committees to allow them to learn firsthand about different parts of the organization. This was not billable time, but the firm reasoned this would help women succeed. They rarely assigned men to participate in these activities (Why not? Shouldn't they know about the parts of the organization too?), so instead men were able to devote more time to what mattered: billable client hours. The firm had the women's best interests at heart, but their approach ended up harming rather than helping them. We pointed this out, but the firm was adamant about the practice; they were doing it to help women, and they would continue.

A friend of ours, we'll call him Ralph, was more amenable to our recommendations. Ralph leads a large division with a number of women who were next in line to assume leadership positions. Ralph had assigned these women a lot of non-promotable work, such as special projects or initiatives, but hadn't assigned this work to the men on his team. When we asked him why, his arguments were similar to those of the professional services firm—he wanted women to have exposure to organizational procedures and players as part of their development for leadership roles. Had the men he recently promoted also served on these groups? He admitted they hadn't, but he told us—with some embarrassment—that he still considered them ready for leadership roles. Ralph's intentions were good, but despite that, he had placed an unfair burden on his female employees. To his credit, he immediately fixed the problem and now assigns the same tasks to women and men.

Organizations need to evaluate whether what they intend to happen actually does. If engaging in these activities makes women better leaders, then it stands to reason that it will make men better leaders too—so everyone should do them. In Chapter 10, we will give you some advice on how to deal stealthily with this type of benevolent sexism.

Many factors influence why we more frequently ask women to do non-promotable work. We're not here to assign blame—we think that people may not realize they are asking so much of women. Even so, it still happens, and the cumulative effect of an ever-increasing load of dead-end work negatively affects women.

The dual phenomenon of being asked more and saying yes more (when asked) creates real gender inequities: in our study, women earned significantly less money than men did. In the first experiment (mixed genders without a manager), men earned 11 percent more than the women did, and in the third experiment (mixed genders *with* a manager), men earned 15 percent more than the women did. Now imagine this phenomenon happening repeatedly in the workplace, with women doing more unrewarded work than men, and the effect it would have on overall compensation and advancement.

Lise and her colleague Professor Rania Gihleb, along with their former student Rachel Landsman, now a professor at Bucknell University, conducted a laboratory study to further understand the effect work assignments have on compensation. In a setting where a manager has two employees, one assigned a less revenue-generating task (an NPT) and the other a more revenue-generating task (a PT), they examined how the assigned task affects compensation and negotiation. The two tasks were randomly assigned, and the manager was charged with distributing pay to the two employees. Although randomly assigned to the task, the employee assigned to the less revenue-generating NPT was paid considerably less than the employee assigned to the more revenue-generating PT. Further, the pay difference between the two employees was exacerbated by negotiation—the gap widened. That's because the only employees who successfully increased their pay through negotiation were those assigned to promotable work. The promotable work gave them a better bargaining position, and negotiating helped them take advantage of it.

Over time, the cumulative effect of an ever-increasing load of NPTs derails women's careers as they miss out on recognition, advancement, and outside offers. Amplifying these costs are the negative effects on women's health, families, and sense of self. We'll focus more deeply on these costs in the next chapter. Brace yourself—it is grim.

EXERCISE 3: UNDERSTANDING HOW NPTS ARE ALLOCATED FOR YOU AND YOUR ORGANIZATION

Now it's time for you to think about how you came to own your current NPTs and understand the processes by which NPTs are distributed in your organization.

EXERCISE 3.1: How Was Your Portfolio of Tasks Created?

You need to understand how you arrived at your current assignment of NPTs, which has bearing on the individual and organizational changes we discuss later in the book.

Step 1. Using Exercise 1.4 in Chapter 2, take the task categories that are either low or medium in promotability and think about the individual sub-tasks that fall into each category. Itemize them so you can see exactly what and how many you do.

Step 2. Note how each sub-task became your task:
- Did you *volunteer* for it when many people were asked to volunteer? (V)

- Did you say *yes* to it when you were asked specifically to do the task? (Y)
- Was the task *assigned* to you without discussion? (A)

Step 3. Think more deeply about how you came to own these tasks. If you volunteered or said yes when asked, *why* did you say yes? Did you think you would enjoy the work, be particularly good at it, or see that it had to be done? Did you feel like you had no choice because everyone expected you to say yes? Did you feel guilty about declining? Were you worried about the effect on your reputation if you said no? If you were assigned the task, why do you think you were asked rather than someone else?

Step 4. Are there other people who could do each task? Write down their names next to the task.

NPTs	How is it yours? V/Y/A	Why did you volunteer, say yes, or why were you asked or assigned?	Who else could do it?
Task 1			
Task 2			

Look at your answers in the table above. Are there any patterns in how you ended up with your NPTs or why you agreed to do them? Jot down your ideas so you can reexamine them later and help determine how best to improve your NPT load for the future.

Maria from earlier chapters did this exercise and filled out the table below:

NPTs	How is it yours? V/Y/A	Why did you volunteer, say yes, or why were you asked or assigned?	Who else could do it?
[Admin work] Summarize data from time-tracking system; prepare report on employees' time by project or activity	A	My boss was having trouble finding someone to do this time-consuming, boring task. He assigned it to me.	Tom, Janet, Roger
[Admin work] Take minutes in staff meeting and distribute	Y	This was one of the first NPTs I was asked to do. I don't know why my boss asked me. I agreed without even reflecting on it. It became my job after that.	Anyone
[Admin work] Organize weekly staff meeting for team of fifty. Create agenda, produce slide deck, arrange logistics	Y	The person who did this left our team and my boss needed a replacement. He asked me because I already was taking minutes and doing a good job. I said yes because I felt honored that he trusted me, but later I realized it was thankless work.	Doug, Andy, Irina, Shawnell
[Coord. others' work] Project coordination for large database projects where I develop project plans	A	We were understaffed and my boss added this to my set of duties. I discovered that I like the project-planning work and I am good at it.	Shawnell, Doug
[Help others] Complete work that team members didn't want to do	V	Work was falling through the cracks so I stepped in to help.	Anyone—or make people do their jobs!
[Help others] Remind people of deadlines and help them with their work	Y	We weren't making some of our deadlines so my boss asked me to help others so we could meet the deadlines. He asked me because I typically make my deadlines. I didn't feel like I could say no.	Janet, Andy
[Admin work] Manage administrative assistants and junior project managers	A	The administrative coordinator who did this left and my boss had me fill in temporarily. Then it became part of my job.	An admin position
[Committee work] Safety and integrity committees	Y	My boss asked my other team members but they said no. I didn't know that was an option.	Everyone should have to be on committee
[Organize social events] Parties and charity events	V, Y depending on event	I volunteered the first time because I wanted to help. The charity events are very important to me. Then I became the go-to person for events.	Anyone

From this exercise, Maria realized that her boss asked her to do lots of NPTs, which she didn't think she could refuse. What about you? Which category is most prevalent? Volunteering? Saying yes? In order to take action, you need to understand what drives you to take on this type of work. You also need to understand how your organization allocates these tasks more broadly, which Exercise 3.2 will help you to do.

EXERCISE 3.2: How Does Your Organization Distribute NPTs?

For the next week, keep track of how NPTs are doled out in your department and organization more broadly (if you have visibility into that level). Observe your manager and other organizational leaders. Even coworkers can play a role in determining who ends up doing NPTs.

- What are your team's NPTs?
- How are the NPTs allocated? Are there requests for volunteers? Are individuals asked to do the NPT? Are the NPTs assigned to a specific person?
- Who volunteers? Who is asked? Women more than men? Men more than women? Both equally?
- If you asked someone to do an NPT:
  - Why did you choose the person?
  - Was it a man or woman?
- What patterns are there in how NPTs get allocated? Is there one approach that dominates?

CHAPTER 6

The Cost of Non-Promotable Work

The many studies and personal stories we've shared show that it does not matter what position you hold, whether accountant, supermarket clerk, professor, TSA agent, or bartender—in all of them, women carry a larger load of non-promotable work than their male counterparts. What are the effects of doing so much non-promotable work?

In this chapter, we will use our own stories and those of other women to illustrate the high human cost of carrying an excessive load of NPTs. It was the hardest chapter for us to write, and we suspect it will be the hardest for you to read. While the material may feel all too familiar to you, we hope that you will come away with a better understanding of the toll NPTs take on your career and personal life. As you read the chapter, keep in mind that there is light at the end of the tunnel, and that the insights you gain will help when we later offer strategies to reduce your load.

At first, it might appear that by agreeing to take on unrewarded dead-end assignments, we bring the problem on ourselves, but as we saw in Chapters 4 and 5, the sheer number of asks we receive and the expectation that women will say yes provide few alternatives. Faced with excessive NPT assignments, what choice do we have? Consciously or not, we end up with a workload that falls into one, or both, of these two unfortunate categories:

- **Work/Work Imbalance:** If you don't want to or can't increase the total number of hours you work, then *you spend fewer hours on promotable tasks*. This will result in work/work imbalance if your load of non-promotable relative to promotable work exceeds that of your peers. This imbalance can manifest as career stagnation, fewer promotions or raises, and dissatisfaction with your job or choice of profession.

- **Work Overload:** If you don't want to or can't scale back on your promotable work, then *you need to put in additional hours* to keep up with the onslaught of non-promotable tasks; this results in work overload. Work overload is insidious and affects your personal life as it eats up time with your family and it may create stress, physical or mental ailments, and emotional exhaustion. Further, it can cause dissatisfaction with your job and choice of profession.

These both seem like terrible outcomes, don't they? In our club, Linda and Lise had the most obvious examples of each of these: Linda ended up with work/work imbalance, and Lise, with work overload.

Work/Work Imbalance

What do you do when faced with demands to take on more and more non-promotable tasks when you can't work extra hours? Perhaps you have children in day care, where there is a firm pickup time. Perhaps your evenings are filled with volunteer work that is meaningful to you. Maybe your work can only be done on-site or you can't work outside of regular work hours. When your worktime is finite, having too much non-promotable work means you don't have enough time for promotable work. You may not realize it, but gradually you shift away from the work that matters the most.

We all understand the elusive concept of work/life balance—the sweet spot where the division of time between our professional and personal lives makes us happiest. But we rarely discuss finding the right balance between the types of tasks we do *at work*, or more precisely work/work balance. If your share of non-promotable to promotable work is greater than your peers', then you are likely to have work/work imbalance. Achieving **work/work balance** helps you reach your full potential.

Work/work imbalance takes a substantial and detrimental toll on you and your career. These negative effects can include:

1) career stagnation,
2) questioning your professional identity and competence,
3) emotional exhaustion,
4) tension with coworkers, and
5) job dissatisfaction, stress, and turnover (from the job, field, or even the labor force).

The stories below illustrate how these play out in real life, and you'll see that most women experience more than just one of these.

Work/Work Imbalance Can Stall Your Career

Linda faced a steady increase in the number of people asking and expecting her to do NPTs. The review board she had agreed to serve on took more and more of her time. The university frequently sought her help with special projects. Her reputation as a problem solver meant that graduate students flocked to her for advice on navigating difficult relationships with their advisors. Women faculty in other departments who had trouble with their department chairs came to her for guidance and support. She had written a popular negotiation book for women, and now she coached numerous colleagues, friends of friends, and even strangers who reached out to her on email for advice. No matter how hard she worked, she could not keep up with these tasks as well as her teaching and research responsibilities. Her daughter was young, and Linda didn't want to lose time with her. Increasing her work hours meant sacrificing time with her daughter, time she could not get back. Her family also liked to travel, and she relished this time off. She had a firm policy of no work during vacations, which she had learned was necessary to refuel her mental energy. This meant that she had to get everything done in her regular workweek and so needed to choose which tasks she would or would not do. She cut back on her research; it was the path of least resistance, so she just kept putting it off. She didn't *consciously* decide to postpone it, but postpone it she did. The committees, mentoring students, providing advice and conducting special projects—all non-promotable work—edged out the work that was most critical to her career.

Linda was feeling the squeeze, which is why she started The No Club. At an early club meeting, she expressed unhappiness with the turn her career was taking. She hadn't been productive in her research program, and she felt it was beginning to show: her publication level was down, she had less research in the pipeline, and while plenty of grad students came to her for personal advice, she was having a harder time attracting good graduate students to work with on research.

As Linda discovered, your career will suffer if you spend less time on promotable work than your colleagues do. The junior female consultants learned this the hard way at the service firm we told you about in Chapter 3. Their larger NPT loads cut into their client time and revenue. Clocking fewer billable hours than their male colleagues likely affected their performance evaluations and raises and could put them at risk, rather than first in line when promotion time came. Their lack of promotable work also had the potential to hurt their marketability at other firms.

Women may not realize that the extra work they are being asked to do is non-promotable, and at first it may not be. This is what happened to Gerri, a software development manager, when she was asked to make presentations at corporation-wide leadership events. She didn't know that the work was non-promotable until her performance appraisal, when her presentations only got a brief mention and her supervisor told her that she was falling short of expectations and not keeping up with the demands of her regular job. When she was invited to give the first presentation, she thought it was a great opportunity for gaining visibility, and it was initially—higher-level managers noticed her. Soon the company took her presentations for granted and asked her to do several more. These assignments prevented her from fully contributing to other work, including the development of her unit's strategic plan, which she later learned was central to her next promotion. Gerri was frustrated: she was working as hard, if not harder, than everyone else, but success eluded her. When she was passed over for promotion, she realized that her work/work balance was out of whack.

Work/Work Imbalance Can Undermine Your Perception of Your Professional Identity and Competence

Work/work imbalance doesn't just affect how your organization perceives you, it also affects how you perceive yourself. When Linda's research productivity dipped, she began to question if her best days as a researcher were behind her. Despite being a renowned scholar, she wondered whether she still could contribute to her field. Was her career stalled or—worse yet—over? She wasn't sure she could be a "real" researcher anymore, and she didn't know if she wanted to be. At one of our club meetings, she deliberated if she should take on a full-time management role and give up her research. The rest of us were stunned. It took us some time to grasp just how negatively work/work imbalance had affected her perception of who she was and what she could achieve in her research.

Studies show that people question their competence when their day-to-day experiences do not match up with the education and training they received for their jobs. Surgical residents who were required to perform work that did not align with their own professional identities as surgeons questioned what their role actually was and should be. They saw themselves as elite specialists, and when they performed an overabundance of non-promotable tasks like making meal choices for patients, they questioned both what it meant to be a surgical resident and the value they added to their place of work. One study found that female engineer interns were "too often relegated to 'female' roles of note-taker, organizer or manager," and that this caused them to question whether they wanted to become engineers. These women were more likely than the men to transfer out of the field and those who remained had lower intentions of pursuing it as a career.

Work/Work Imbalance Can Cause Emotional Exhaustion

Working hard on less satisfying work than your colleagues and advancing at a slower rate is frustrating and emotionally draining. Having to hide your true emotions or regulate them to perform your job further amplifies the emotional exhaustion. Sociologist

Arlie Hochschild calls this *emotional labor*. Indeed, sometimes it isn't just the load, but also the types of NPTs you perform that become a problem. The female grocery clerks had more difficult jobs than their male colleagues because they only worked at the cash registers, where they constantly interacted with customers and had to be pleasant on demand. Likewise, the female TSA agents who did more pat-downs than their male colleagues had to be congenial in the face of angry passengers. And a recent study of health managers shows that females more than males engage in *surface acting* when managing senior staff, displaying stereotypical female emotions like calmness, empathy, and optimism, even though that isn't what they are feeling.

Other times the emotional exhaustion comes from helping others with their problems. Linda spent a great deal of time advising students and faculty on their work and personal conflicts, and by the end of the day, she felt emotionally drained and had a hard time shaking it off. The work followed her home.

Work/Work Imbalance Can Cause Tension with Coworkers

Both the female TSA agents and female grocery clerks were bitter about the gender-based allocation of tasks, so it is not surprising that they had a lot of tension with their male colleagues. Our club was no stranger to this problem. Brenda's close male colleague spent his time on the tasks he thought mattered, and she had to pick up the slack. Far more than she would have liked, she found herself feeling not just frustrated, but enraged, that he was able to avoid the tasks that didn't interest him. It made her even crazier that other people didn't see the inequity. Brenda did take some actions to lessen the problem (which we'll discuss in Chapter 7), but she couldn't understand why no one else thought it was an issue. He got credit for being visionary, while she kept the critical administrative pieces together. Here's the real killer—she liked him anyway! As frustrated as she was, she was also friends with him, and this created a lot of conflicting emotion—anger, resignation, and guilt for feeling the way she did.

Work/Work Imbalance Can Cause Job Dissatisfaction, Stress, and Turnover

A snowball effect happens with work/work imbalance. First, you feel bad about yourself, then you feel bad about your coworkers, and finally you feel bad about your job. A study of over three hundred members of the National Association of Women in Construction showed that dissatisfaction grows with an imbalanced workload. The study included tradeswomen, construction company owners, engineers, architects, and administrative assistants—it ran the gamut of jobs in the industry. In environments where men had more opportunities to engage in promotable work than women did, women reported lower job satisfaction and greater job stress than women who worked in environments with more gender equity in work assignments. Similar evidence of dissatisfaction with work assignments is seen across five Swiss studies involving eleven hundred white- and blue-collar workers. The studies examined employee reactions to task assignments that they saw as unreasonable or unnecessary, tasks that they didn't think should be part of their jobs. Examples include nurses who cleaned toilets and programmers who reentered data because the company had incompatible computer systems. Employees who reported performing these tasks more often had more resentment toward their organization, experienced more internal stress, strain, and burnout, and were more likely to act out against coworkers, their supervisors, and their organizations.

Work/work imbalance contributes not only to dissatisfaction, but also to stress and turnover. This is what happened to Maria, the database analyst from earlier chapters whose progress we've been following in the exercises. Maria's dissatisfaction grew with her load of non-promotable tasks. Five years before, she and her colleague Doug started in the same position at the firm. They had the same background and aptitude, were on the same team, and became friends. Early on, it was evident that Maria had great people skills, and everyone asked her to "help out" on tasks outside of her core job responsibilities. She planned birthday parties, often completed projects that had fallen through the cracks, and served as her team's representative on both the safety and the integrity committees. Maria and Doug met for drinks once a week and compared notes. She filled him in on the monotony of her work, and he talked about the algorithms he wrote. His work seemed a lot more innovative and important than hers, and Maria wondered why she wasn't getting the same assignments.

To make matters worse, Maria's boss asked if she would coordinate projects for their team since he lacked support staff. While he would do the high-level managerial work, she would organize the weekly team meeting, help other people with their work, and ensure that the team met its deadlines. Her boss knew she was a team player and appreciated that he could count on her to keep the team moving forward. This wasn't really Maria's interest. She wanted to stay on the technical side, not organize or correct other people's work, but her boss needed her help, and she felt she had to provide it. That was the beginning of the end for Maria: she didn't enjoy the new work, and over time she became dissatisfied with her job. More and more, her colleagues thought of her as an administrator, not the technical and creative person that she was. She became isolated—

no longer doing the work she loved and not really a manager in her own right. When the VP praised her boss for his success in managing the department, the large role Maria played in its success was never acknowledged.

Her accomplishments were hidden and her talents unused. She was unhappy and told her boss that she could contribute much more by going back to her technical role. He wouldn't hear it; she was too valuable in her current position. Maria had exhausted all her options—she couldn't do a job she hated, and she couldn't have the job she'd once loved. Her organization had left her no choice, so she resigned. Given her administrative load, she did not have a technical track record that corresponded to her years of experience, and she ultimately had to accept a lower position and lower salary to secure a job at another firm. Her career was derailed, leaving her disillusioned, discouraged, and disempowered.

All of these are dreadful outcomes for any woman, so the question is "Would it be better to hold on to the promotable work and just work more hours?" That's what Lise did. Let's see how it worked out for her.

Work Overload

You may try to keep your career on track and handle your load of non-promotable work by increasing the number of hours you work. That's what the senior female consultants at the professional services firm we discussed earlier did. They spent many more hours on non-promotable tasks than the men, but they logged the same hours of promotable tasks. The only way to keep up with the work that was most important to the organization—and their careers—was to work longer hours, resulting in **work overload**. To remain successful, they just did it all. Working long hours as a result of an excessive load of NPTs can have its own set of detrimental consequences for your life, such as:

1) negative impacts on family,
2) social isolation,
3) mental and physical problems, including stress, poor sleep, and negative health outcomes such as hypertension, and
4) career stagnation.

None of us wants this, and yet so many of us, like Lise, end up here.

Some of the consequences of non-promotable work overload are similar to those of having work overload from too much *promotable* work. Indeed, certain professions, the *greedy professions*, require an enormous number of promotable work hours to advance, like consultants, accountants, investment bankers, surgeons, and lawyers. While the consequences of having too much promotable work are troublesome, they are more severe if your work overload results from NPTs: paying the physical and psychological cost of excessive work hours, without the prospect of advancing your career, exacerbates the costs. And as you might imagine, the challenge of excessive NPTs is even greater if you are in a greedy profession, because they compound the problem.

Work Overload Can Negatively Impact Family

By having more work than you can handle in a regular workweek, your work will creep into early mornings, late nights, or weekends, and eventually impact your personal life. Lise was passionate about her research, and she was good at it, but she was also a dedicated teacher and a good organizational citizen. Every year her service commitment to her department, university, and profession grew. Adding these excess demands for NPTs to her active research program caused her to fall further and further behind; she struggled to meet deadlines and ran ever faster in a desperate attempt to catch up. Preoccupied with work, her physical and mental presence decreased at home. When her youngest would explain his latest invention in minute detail, her brain would wander off to her to-do list. While she tried to be patient with students and colleagues at work, her fuse was short when she got home. Far too often, a few dishes in the sink or a gym bag on the floor resulted in angry (and unjustified) outbursts. Her loved ones got the least of her, and while she knew it, she didn't know how to fix it. All her attempts to reset only got her off the treadmill temporarily.

Years earlier, she had sworn that she would change her ways. Work had been nonstop, and she and her family were taking a vacation with her in-laws. She was looking forward to kicking back, reconnecting, and enjoying herself. Staying at a hotel near the airport to catch an early morning flight the night before their trip, she put her two young kids to bed, said good night to her husband, and retreated to the bathroom (!) with her laptop to work on an outstanding committee report. Climbing into bed hours later, she realized that she had yet to prepare a research talk, which was due at the end of vacation. She had promised her husband that, starting tomorrow, she would be in full vacation mode, and so she lay there stressing about how to do both. The next morning, before boarding the plane, a journalist emailed, asking her to weigh in on a local policy initiative. Media attention was important to her institution, so she agreed and ended up withdrawing from her family on the flight to prepare for the interview. At the hotel, she got ready for the call, sending her sleeping baby off in the stroller with her husband and her four-year-old daughter to her parents-in-law's room. Nervous about keeping the phone line free, her pulse spiked when it rang and she realized her four-year-old was calling. Her daughter giggled and asked her to step outside so they could wave to each other from their separate balconies. Eager to get her off the phone, Lise complied. As she stepped out, she was hit by the sun's warmth, the view of the glistening blue ocean, and the look of joy on her daughter's adorable face. If only she had more time—but work was calling, so she quickly waved to her daughter and told her it was time to go. Her daughter's smile vanished as she said, "Mommy, why are you always working?"

Lise paused. In that moment, looking at her daughter, she understood that she was sacrificing something precious. And for what? Were a committee report and media interview important enough to interfere with quality time with her family? She wanted to be present for her family and herself, and realized then that she would need to take some drastic steps to change. She called off the interview and spent the rest of the vacation focused on her family and relaxing.

The trip provided a glimpse into what might be possible. But once she was back in the office, Lise slipped back into juggling mode. There was just too much to do. Keeping up with her research, teaching, and ever-growing service obligations, while carving out time for her young family, was a continuing struggle.

While we know little about the direct causal impact of work overload on families, there is evidence that people with work overload face more challenges in their family life. For example, *long hour* workers report that they often miss important events in their personal life because of work and that their irregular hours have a negative impact on their children. We do not want to miss out on events with our children, and we worry about the consequences of doing so, but there is evidence that we often find effective ways of compensating for our time away from our kids. Parents who work more hours tend to carve out quality time with their children, and while they have fewer hours available, those that they do spend are often more focused on the child. With the latter being the key driver to child development and well-being, work hours need not negatively impact our kids.

Unfortunately, an extended workday affects not just the hours you spend with your children, but also your behavior during that time. The stress you feel from being overworked may very well affect the relationship you have with your children. And the stress is likely to be greater and negatively impact your behavior if you are working long hours to keep up with an excessive NPT load. That is precisely what happened when Lise snapped at her kids for leaving a gym bag in the hallway. Working long hours and not getting to the work that really mattered caused her frustration and exhaustion.

Work overload may impact your relationship with your partner as well. People who work long hours are more likely to report being unhappy with their work/life balance and see it as having a negative impact on their domestic relationships. One study shows that partners of individuals with higher workloads at one point in time report lower marital satisfaction at a later point in time, compared to the partners of individuals with lower workloads. A survey of managers revealed that one-third would change jobs if it meant improved work/life balance, and work/life balance is frequently cited as a determining factor in an individual's choice of occupation or place of employment.

Little research exists on work overload consequences in lesbian and gay relationships. Not surprisingly, the work to date shows that same-sex couples suffer the same negative consequences to work/life balance that opposite-sex couples do. Homosexual and heterosexual women give the same assessments of their work/life balance, and face similar struggles in balancing the demands of work and home. The challenges are, however, more severe for homosexual parents if they are not "out" in their professional lives and are fearful to reveal their family demands. Work interfering with family is more pronounced among lesbian mothers who are not out at the office.

Work Overload Can Create Social Isolation

Working long hours spills over to other relationships as well. You might limit what you do at work—you don't have time for a casual chat, you turn down the invitation to grab drinks after work in order to meet a deadline, and rather than having lunch in the break room, you resort to eating alone at your desk. Little by little, you cut yourself off from the people you work with.

This social isolation may extend beyond the workplace. People who work longer hours spend fewer hours socializing. Of course, having less leisure time reduces social interactions, but the pressure you feel from being overworked can reduce it even more. If you pour every ounce of energy into your job, then there isn't any left for socializing, and what used to be fun—events with friends—moves from being the highlight of the week to yet another obligation.

But keep in mind that social interaction affects the enjoyment we get out of life. Individuals who eat with others and talk with their neighbors report being happier, and have higher well-being. We have seen dramatic effects of social isolation during the COVID-19 pandemic when, in attempts to overcome the seclusion, families gathered over Zoom, friends held online happy hours, and neighbors checked in on each other from six feet away. Social interactions improve our physical and mental health, with research suggesting that the effect of social isolation on mortality is comparable to that of smoking and alcohol consumption.

The opposite of social isolation—connection—has real benefits for us. The Harvard Study of Adult Development aimed to understand what leads to healthy and happy lives. Started in 1938, it is now one of the longest longitudinal studies of adult life. The study includes two cohorts: the first, 268 white young men from Harvard's classes of 1939–1944, and the second, 456 economically disadvantaged white boys, ages 11–16, from neighborhoods in Boston. Health information along with repeated surveys and interviews of these cohorts revealed that more than money or fame, connections to others were the key to keeping people happy throughout their lives. For both groups of men, personal ties helped delay mental and physical decline and were better predictors of long and happy lives than social class, IQ, or even genes.

If work overload cuts into the time and energy you have for social interactions, then you are losing one of the most valuable things in your life—the joy that comes from being connected to other people.

Work Overload Can Cause Negative Impacts on Health and Well-Being

Lise was concerned about how much her workload affected her family, but she never stopped to think of the effect it had on her. That is, until it was almost too late. Her department needed a new chair to manage the department, and everyone was asking Lise to do it. Reluctantly she took on the assignment, which increased her already heavy workload. On top of her research, teaching, and external service, she was now administering the department's research and education program, as well as overseeing close to a hundred faculty, staff, and graduate students. She cared deeply about her department, the university, and its many students, so she dove into the job and worked tirelessly to improve the department. She took on several large special initiatives: an external review, a five-year strategic plan, a revision of the undergraduate curriculum, an extensive plan to recruit new faculty, and a complete remodeling of the department.

None of these efforts were promotable for her. As counterintuitive as it may seem, serving as chair was a non-promotable task for Lise because she was hired and rewarded as a researcher, and she had no intention of changing career path and moving into university administration. Being chair took time away from the work that mattered most for her future success: the research that justified her salary and research budget. Even though serving as chair was a full-time job, Lise had to keep up with her research because her studies were ongoing and her collaborators were counting on her. Early mornings, late nights, and weekends were part of her workweek. One day, having just returned from a hectic business trip, she started work extra early to prep for back-to-back meetings and a five p.m. school-wide faculty meeting to discuss a controversial new policy. Angry and determined to secure a vote against the policy, Lise stepped up to give her statement, looked out over hundreds of her colleagues, and started to speak. Out of nowhere, she was hit by the most severe headache she had ever experienced, as if a giant nail were being pounded through her skull. She knew it was bad; in fact, she even thought, *This is it*, and yet she finished her statement. She was rushed to the ER, her thunderclap headache revealing severe hypertension, and with that began a long and bumpy road to recover from stress.

Maybe, like Lise, you think you can do it all, and maybe you can, at least for a while. But here's what's likely: over time, the work overload will become too much, harming your health and well-being, causing stress and burnout. Lise has plenty of company in battling increased blood pressure; hypertension and cardiovascular problems are more likely for those who work long hours.

Study after study shows that those working long hours are more likely to have poor and interrupted sleep, poor physical health, and unhealthy habits, including irregular and unhealthy meals, infrequent and poor physical exercise, higher alcohol consumption, and greater painkiller use. Disturbingly, the health impact of long work hours is particularly severe for women in heterosexual relationships. While Lise was fortunate to have an incredibly supportive husband, women often carry more of the load at home. Women who work long hours and have a male partner are often the ones responsible for the central household tasks (e.g., cleaning and cooking), while men who work long hours and have a female partner rarely are. In summarizing this large body of research, one study concluded that "long hours working puts women under greater amounts of pressure and has a greater negative impact on their health, well-being and satisfaction with life than it does for men."

Overwork also correlates with poor mental health, with increased likelihood of depression and feelings of distress, anxiety, frustration, and fatigue. Women are twice as likely as men to be diagnosed with stress and anxiety, and while this stress gap is confounded by physicians being more likely to provide such diagnoses to a female than a similar male patient, there is evidence that stress and burnout differ by gender. For example, women more than men experience burnout in the form of emotional exhaustion, feeling overextended, and being emotionally and physically depleted at work. On the other hand, men more than women experience burn-out in the form of feeling *depersonalized*, experiencing distant, indifferent, or impersonal engagement with colleagues and clients. Nonetheless, research reveals that men and women have similar physiological responses to stressors, and this finding has caused scholars to conclude that women's greater incidence of stress must result from men and women being subjected to different stressors, stressors that are hypothesized to be closely tied to different gender roles and expectations.

Lise's battle with stress didn't just come from the many hours she worked and the hours she was missing with her family. It also came from her guilt about not delivering and not helping others when needed, her fear of the consequences for declining a request or not keeping up, and her eagerness to prove that she qualified as a scholar—factors that may have been exacerbated by her role as a female in a male-dominated profession.

We could cite so many more studies that show the deleterious effects of overwork on physical and mental health, but we think you get the picture. It is not good for you!

Work Overload Can Create Career Stagnation

If work overload results from too many NPTs, then it may harm your career. Even if you get all your work done and you do it well, your reputation as being the "NPT person" may overshadow all the good work you do on your PTs. When you work extra hours to hold on to your promotable work, you're *still* handling a larger share of NPTs, and this may influence how your colleagues perceive you. Also, long hours may decrease the quality and, at the extreme, even the quantity of your work, with one study showing that those working seventy hours a week get the same amount done as those putting in fifty-five hours. Together, these factors can result in poor performance evaluations and interfere with career growth. While we can justify temporarily taking on promotable overwork—tasks that lead to advancement or improved compensation—it is hard to justify overloading on non-promotable work, where there is no upside for your career.

The Potential for a Double Whammy

Are you as depressed as we are? It feels like a pile-on here. The two outcomes of women handling too much non-promotable work—**work/work imbalance and work overload**—are extremely disturbing. Not to make matters worse, but it is possible to have both. You might have so many NPTs that you cut back on your PTs. Then you realize that you still don't have enough time to finish both, so you work extra hours as well. This happens, and it happened to us.

What does your workload look like? Are you facing challenges similar to ours? Take a moment to close the book, close your eyes, and think about your situation. The research we cite confirms how destructive it is for women to be overloaded with NPTs. The stories and studies may paint a bleaker picture than the one you've experienced. We hope so. We suspect that if you are like us, you had moments where you recognized that you suffer from the negative consequences of an imbalanced and overly heavy workload. We want you to examine that a little more because knowing how deep you are in this hole will matter when the time comes to reduce your NPT load. We will finish off the chapter with a brief exercise to help you understand your situation—which we'll help you improve in coming chapters. As promised, there is light at the end of the tunnel!

EXERCISE 4: ARE YOU EXPERIENCING WORK/WORK IMBALANCE, WORK OVERLOAD, OR BOTH?

In the questions below, identify the issues that apply to you. As unpleasant and unsettling as this may be, try to be brutally honest with yourself, and jot down brief responses to the issues that are relevant. At the end of the exercises, take a look at your responses to assess whether you think non-promotable work is causing work/work imbalance, work overload, or both.

EXERCISE 4.1: Are You Showing Signs of Work/Work Imbalance?

First, answer this: *Do you feel like you are spending too little time on promotable work?*

If the answer is yes, then look at the list below and see which, if any, apply to you and how. (Note: you may have only some of these or none at all.)

1. Career stagnation
   a. Were you disappointed by your last performance evaluation?
   b. Do you feel like you are overdue for a promotion?
   c. Are your coworkers advancing at a faster rate than you?
   d. Did you get a smaller raise than you expected?
   e. Has your boss met with you to discuss problems with your performance, like not prioritizing your tasks, not completing your tasks, doing a poor job on your tasks?
   f. Are you getting the right set of experiences to help improve your skills?

2. Questioning your professional identity and competence
   a. Do you question how good you are at your job?
   b. Do you wonder if you made the right career choice?
   c. Do you feel you are not using your skills in your job?

3. Emotional exhaustion
   a. Do you feel drained when you come home from work?
   b. Do you have trouble sleeping?
   c. Are you indulging in bad habits—more alcohol, less exercise?
   d. Have you called in sick more than you used to? Why?

4. Tension between coworkers
   a. Do you feel resentful toward your coworkers? Why?
   b. Do you want to do the work that your coworkers do? What is that, exactly?
   c. Have you gotten into an argument about task allocation with any of your coworkers?

5. Job dissatisfaction, stress, and turnover (from your job, your field, or even the labor force)
   a. Are you sick of your job?
   b. Is it difficult for you to stop thinking about problems from work when you get home?
   c. Have you thought about looking for a new job?
   d. Have you thought about changing careers?

EXERCISE 4.2: Are You Showing Signs of Work Overload?

Now answer this: *Are you working excessive hours? Do you feel like non-promotable work is contributing to your excessive hours?* If the answer is yes, see if any of the following apply to you and how. (Note: you may have only some of these, or none at all.)

1. Negative impacts on family
   a. Have you missed family events you were looking forward to?
   b. Have you canceled or postponed engagements with family?
   c. Do you feel guilty about how much time you're spending at work?
   d. Do family members mention how much you're working?

2. Social isolation
   a. Have you canceled or postponed engagements with friends?
   b. How often do you eat lunch alone?
   c. Do you feel out of touch with your friends?

3. Mental and physical problems, including stress, poor sleep, and negative health outcomes such as hypertension
   a. Are you staying up late to finish your work?
   b. Do you have trouble sleeping because you're worried about how much you have to do?
   c. Are you taking medication for stress-related ailments?
   d. Has your health declined?

4. Career stagnation
   a. Are you making more mistakes at work lately? Are you falling behind on deadlines?
   b. Do your coworkers and/or boss see you as the person who will always pick up the slack on the NPTs?
   c. Are you getting recognition for the promotable work that you do?

CHAPTER 7

The No Club Playbook

Once we identified non-promotable work as the source of our challenges and started to understand our struggles with work/work imbalance and work overload, we thought the answer was simple—we just needed to say no to any and all NPT requests. After all, our club began as the I Just Can't Say No Club, so improving our skill at saying no became our top priority.

We needed to get our lives on track, and as "yes" became a dirty word, "no" became the goal we stood united behind. We shared proclamations we found online with one another: Brenda sent a screenshot of Katie Couric's Instagram post that read: "NO means Nourish Oneself." Laurie shared a picture with the caption "She could speak five languages but couldn't say 'No' in any of them!" and we all recognized our prior unenlightened selves who always said yes. We didn't want to be like that anymore! Lise gave us mugs that said, *Stop me before I volunteer again.* And Linda was given a big red button with *NO* printed in giant capital letters, which, when pressed, shouted, "No!" in a booming voice; it sat prominently on her desk. We were trying.

We spent our No Club meetings sharing stories of requests that we didn't know how to turn down and our struggles to keep up with the demands on our time. We helped one another identify why it was so difficult to say no to non-promotable work and how to do better next time. Laurie worried that people would think she wasn't a team player if she said no. Brenda knew that the task wouldn't get done, and wanting to be a good organizational citizen, she picked up the slack. Lise ignored the consequences of saying yes and thought that if she just worked a little bit faster, then she would be able to fit in all of her requests. Linda worried about disappointing someone, especially when that someone was another woman coming to her for help. Although we didn't recognize it at the time, we had internalized others' expectations of us to say yes, and we needed to come to terms with our individual reasons for saying yes before we could begin saying no.

Learning to say no did not come easily to us. While it was easier to identify and say no to the obviously crappy dead-end tasks like office housework, we didn't really know when and how to decline requests that were not as clear-cut, and our lack of experience made us uncertain and wavering. We spent too much time talking about saying no and too little time doing it. And when we did, we did it poorly. But we kept at it and eventually developed strategies to evaluate requests and effectively say no in a way that reduced both our own feelings of guilt and others' negative reactions. In this chapter, we share our insights and best practices, honed over years of working together. We present to you The No Club Playbook, your guide for how to handle NPT requests and avoid pitfalls along the way.

Getting to No

The requests we brought to The No Club were always the hard ones. It wasn't just difficult to say no, but also challenging to make sure we said no when we should. We used three steps to assess whether a request for an NPT warranted a no: 1) get the information you need to understand the task, 2) consider who is asking you, and 3) eliminate the wrong reasons for saying yes.

Step 1. *Get the Information You Need to Understand the Task*

Suppose that Joe comes into your office and asks you to organize the annual sales meeting for the global task force that will be held eleven months from now in Chicago. Should you say yes or no? To decide whether to take on this task, you need much more information than Joe provided:

- What, exactly, does it mean to "organize the meeting"? What does the task entail? What resources do you have to help you?
- How much time will it take to handle this task? When should you expect to do the bulk of the work? Do you have the time to take this on?
- Where on the promotability continuum does this task fall?
- Are there things you won't be able to do if you take this on? Will it affect your performance on other tasks?

How can you get this information? Maybe Joe has some of the answers, or better yet, maybe he can refer you to the person who organized the meeting last year (and you can ask them why they aren't doing it this year). Maybe you can ask the senior VP of sales what her expectations are for the meeting. If you attended last year's meeting, maybe you have some recollections and insights of your own. These sources can provide you with a good deal of information, which, together with an assessment of your current workload, will paint a complete picture of what's being asked of you.

You need this information to make the right decision. But Joe is hovering in your doorway, staring at you, expecting an answer now.

If you already know the request is worthy of a no, decline now (see our suggestions below for how to craft an effective no). Otherwise, buy some time; don't be Brenda and blurt out, "Happy to." Instead, tell him that the task sounds like an interesting opportunity and you'd like to learn more. Ask Joe not only for details on the request, but also for time to think about it. Schedule a follow-up meeting to show that you are considering it. Then take the time to gather and review the information needed to consider your options. Once you decide, don't delay in closing the loop. The sooner you say no, the sooner Joe can start looking for someone else.

Step 2. Consider Who Is Asking You

Can you say no to Joe? What are the risks? What is Joe's job? Is he a peer? A superior? If he's not your supervisor, then on whose behalf is he asking? Would there be repercussions if you said no? Will others learn of you declining? Are Joe's preferences aligned with yours? Will he give you an honest assessment of the task and whether you should take it on? Saying no to an NPT request carries its own set of risks and depends on who is asking. If you decline, a colleague may not see you as a team player, and your supervisor may consider you as insubordinate.

Deciding whether you can say no requires an understanding not only of who is asking but also of your organization's culture. A very hierarchical organization may not be the place where you can decline a request from a supervisor. And if you do, you need to be careful in communicating the reason why.

Step 3. Avoid the Traps that Lead to Yes

Our club spent a lot of time talking about why we felt we needed to say yes and realized that not all of our reasons were good ones. Many of them grew out of our internalization of people's expectations of us; others were driven by biases that crept into our decision-making when we didn't fully think through what was being asked of us. In order to eliminate the wrong reasons for saying yes, you need to avoid the temptation to immediately accept the task.

Your best defense is to impose a waiting period before you respond with an automatic "yes." It will buy time to gather information to evaluate the task and will let you think about what you really want without the pressure of an immediate decision. Linda made a rule for herself: she could say no to anything straightaway, but if she was going to say yes, she had to wait at least twenty-four hours and her immediate response was simply: "I'll get back to you."

Waiting periods also apply when someone asks for a volunteer. If you are in a meeting, resist the impulse to raise your hand. Distract yourself. If the request for volunteers comes via email, hold off and give others a chance to respond. Our research found that women were 60 percent more likely than men to write back to the requester and say they can't do it, rather than just ignore the email. If the email is widely distributed, you may not have to write back to decline, and doing so signals that you have considered agreeing to it and so might be persuaded to take it on. Give yourself some breathing room to make sure you are not saying yes for the wrong reasons. That will make it easier to say no.

Don't Underestimate the Cost

It is easy to fool ourselves into saying yes because we often underestimate how costly it will be to take on NPTs—both in terms of the time involved and impact on our other work. Far too often we think that we can knock it out in thirty minutes, when the task is actually hours' worth of work. If you've ever painted a room in your home, you'll understand the concept of miscalculating how much time a "small" task will take. Linda's rule of thumb to more realistically assess how long a task will take is to multiply her initial estimate by 4. Consider your past estimates and how far off they were and adjust accordingly.

Another factor that conspires against us and makes us think that saying yes to an NPT won't be so bad is our limited ability to anticipate its impact on other work. One problem is that a task with a short deadline will trump a task with a longer one—no matter how insignificant it is. The big tasks—strategic, important work—rarely are as time sensitive, so taking on an NPT likely means that you will put off these big initiatives. Of course, you can try to protect yourself by blocking out time on your calendar to work on your promotable tasks, but if you're like us, you'll reschedule them to tackle the NPT that needs to be done by day's end. In other words, you'll fail to see that the NPT will overshadow your more promotable work.

Consider Your Implicit No

When Lise considers requests for NPTs, she now thinks about what she is implicitly saying no to if she agrees, because she knows she can't add more tasks to her already packed schedule. Her implicit no is what she forfeits by agreeing to the NPT request. Since she can't reduce her time spent on teaching or research, what she gives up to take on another task—her implicit no—is time with her family. With that in mind, when she got a desperate plea on a Friday afternoon (for a Monday-morning deadline), she responded with a well-deserved no. How she did it was simple and effective. She visualized her two small children and said to herself, "Laura and Jacob, I know I've been working late all week, but I am going to spend this Saturday and Sunday commenting on a research paper of someone

I barely know rather than going to the park with you." It was a great reality check, and it had an added benefit. It changed her perception of herself for saying no. No longer did she see herself as selfish, but as distributing her time to those who most deserved it, and that was easy—her kids and husband were at the top of that list. Thinking about her implicit no helped her make better decisions and alleviate the guilt she felt when doing so.

Remember the Future You

Joe's request to organize the annual sales meeting is eleven months away, far in the future, when your schedule is wide open. Today's yes doesn't seem so bad, but suddenly it's eleven months later. Will you still be happy with the task? The future isn't busy—yet—but it will be once you are there. Here's a trick we learned from Richard Thaler, a Nobel Prize–winning economist: Imagine that Joe's request is for tomorrow, not eleven months from now. Would you be as excited to do it tomorrow as you think you will be in the future? In eleven months, your day is likely to look just like tomorrow, and the task will seem much less appealing viewed through that lens.

Beware of Your Triggers

In this chapter's opening, we shared our own triggers for why we said yes. It took a lot of soul-searching to uncover these, and we needed the help of the club. Where we were blind, others were not and helped us see how we could get back on track. As we gained awareness of our own struggles, we worked on them, and, in all honesty, we continue to do that work today.

Your triggers prevent you from clearly seeing the consequences of NPTs; being aware of them will stop you from falling prey to your own reasons for saying yes. Why do you usually say yes? Look back at Exercise 3.1, where you reflected on how you ended up with your current NPTs. Reread what you wrote in the situations where you volunteered or said yes but could have said no. Look for themes. Do you automatically say yes? Do you say yes because you feel it is the right thing to do? Dig a bit deeper and ask yourself why. Now flip the script. Imagine you said no in each of those situations. How would you have felt? What might have happened? What were you trying to avoid by not saying no? This introspection can illuminate the "triggers" that push you toward yes.

As we discussed, you're likely to have internalized others' expectations for you to say yes, and you might find that guilt and the worry of disappointing other people make it difficult to say no. This might be your trigger, as it is for Cheryl Strayed, cohost of the *Dear Sugars* radio show on Boston's WBUR. She shares, ". . . what I've come to realize is that if I don't learn how to disappoint people by saying no to them, I myself will be devoured. And that is the circumstance I found myself in. I finally am learning because I had to. I had to learn how to not be the people pleaser, not be the person who says yes to everyone."

Ignore the Diva Moment

What happens when you are asked to do something prestigious, but it comes at the exact wrong time? We described Lise's experience with this in Chapter 1, when she was invited to serve as editor of an academic journal. This was a hard decision because, as she told us at first, she thought that she owed it to the profession to say yes. What she didn't confess until almost a year later was that she felt honored to be asked and was worried that if she said no, they might never ask her again. Like Sally Field at the Oscars, we all have the surprised reaction of "You really like me!" We named this the *diva moment* because you are so flattered that you don't see the potential downside. Lise fell victim to wanting to be wanted, and she underestimated the cost when she took on the time-consuming editorial role on top of her already intense workload. Remember, you still get to be a diva even if you say no; they asked you, so your ego can do a little dance.

Don't Get Cornered into Saying Yes

Recall Rachel from Chapter 4, who ended up organizing the annual charity fundraiser two years in a row. She tried to avoid the task by not offering when the senior vice president asked for a volunteer. But her body language sent a different message. She made eye contact with the senior VP, hoping that he'd remember she had already taken her turn last year. Rachel missed seeing that almost everyone else was looking at their phones, shuffling their papers, or gathering their coats. In other words, they were doing everything to signal disinterest in the task. In online meetings, people signal disinterest by suddenly looking away from their cameras as if someone has just entered the room or an important message has popped up on their second monitor. Do the same. Mimic the behavior of those planning to say no.

When Peter 'volun-told' Rachel to again take on the charity fundraiser—in front of everyone—she felt all eyes on her. Her resolve crumbled, and she agreed. Could she have done something else? Saying yes in the moment because you don't know what else to do is not a good reason for saying yes. Instead, have a general strategy ready for saying no or deferring your response until you know more about the task. If you see "charity fundraiser" listed on the agenda, then you know there's a good chance someone is going to leave the meeting with a new assignment. Perhaps go to your boss ahead of time to avoid being cornered—help him see that it is someone else's turn. Or, if you are asked, suggest that you and your boss grab ten minutes after the meeting to discuss this privately. That can make it easier for you to decline.

Now that you are aware of the severe personal implications of NPT overload, we hope it will be easier to give yourself permission to say no. In a nutshell, if you are taking on work that doesn't fully utilize your skills, then you are not contributing as much as you can to your workplace (more on this in Chapter 9). The person asking you to take on a dead-end task may not fully appreciate what other work you have, and you need to make that known if you are assigned too many NPTs. A friend of ours struggles with giving herself permission to say no, so before attending any meeting she puts a note in her pocket upon which she has written that elusive word, *No*. It helps her remember it's okay to say no.

Crafting an Effective No

It's time to give Joe an answer about whether you'll organize the sales meeting in Chicago. You have taken the time to understand the nature of the task (time-consuming and, really, a full-time job that will compromise your current assignments), who is asking and can you decline (Joe is asking, and he's your boss, but declining is an option), and to recognize your triggers for saying yes (when your diva moment arose, you shut it down). Armed with all this information, ask yourself, do you want to do this task? You realize there is little to gain by doing it and it will come at a substantial cost. The smart choice is to say no, but how do you decline Joe's request?

You need to craft an effective no. That should be easy, shouldn't it? Well, if saying no were so easy, our club wouldn't still exist. The blogger Suzanne Gerber put it this way: "Even for the most stalwart women, there comes a moment when our inner resolve fails us, and one of the simplest sounds in the English language (n-o) comes out as 'OK,' 'sure,' 'why not,' 'all right,' 'I suppose,' 'if you really think so'—or just as a sigh of resignation." Saying no can be complicated, emotional, and it has a lot more subtleties than we ever imagined.

There are two big issues to consider as you craft your no. The first is to have your no accepted, and the second is to avoid backlash or negative implications to you. The effectiveness of your no depends on both.

Ensure They Take No for an Answer

The person who you say no to needs to understand that you really mean no. We were so guilty of not saying it directly enough in the early days. "Oh, I would so love to do that, and I love working with you, but I don't know, I'm just so, you know . . . is that okay?" Brenda found herself twisting one word into incomprehensible paragraphs to avoid being direct. Now she knows that "No is a complete sentence," which she learned from author Anne Lamott—so that is what she says: "No." Shonda Rhimes takes that a step further with three unambiguous ways of saying no: "I am going to be unable to do that." "That is not going to work for me." "And there's simply: 'no.'"

Hedging your no can make it seem like you might be convinced to say yes. For example, saying, "I'd like to help, but I've got a lot on my plate right now," leaves the door open for the other person to spend time persuading you, and the phrase "right now" opens the door to negotiate a later date.

You might trap yourself by saying no in the wrong way. Linda did this when she gave an excuse that backfired. She was asked to run a negotiations workshop on campus the following month. She responded with: "I am so sorry. I am jam-packed with travel and other commitments next month so I can't." The requester said, "Oh, you know what? That's not a problem. I can push it out for another month or two. Thanks so much!" What could Linda do now? Say she's busy for the rest of her life? Another pitfall: instead of just saying no, saying something like: "Wow, that is not in my wheelhouse. Thanks for asking, but I'm not good at that at all." The requester then sings your praises: "Are you kidding? You are the perfect person for the job! You're the first one I thought of!" Now you're trapped again. The key to a good no is that it sticks. It has to be clear, concise, understood, and airtight.

Avoid Negative Repercussions from Saying No

Some ways of saying no are better than others. Research demonstrates that how people say no doesn't always align with how people prefer to receive a no. This discrepancy is important, as saying no the wrong way can negatively affect your relationship with the requester, as well as your reputation.

How do people actually say no, and which approach works best? To study this, researchers surveyed a group of employed college graduates and asked them to recall a time that they had declined a colleague's work request through emails. The participants submitted their actual email response declining the ask. The researchers then created a list of the most common ways people said no (each email could contain multiple ways): Gave a rationale for why they couldn't help (87.5 percent); apologized for not being able to help (39.1 percent); deferred to helping in the future (35.3 percent); offered to do part of the help but not all (11.4 percent); provided a referral to another person who could help (10.9 percent); pure decline (1.6 percent).

They then asked another set of people how they felt about someone who declined their request for help and used one of the approaches listed above. This is where the discrepancy showed up. People felt most positively toward a decliner when they gave a referral to someone else who could help, yet decliners used this strategy only 10.9 percent of the time! Another successful strategy was offering to help at a later date, yet this was used only 35.3 percent of the time. The differences between what decliners do versus what requesters want is not surprising: decliners engage in strategies to alleviate their guilt (by using an excuse), whereas requesters are more interested in getting the help they need. So how do we get to an effective no?

Use a "Yes, No, Yes" Strategy

William Ury, author of numerous bestselling books on negotiation, articulates a good recipe for saying no. He recommends responding with a *positive no*, which considers your needs while safeguarding your relationships. A *positive no* is a "yes, no, yes." The key is respect—for yourself and for the other person.

Yes: Say yes to yourself by recognizing and expressing your needs and values.

No: Assert your agency and personal power by saying no and providing a brief explanation why (but keep your baggage to yourself).

Yes: Further the relationship by finding something to say yes to; for example, get them the help they need without suggesting others who are already overburdened with NPTs.

You could use this strategy in your response to Joe. "Thank you for thinking of me, Joe. I have so much on my schedule the next two quarters with leading the new product launch that I won't be able to devote the time that organizing the meeting really requires, so I'm going to have to decline. But Don would be a great person to take on the task, and he could benefit from the opportunity to interact with others from across the company. I am confident he'd do a fantastic job."

The "yes, no, yes" formulation is a simple recipe that shows you are declining, *but* that you are helping by recommending a solution. Note that in our quest to redistribute NPTs more equally, the solution was Don—not you, not another woman, but a man short on NPTs. You can easily tailor the "yes, no, yes" decline to your circumstances. We provide a number of examples below, where the last yes recommends someone else who is not overburdened with NPTs.

- Note your implicit no. "This is a big job that will take a lot of time to do properly. It would cut into my time with clients if I take on any additional assignments, so unfortunately, I can't take this on. See if you can get Rajiv; I know this would be up his alley."

- Blame us. "I just read this book on how it is important to have a well-balanced set of work assignments. I'm trying to put the ideas into practice to ensure I can devote the time needed to our new product launch. Is there someone in the department who is doing less of this type of work right now that you could ask? Or is there someone who would benefit from doing it? Perhaps you can ask Greg, Mark, Dan, or Bill?"

- Note the inequity. Most people who ask you to take on a new NPT don't know all the other things you are doing, so you can mention the one or two major projects that prevent you from helping them. "I'm not sure you're aware that I am responsible for the weekly office newsletter. Brett doesn't seem to have the same commitments. Perhaps he could help?"

- Use others to run interference. We've given plenty of women the following advice with a great deal of success. Here's what to say (after actually speaking with your boss): "I had a recent discussion with my boss and they want me to prioritize other work, so I'm afraid I can't do this for you." If you have an assistant, you can use them to run interference for you and protect your time. (And those of us who don't have an assistant might wish we could use the strategy that journalist Anne Helen Petersen dreams of—creating a second email account that can pose as your "assistant" and say no, repeatedly and firmly, for you.)

Have the Requester Justify Why You Are Being Asked

When Linda was asked to serve on a committee, she followed up with the requester to see if this was a project that required her expertise in the barriers to women's advancement. The requester said that they just needed a senior faculty member, and so Linda declined by saying that she could better serve her employer in other ways. By having the requester articulate why she was asked, Linda secured a sound explanation for saying no and eliminated potential backlash. Caty, a manager at a tech company, suggests: "Have them tell you what unique and/or specific traits make you best suited to do this work. This will help the requester think critically about why they requested you do the labor as opposed to others who are also capable." This answer can help you identify other people who can do the task, so you are giving the requester an alternative when you decline.

Get Outside Help to Evaluate (and Decline) a Request

It is so easy to give advice to someone else, isn't it? It was a snap for any one of us to tell the other club members what to do, but just a teeny, tiny bit harder to solve our own problems. We relied on one another a lot for help, especially in the early days, like when Linda sent out an SOS to the club:

> **From:** Linda Babcock
> **Sent:** Friday, 8:24 AM
>
> **To:** Brenda Peyser, MJ Tocci, Laurie Weingart, Lise Vesterlund
> **Subject:** FWD: negotiation
>
> Help!!! This is the type of request I find IMPOSSIBLE to say no to. Help!!
>
> Linda
>
> **From:** Jane Doe
>
> Dr. Babcock,
>
> It is unlikely that you will remember me, but I am one of your former students. Through taking your course and reading your book, I had the knowledge and courage to negotiate my starting salary at my current job. I also used these skills when participating in a women's leadership program last year.
>
> I am excited to see and/or hear what your current research is telling you. I'd also like to ask if you would agree to speak to my leadership class. We have breakfast meetings every other month, where we hope to learn from other

strong women role models in the community. Many of my peers mentioned a desire to know more about negotiation. While I understand your time is precious, I can think of no one better to speak with us about this topic, so critical to advancing women in the workforce.

Our hope would be that you would consent to speak with us during a breakfast meeting in September. I ask many months ahead of time, in the hope that it would provide you with whatever time you needed among your other obligations. If you should need additional information to make a decision, I would welcome any questions you have. Thank you so much, for your work, for your dedication to learning more about this topic, and for considering my (our) request.

Sincerely,
Jane

In just under three hours, Linda had responses from all the club members. Laurie was first:

—**On Friday at 9:18 AM, "Laurie R. Weingart" wrote:**
This one is easy! You can't give a negotiation seminar to any group who asks. I only say yes if it's inside the university. This is way outside your job description. While you don't need to give a reason, I find that softens the blow. A reason like "no time" or "will be traveling" or "sorry, I don't do these types of outside seminars." Or name your price for which you'd be willing to do it.

Just say no (thank you).
Laurie

—On Friday at 9:33 AM, Brenda Peyser wrote:
I actually think this one is hard and that's because it's a former student upon whom Linda made a big impact. So she's appealing to Linda as a mentor—and she incorporates all the right "flattery" into her request. She's asking well in advance and we all know the danger in that because our calendars look clear, at least now. But Linda, you'll be teaching three morning classes in the fall, which means you won't be able to do a breakfast talk. I agree that you should say no (very nicely), and if there's someone else you can recommend, then do that.
B

—On Friday at 10:18 AM, Vesterlund, Lise wrote:
Dear Linda,

I agree this is a tough one—but despite sounding like a relatively easy invite to accept—it will take you time to prepare and be a major interruption to your week—and while satisfying and rewarding, you will be giving up more rewarding activities to do this.

Beginning to think that these smaller temporary requests are far more taxing than I used to. Just declined requests for two committee assignments and postponed a lecture. Never thought saying NO could feel so good.
Best
Lise

—On Friday at 10:47 AM, MJ Tocci wrote:
Linda and all-

Sorry to weigh in so late but I have a thought. I agree that this is a slippery slope and in the end, it will not be satisfying for you. You would accept thinking it's different from the daily fare, but walk away from the presentation realizing that it is more of the same. I recommend that you advise your student to give the presentation herself—based on your work, which she has embraced so enthusiastically and her successful experience negotiating her salary etc. She's got plenty to say and she can incorporate aspects of her leadership training too. It's time for her to step up and claim her expertise and successes.

This email stream is fantastic.

Cheers

MJ

Did you notice the various issues that we each raised in the email chain? Laurie was strategic about what to say yes to and gave advice on how to say no. Brenda encouraged Linda to find an alternative, warning her that the future always looks wide-open. Lise pointed out the impact on other work and Linda's implicit no. MJ put all the pieces together by providing the best solution—empowering the student to do this, and in doing so, unknowingly providing an effective no in the format of a "yes, no, yes" decline.

This was not an isolated incident—we often had emergency emails that helped us wrestle with a decision and provided support as we learned. Helping one another didn't just give us courage to say no, it also gave us knowledge and insight to craft effective nos that were accepted with limited, if any, repercussions. We hope that you, too, will get the support needed from friends and colleagues, perhaps by forming your own No Club (we'll provide advice on how to do this in the Appendix).

Successful strategies for saying no are especially important for women. In earlier chapters, we cited research that shows that there are situations where it is perfectly acceptable for men to say no to a request, while a woman who says no would face negative consequences. And this is particularly true for women of color. Women are expected to say yes, so when they say no it violates expectations and may trigger a negative response. Having the right words when you decline can mitigate the repercussions.

Say Yes While Saying No

Sometimes it isn't possible, practical, or wise to decline an NPT. This is often the case when you get a direct assignment. In these instances you need to get creative—can you fulfill the request in a different way that is better for you? Like Ury's "positive no," you need to figure out how to make the situation work to your advantage. We called these our plan Bs.

Offer an Alternative

Putting together the schedule of courses dogged Brenda every semester. It took a lot of work and always occurred at the busiest time of the year. We described earlier how her male colleague had avoided the task. She finally decided to address the situation and designed a solution that she presented as a fait accompli. Brenda: "We need to do course scheduling, and I've divided the job in half. You can pick the half you want and I'll do the other." Her colleague: "Oh, okay. I'll do the first half." Point goes to Brenda! But she sure waited a long time to ask, and when she did, her colleague readily agreed and then completed his half of the work on time. The lesson here is that people (men) may not volunteer to help, but if you give them a defined and fair scope of activity, it becomes much harder for them to decline.

Put Conditions on Your Yes

When Lise was encouraged by her institution to serve as a panel member for the National Science Foundation, she asked that she get a course reduction to free up time to do the extra work.

Consider Asking for Additional Resources

If you agree to take on the task, you may want to ask for staff or colleagues to help lighten your load and complete the task more expeditiously. When Laurie was asked to lead a curriculum review committee, she agreed upon the condition that the school hire an outside consulting firm to run focus groups and synthesize the results. Her insistence that her school hire an outside firm relieved her committee of a burdensome task and allowed them to focus instead on other important activities. While chairing the committee would still be a lot of work, she would have an outside partner support the committee.

Set a Time Limit

The task doesn't have to be yours forever. Negotiate a timetable for when the task should move to another person.

Do a B+ Rather than an A+ Job

For some NPTs, there are diminishing returns—that is, spending two hours on the task rather than one will only incrementally improve the quality of the outcome. Think about taking minutes in a meeting. Keeping A+ minutes may be a good strategy if you are junior, but if you are among peers it means you aren't participating as fully as everyone else (you're too busy looking at your laptop), and all the time you spend on a detailed three-page summary won't matter much. Instead, a quick list of bullet points outlining the decisions achieves the same result.

Turn a Request for Help into a Negotiation

Instead of doing the entire NPT, you might negotiate doing a part of it—the part you find most interesting. When the person requesting a new NPT is your boss, ask which of your current NPTs they can reassign so you have time to take on the new one. Let them know that you want to keep doing a good job on all your PTs and becoming overburdened won't allow that. Or you could point to an NPT that you would prefer to do instead. When Lise was asked to be on the website committee because she "had a good sense of colors," she asked if she could be on the recruiting committee instead.

These strategies and tactics have helped us navigate requests and reduce our NPT workloads, and we hope they will help you as well. Our patterns for saying yes are deeply engrained, and it takes determination and persistence to get your NPT load under control. In fact, simply saying no to new NPT requests is unlikely to get you the right work assignments. You can't just say no to all NPT requests; everyone needs to carry part of the load. You might also get NPT requests that you really want to take on and you need to consider how to make room for those. To get this right, you need to do a bit more work. You need to take a more comprehensive view of what you do and what you *want* to do, and we will help you with that in the next chapter.

CHAPTER 8

Optimize Your Portfolio of Work

·Our club got *really* good at saying no. We came to club meetings ready to share our victories. We toasted saying no to small and large asks—from a request to review a student's conference submission two hours before the Saturday-evening deadline to chairing a university-wide task force. But we need to come clean: while we eagerly celebrated our nos, we were embarrassed to admit to one another that there were times we wanted to say yes.

Laurie was the first to confess. She cared about several of her NPTs and enjoyed them, but she felt like she was falling off the "no" wagon when she agreed to do them, and was afraid to tell us. When she finally did, we recognized that we each had NPTs we were genuinely happy to do. But we had been so busy lightening our load to make time for our promotable work that we hadn't considered there were NPTs we enjoyed and that mattered deeply to us.

We knew we had to do some NPTs—everyone does, women and men. Organizations can't survive if we don't. So, while doing lots of NPTs may not help you advance, doing none could very well get you fired. Understanding this and wanting to do our share, our focus solely had been on not increasing our load any further. But it became clear that to improve how we spent our time at work, we needed to be intentional about *all* the work that we did. We had to move beyond giving new requests a simple thumbs-up or thumbs-down and instead think holistically about our entire portfolio of work, both promotable and non-promotable.

You should evaluate and reallocate your work assignments as you would the assets in your retirement portfolio. Imagine if your retirement portfolio changed over time with your high-return assets replaced by low-return options. You wouldn't let your financial future suffer if you saw your returns falling further and further below the market average—you would take action. Your time is also an investment and you can apply the same thinking to your work assignments. If you keep piling on NPTs (low-return assets) and these replace your PTs (high-return assets), then you will have work/work imbalance, and neither you nor your organization will see the full return from your efforts.

As we considered our portfolios of work along these lines, we saw that ours were poorly balanced, and we needed to change that. This chapter will walk you through four steps we used to create an *ideal portfolio of work*—the set of promotable and non-promotable tasks that allows you to be successful, reach your potential, and secure work/work balance.

The first two steps entail determining how much time to spend on NPTs and which NPTs are right for you. Your target will be your *optimal set of non-promotable tasks*. Think of this as the design phase—you are creating your ideal portfolio of work. The exercises at the end of the chapter will make this process concrete.

Next comes the execution phase, where you first change your current assignments to better align with your ideal work portfolio.

To do this, you are likely to cut back on the hours you spend on NPTs as well as change the types of NPTs you do. You might want to make dramatic and immediate revisions to reach your goal, but it's more likely you'll need to make changes gradually. You'll need to involve your supervisor to get your changes accepted and approved. The final step involves maintaining your ideal work portfolio. Requests will keep coming—see them as opportunities to keep moving closer to your goal. When your organization, or your career, undergoes changes, you have yet another opportunity to revisit where you are and where you want to be.

You will need outside help to succeed with this entire process. We certainly did, and our club was invaluable. We'll help you consider your own sources of support: how your supervisor can help and how you might involve friends, colleagues, and mentors in deciding what to do and how to do it.

How Much Time Should You Spend on NPTs?

The first step to best using your time at work is to understand how to split it between promotable and non-promotable work. If, like us, you struggle to get enough time for promotable work, you will benefit from determining how much time you need and want to spend on NPTs.

What NPT Load Does Your Organization Expect?

There will always be work that goes unrewarded, and organizations have norms for pitching in to get it done. We've heard many stories about "shirkers" in the workplace—colleagues who always seem to weasel out of doing certain tasks, the non-promotable work. They are always too busy or they do a mediocre job when assigned an

NPT. You don't want to be that person. So what is the minimum number of hours you should spend on NPTs? What is the expectation in your organization? Look around you and have your colleagues help answer this question.

Your organization is unlikely to have considered work assignments directly through the lens of promotability, and they are equally unlikely to have determined, let alone shared with you, the precise amount of time they think you should be spending on NPTs. While employee handbooks and job descriptions might provide detail regarding tasks that are core to a position, they rarely address non-promotable work. Highly regulated jobs, like those that are unionized, carefully lay out the activities that are within one's responsibilities, but even those often fail to specify NPTs.

Expectations for how much time you should be spending on NPTs are usually implicit, so you'll need to put in effort to figure out what the norms are in your organization. Expectations will vary across organizations, jobs, and people (because we have unique skill sets). What works at Google might not work at Amazon, what works for lawyers might not work for nurses, and what works for a seasoned employee might not work for a new hire. That means you need to account for the type of business you work for, the position you hold, and your rank to determine the load of NPTs you should carry. A word of caution here. We've seen in earlier chapters that expectations for NPTs vary by gender, and ideas (our own and others') about an appropriate load may be influenced by these biases. So be sure to look at everyone (women *and* men) with your position and rank to get an accurate picture of expectations. Further, keep in mind that these norms are likely to be more important for women than men. While men might have some leeway on meeting the expected NPT load, there is a stronger expectation that women should do their share. This is not to say that you need to live up to the higher expectations for women, but rather that knowing the norms will help you address these differences and reduce negative consequences for falling short.

You'll probably have to ask around to gauge expectations, and at this point, a general sense will do. Start by asking your mentors and friends in the organization, especially those who are highly successful, what they think might be expected. Try to get a sense of how your peers spend their day. If you work remotely or, for other reasons, can't observe them directly, be proactive. Offer to take them out for lunch or set up a call and ask if you can chat about how they spend their time at work. Maybe your female coworkers are reading this book too. Compare your completed exercises in Chapter 2 to their distribution of tasks and the amount of time they are spending on NPTs. Be sure to also check in with your male colleagues to see how they spend their time. This will give you an accurate picture of the full range of NPT loads among your peers.

If you feel comfortable, you can assess expectations by (carefully) asking your supervisor, who, remember, may not be familiar with the term *non-promotable tasks*. Find other words to talk about NPTs, perhaps "extra work" or "administrative tasks" or "support tasks" to avoid them inaccurately equating *non-promotable* with "not important." Assure them you are not trying to avoid this work, and that your goal is to contribute to the organization in significant ways (your PTs), while carrying an NPT load that conforms to the organization's expectations, and no less. Your colleagues and your supervisor may not have considered what work is or isn't promotable, or even be willing to discuss work as being non-promotable. For them, you might want to frame the question in terms of the specific PTs and NPTs that you have identified—for example, you could ask how much time someone in your position should plan to spend on client- versus non-client-related work. These sources of information will help you gauge how much time you should be spending on NPTs.

What NPT Load Is Best for You?

Determining the right amount of time you should spend on NPTs involves assessing the best use of your time and knowing what others expect of you. You need to know what is feasible in your organization (you've done that above), how you actually spend your time (you did that in Exercise 1.4, Chapter 2), and how you would like to spend your time.

The accumulation of more and more NPT work can be gradual, so it's easy to miss how you've suddenly become overburdened. Like the proverbial frog in a pot of slowly heating water, you don't realize you're in trouble until it's too late. We suspect that you are not spending too little time on NPTs and are probably spending more than your male colleagues are. If so, and if you show signs of work/work imbalance or work overload (from Exercise 4 in Chapter 6), then you need to decrease your NPTs to improve your health and well-being and to do the promotable work that your organization values most.

Think about alternative uses of your time. What would you do differently with your work and personal time if you spent less on NPTs? Understanding the consequences of your NPT workload can help you identify the opportunity costs—that is, the value of opportunities you missed while doing those NPTs. You may find that you want to spend more time on your promotable tasks (you have your PT hours from Exercise 1.4 in Chapter 2). Would you be better off moving some of your NPT time to specific PTs? Or do you simply want to free up time so you are able to pursue new and more rewarded tasks? Knowing that: How much time are you willing to devote each week to NPTs? You'll want to be objective, and a bit ruthless, in your analysis to end up with the right mix of promotable and non-promotable work.

Which NPTs Are Right for You?

Brenda, Linda, and Lise were stressed out about the time they spent on their NPTs, but Laurie felt less pressured. At first we were perplexed by this, but then we realized that Laurie had been careful about which NPTs she did. This lowered her stress level because she *liked* many of them and they felt right for her, which helped her avoid the resentment, anger, and frustration the rest of us felt when we were overloaded and had little time to do our promotable "real" work.

While Laurie was spread thin and pressed for time, she didn't reach the breaking point like the rest of us did. Besides her research and teaching, she also spent a lot of time serving her profession and university. Over the span of her career, she led professional associations, organized conferences, served on committees, led project teams, worked as a journal editor, and helped her department navigate difficult situations that arose. Her workload was heavy, but it didn't feel overwhelming.

Upon reflection, Laurie realized that her NPTs typically fell into one or more categories: 1) the task fulfilled her personally; 2) the task was appropriate for her position and rank and leveraged her expertise; 3) the task provided a good return on her time spent; 4) the task gave her a mental break; 5) the task fit with her current assignments. She gravitated toward tasks that fell into these categories and when possible steered clear of those that didn't. While she still had some crappy dead-end tasks in the mix, her NPTs were generally right for her. By considering your tasks along the lines of Laurie's five categories, you, too, can find the NPTs that are well suited for you.

NPTs That Fulfill You

In a perfect world, which NPTs would you want to do? Which do you like or dislike? Do you know why? Which correspond to your values?

Many of Laurie's NPTs fulfilled her. She had a sense of what resonated within, and that guided her responses to the work she took on. She enjoyed being in positions where she could innovate and have a positive influence. Leading the curriculum redesign for her school's MBA program was a task she carefully deliberated doing before agreeing, understanding that it would be a time-consuming and challenging NPT, especially in light of all her other commitments. She expected the task would last more than a year and require serious effort and knew that the time would need to come from somewhere. But the task appealed to her values—she wanted her school to provide students with a curriculum that included more big-picture thinking and opportunities for leadership development, and she believed her involvement could make a difference. This alignment led her to say yes, and for the eighteen months that followed, the demands on her were high. Her research productivity suffered—she had less time for it during the day, and it spilled over into evenings and weekends. She thought carefully about how to balance her portfolio, rolling off some long-standing committee assignments that others could do (all NPTs) while retaining the ones that were most interesting and impactful, and whenever she could, she delegated other tasks. The workload was exhausting, but at the same time, she found it energizing. The curriculum redesign created work/work imbalance and work overload, but Laurie knew that was temporary, and enjoyed her role in leading the effort to improve the education of future generations of students.

Camille, an epidemiologist for a public health agency, also chose the NPTs that were aligned with her values and goals and where she could make a real contribution—for her it was mentoring junior colleagues. Camille was in her mid-thirties, so she had solid experience but could relate easily to the younger women in her group. She was the only Black woman in her division, and many of the younger women of color, who were just starting out their careers, came to her for advice. Having successfully faced the challenges they were confronting, Camille knew how to help them navigate their paths, including the NPT requests they faced. While serving as a mentor was non-promotable, it was important to her, and she enjoyed the time she spent with her mentees. Camille told us that her personal mission statement guided her decisions about what NPTs to take on, and it kept her focused on what she cared about and found most fulfilling. She consulted with a group of more senior women about what to take on, and their advice ensured that her tasks were a good match for her values.

NPTs That Leverage Your Expertise

Which NPTs are best suited to your skills and abilities? Are there tasks that are better for you rather than someone else because of what you bring to the table? Laurie's research on teams and conflict management, along with her leadership experience in several professional associations, made her a particularly good candidate to lead the MBA curriculum review. She brought valuable knowledge and skills to the committee, and she was glad to perform NPTs that allowed her to use those assets in service of the school. At the same time, Laurie didn't want to take on NPTs that could be handled by someone who had more relevant expertise than she did or would benefit from doing the task (remember, an NPT for you might be a PT for someone else). While it would be easy for Laurie to organize the logistics for a conference she was hosting (she'd done it before), Brenda pointed out at a club meeting that one of the administrative support staff could handle the task more efficiently. The solution worked out for her and for the staff member, who received recognition at the conference and within his department for his exemplary performance on the task.

NPTs That Provide a Good Return on Your Time Spent

Which NPTs provide a better return to you and your organization? There are two ways to maximize the return on your time on NPTs: one is to select NPTs that are more beneficial than others, now or in the future; the second is to choose NPTs that limit the time you spend on them.

We talked earlier about the range of promotability of tasks, the continuum along which all tasks fall. While the promotability of some tasks is apparent, others fall into a gray area: they are not really promotable, but are more promotable than other NPTs. Tasks that have some degree of promotability will provide you with a better return on your time spent. They can provide a potential boost—though perhaps small or down the road—to your career. These tasks can help develop your skills, increase your exposure to leadership, provide important connections, or open up new opportunities for the future. We call these tasks *indirectly promotable*, as discussed in

Chapter 2, because they will not help you in the short run, but they might later on.

Serena was a hairstylist who took on a non-promotable task with an eye toward the future. She worked on commission at a salon—receiving a share of the fees collected from the clients she cut, colored, and styled each week. The salon was expanding to a new, larger location, and the salon's owner needed a few of the stylists to help design the layout of the new space. Even though this would take time away from her client work, Serena someday wanted to own her own salon and thought this would be useful experience, so she volunteered. She recognized that she was taking a short-term loss (lower client commissions) for a potential benefit longer term. She learned about space and equipment needs and saw the cost side of the business, which gave her knowledge that would pay off later.

The potential for future benefit should factor into your decision process, but consider carefully what those future returns might be. Don't be fooled by non-promotable work that *might* pay off later, when there is promotable work that will *definitely* have returns in the future. Know, too, that indirectly promotable NPTs often have diminishing returns; that is, they can be valuable at first—maybe you meet new people or develop new skills—but after a while, the benefit decreases dramatically. Remember Gerri, the software development manager, who was repeatedly asked to make in-house corporate presentations? Initially, she received recognition, but over time, the novelty wore off, and it cost her more than it benefited her. In assessing your portfolio, watch out for this "NPT creep," where a task that started out as indirectly promotable now is a full-blown NPT. An indirectly promotable task should not be a permanent part of your NPT load, and if you have one now, then consider off-loading it as you align your current assignments with your objectives.

NPTs that you can complete quickly can be a good option. Here, you spend a little time on the task while receiving credit or gaining other benefits. Maybe the task highlights you doing the right thing, or gives you visibility with the right set of people, or even uses your position to give others visibility. These activities are different from Laurie's curriculum redesign in that they require little effort for a noteworthy payoff—so they have a larger return. For example, our friend Kirsten is a graphic designer at a large sporting goods firm. Her boss asked her to serve on one of several employee health and wellness initiatives and let her choose which one. She knew she needed to say yes, but with a full schedule, she needed a lighter assignment, one that would require fewer hours. She asked us what to do. We suggested she contact people who had previously been involved to understand the time and effort expected for each, and then choose the one that required the least amount of time. She was able to meet the request, be a good corporate citizen, and, by selecting the assignment with the lightest number of hours, she salvaged time that she needed for promotable work. Like Kirsten, consider NPTs with a relatively low cost in terms of time and effort, or where the benefit is greatest.

NPTs That Give You a Mental Break

Are there some NPTs that you can complete without much thought? Ones that are straightforward and not too demanding can give you a much-needed break, and because the stakes are lower, they are less stressful. The change of pace allows you to feel a sense of accomplishment and, with that surge of positivity, go back renewed to more challenging work. Although NPTs are less rewarding careerwise, they often come with immediate positive feedback and appreciation. When challenging work has worn you out, these NPTs can be a welcome respite.

Laurie chose some of her NPTs because they were so different from her PTs. While she found research stimulating, the projects had unknown horizons, uncertain success, and a time span of years. Her NPTs were the opposite: they had well-defined objectives and established end dates. She felt appreciated when she delivered work that—while not rewarded with the status of a top publication—garnered gratitude and enthusiasm. She enjoyed having a mixed portfolio, and she felt proud when she was appreciated for doing a great job with shorter-term and easier-to-achieve objectives.

NPTs That Fit in with Your Current Assignments

Consider how your assignments complement one another within your portfolio of work. Do your PTs give you insights that are beneficial to your NPTs, or vice versa? Does the timing and type of work fit with your other assignments? For Laurie, NPTs that provided a leadership role were attractive, and they complemented her other activities. She kept an eye on the overall load she was balancing and the timing of her assignments. She tried to stagger the timing of her NPTs so that she wasn't dealing with too many at once, still had time for her PTs, and could meet deadlines on both.

The guidelines above and the exercises at the end of the chapter will help you determine how to allocate your time and which NPTs are best suited for you. Once you have a blueprint for your ideal portfolio of work, and more specifically, the amount of time you want to spend on NPTs and which are right for you, it is time to put your plan into action.

154 | THE NO CLUB

Align Your Current Assignments with Your Ideal Work Portfolio

Laurie had intuitively secured NPTs that were both a good match for her and a reasonable load given the amount of time she wanted to spend on both PTs and NPTs. The level and types of tasks reflected her preferences, aspirations, and the needs of her organization. We expect that as you start this process, you are unlikely to find your work portfolio as optimized as Laurie's. Instead, like Brenda, Lise, and Linda, you may find a vast distance between your ideal work portfolio and your actual one. If so, you need to make significant changes to close the gap. You'll need outside help to determine what you should change and how to go about it.

Whether you rely on a mentor, a friend, or a No Club, use this support to prioritize the tasks that are easiest to change and to guide you in how to do it. Are there smaller changes that would be uncontroversial? Do you have assignments that naturally belong to someone else and should be transferred or tasks where you can suggest taking turns or randomly assigning them? Your support network will help you identify creative ways to make small adjustments to your current workload. They also can help you prioritize and strategize larger changes that require your supervisor's involvement.

Engage Your Supervisor in the Conversation

While there may be work that you think you can readily hand off, reassigning it will generally require your supervisor's approval, so you'll want to solicit her feedback first. We recognize that not everyone has a positive, forward-thinking boss who understands how to keep employees motivated and engaged. Do you? Can you introduce the topic of NPTs? Can you speak with your supervisor without negative repercussion? If so, then discuss your work portfolio at an informal meeting or during your formal performance evaluation. You'll want to frame it as a collaboration about shared goals, where both you and your supervisor want to maximize the contribution you can make to the organization. If this sounds like negotiation advice, it is. This meeting with your supervisor is, after all, a negotiation that has the potential to be win-win. Laurie's and Linda's many years of teaching and researching negotiation provide the basis for our recommendations for how to have these conversations.

Introduce the topic by pointing out what you have accomplished in the last year, starting with promotable tasks. Your supervisor will appreciate hearing about your achievements—especially the PTs you are invested in and how you see them adding value to the organization and advancing your career. Then move on and describe the concept of NPTs. *Non-promotable work* is an easy concept to grasp, and it resonates with everyone we have spoken to over the last decade, including many executive teams. Your objective is to help your supervisor understand the dangers of being overloaded with non-promotable work and the benefits of you having work/work balance, where you will have more time to do the work that is most valued by the company (more on this in Chapter 9).

But you'll need to start slowly. Though you know the full list of NPTs that you want to remove, only introduce a few strategic ones in your first discussion, perhaps sharing some less-controversial tasks that are easier to take off your plate. Start with tasks below your skill level or that don't make sense for someone at your rank. Your supervisor might be surprised to see how much time you spend on these tasks. Realizing that they do not directly tie to the currency of the organization and do not best utilize your skills can motivate her to act. Suggest other tasks you will pick up—here's where having developed your ideal portfolio of work and a well-defined goal will help. Offer to pick up some new NPTs (ones that you want) or use the newfound time to focus on promotable tasks. Show that you are thinking strategically about maximizing your contribution to the organization, both in terms of PTs and NPTs. Make clear that you are not trying to decrease your contribution, but rather *increase* it by spending more time on the tasks where your value added is greater. Ask for her feedback on your ideas: Which changes seem most beneficial to the organization from her perspective?

Despite gradually introducing the tasks that you want to have reassigned, recognize that your supervisor could balk at making changes. Knowing how she might react can help you frame your conversation. You'll want to be respectful and objective. Suggesting, "I'd like to dump this dead-end task," is unlikely to have the same effect as "I'd like to talk about how to open up time in my schedule to do the work that matters most to the organization."

Having this conversation is, of course, more challenging if your supervisor is the reason you are overloaded with NPTs. Only you can judge whether the conversation is likely to be successful. If you anticipate objections or think your organization or supervisor is not ready for a discussion of NPTs, then *hold off*. Your manager might object to the notion that any task is non-promotable. In that case, soften the discussion by suggesting that some tasks are *more critical* to the organization (rather than using terms like *promotable*, *non-promotable*, and *currency*). If you can't have the conversation about task allocations now, don't give up. The next chapters will give you some ideas and actions to help you change the culture and enable you to introduce the topic in the future.

The goal of this conversation is to help your supervisor see how your assignments can change over time—to move them toward your goal. If you're lucky, she will grasp the problem and help remove or redistribute some of your unwanted NPTs, but more likely, you'll need to guide the conversation about how to reallocate work. To do that, you can identify someone else who would benefit from the task, help her reimagine the department or role that should be responsible for the work, or offer to prepare someone else to take it on in the future. Be ready with potential solutions for each of the NPTs you wish to remove. You might find one or more of your colleagues already doing similar work, and someone might take it outright or offer to swap one of their assignments with you. The process of changing your workload is gradual—get some activities reassigned now, and keep others on a list and try to off-load them later in return for taking on new tasks that are better aligned with your goals.

Be Strategic When Realigning Your Portfolio of Work

Chapter 7 focuses on saying no to new requests, but it also contains plenty of advice that you can use to change the tasks you currently have. Consider options like asking for additional resources, or setting a time limit to turn the task over to someone else ("how about if I handle it for another two months while I train a new person to take it on?").

Remember Francesca (Chapter 2), who worked at a law firm, and had gotten stuck assisting in reviewing, interviewing, and assessing summer associates? At her sixth-year review, she learned that her efforts in securing new recruits had thrown her off track for making partner. It was evident that she was spending more time on non-promotable work than her colleagues were. She now saw that recruiting summer associates was not a development opportunity for her, and so she should transfer the work to someone else as quickly as possible. Everyone else saw the recruitment process as her responsibility, so she needed to be strategic in getting it reassigned. She assessed all the components of the task and saw that certain parts should have been handed off long ago, so she started with those. No one questioned when she asked a newly hired staff member to solicit résumés and schedule interviews. More important, Francesca recognized that the recruitment process needed to be revised and improved; the screening and interview process were neither fair nor effective. Francesca easily rid herself of the administrative side of the job, but it was more complicated to withdraw fully. She recognized that improving the process would be her path out, and so she created and presented new recruitment procedures and offered to lead the implementation—with the clear agreement that she would transition out of recruiting at the end of the year. Under her proposed process, with clear qualification criteria in hand, staff could perform the initial screening. Then a small team could interview and rate qualified candidates, with staff summarizing the scores for each candidate. This put the tasks in the right sets of hands and used everyone's time well. Management readily embraced the plan and recognized Francesca for vastly improving the recruitment process. Francesca benefited too—she got credit for her initiative and successfully transitioned out of recruiting. With more time for promotable work, she increased her billable hours, and she and the firm were able to take full advantage of her legal expertise.

Maintain a Well-Balanced Portfolio of Work

Aligning your current assignments with your ideal portfolio of work will bring you closer to your goal, but it is always a work in progress. To keep pace, you need to keep moving closer to your goal, but also be ready to revise your vision of where you want to be. Opportunities will keep coming, your career will advance, and your organization will change. Make sure your tasks—PTs and NPTS—change in sync with these.

It takes effort to maintain the right load of NPTs, but don't be daunted by it. The support and good advice from our club helped us navigate this process. As you shape your ideal portfolio of work, identify your optimal set of NPTs, align your assignments accordingly, and, *finally*, reach the point of maintaining them, you will benefit from having outside support. Obviously, for us this was The No Club, but there are other options to help you keep your NPTs in line.

Form a No Club

In case you haven't noticed, we *love* our club. It has been invaluable in identifying the work we should do—both PTs and NPTs, honing strategies for aligning assignments with our objectives, and maintaining the right balance of tasks over time. For more than ten years, we've been able to rely on one another to tackle challenges with NPTs and navigate difficult requests and situations. The club is a safe space where we can bare our souls about our workload, help support each other's career progression, gain insight into why we agreed to take on too much, and receive understanding, not judgment.

We provided hours of help to one another over the years—we offered shoulders to cry on, strategies for saying no, and ideas for rebalancing our workloads. It was time well spent. For every hour we met, we saved many more, thanks to our greater confidence in saying no and better-balanced workload. Our colleagues, seeing us at the Union Grill drinking wine and engrossed in conversation, knew we were in a club meeting and left us alone. Some of them came to us later, though, and asked if they could join. Word got out, and we got more inquiries about the club. We shared our experiences with other women, and they started clubs in New York City, Berkeley, Philadelphia, and our hometown of Pittsburgh.

It didn't occur to us that what we were doing was special. On the contrary, we felt more like members of a "loser club" who needed help managing our lives. When we told people about the club, it was with mild embarrassment even though we knew how much it helped us. Brenda was in a cab in Washington, D.C., with a male colleague, and he asked what she had been up to. When she told him about the club, he begged to join. The cabdriver, who had been listening to the conversation, said that *he* needed a club too. Everyone in his family asked him to fix things, and he didn't know how to say no to them. Brenda was a little surprised—and puzzled—by their responses because, in our experience, it didn't seem like men really needed a club to strategize about saying no. Our research made it evident that, on average, women do more NPTs than men do, but that some men can have an excessive load. Our laboratory study revealed that while the majority of men rarely volunteered, some men did, and a few did it almost as often as women. These men could also benefit from being more strategic about how they spend their time.

Enlist a "No" Buddy

Is a club the best way to keep your NPTs in check? For us, the club was the right answer, but other effective options exist. What if you could go to a "no" buddy for advice? Could you use your mentor as a sounding board for strategizing about which NPTs are right for you? We've each served as a "no" buddy at some point for friends and colleagues as they needed help navigating NPTs.

Laurie received a call from Daniela, a former student, now working as a program manager for a large foundation. Daniela had to duck out of a department meeting ten minutes early, and, in her absence, her colleagues named her as their department's representative on a task force to review the foundation's grant-making guidelines. Laurie helped her with questions to identify the time commitment and consider issues like how this fit into her career path, what visibility she would gain by serving, and the risks of saying no. Importantly, she asked whether the assignment aligned with her preferred portfolio of work. Daniela was able to make an informed decision about how to proceed as a result. She learned that although there was a lot of work involved, it was a high-visibility assignment working with the top leadership of the foundation. She would be able to showcase her skills, interact with high-level decision makers, and have an effect on how monies were granted. With Laurie's help, she decided it was the right type of NPT to take on. Recognizing that if we add a task we also need to remove one, she identified her dreaded dead-end assignment on the holiday committee as something she could off-load to make time for the new task. A win-win that got her closer to her preferred set of assignments.

While a "no" buddy can ensure that you have some support and are not going it alone, consider the downsides. What if the person offers bad advice? This is a greater risk with a "no" buddy than with a club because you are soliciting only one person's opinion. Right out of college, our friend Anna received multiple job offers and chose the marketing department of a nationwide chain of hotels. Soon after joining, she connected with a "no" buddy who was senior to her and had a long tenure with the organization. He had joined when the company was much smaller and there were fewer administrative obligations. Whenever Anna asked him for advice on a new request, he said that it was a great opportunity and worthy of a yes. Anna figured he knew what he was talking about—he had an impressive career, but he was a bit out of touch with the types and number of tasks being handled today. Anna heeded his advice and took on a lot of extra unnecessary work; a year into her job she was doing far more NPTs than her peers. Her "no" buddy hadn't taken the time to dig into the consequences of each request, her ability to keep up with the work she had been hired to do, or the impact each assignment had on Anna's portfolio of work.

Our club insights, in contrast, resulted from deep discussions on how one of us should handle an issue. While Linda thought one approach to Laurie's conference-planning problem would work, Brenda had another idea. Those debates helped us sharpen our thoughts about whether to say no, and the best idea won out. And while a "no" buddy is there when you need them, a club also provides camaraderie and accountability that is difficult for a sole individual to provide.

Form a "No" Advisory Council

We were introduced to Camille, the epidemiologist we described earlier, after learning about her use of a "no" advisory council to help her be strategic about her NPTs. She was kind enough to say yes to us when we asked for some time to learn more about the group.

Camille's other Black colleagues warned her that due to her gender and race, "Everyone will ask you to do everything." And while she was comfortable saying no, she didn't know what she should say no or yes to. She followed the advice of a senior mentor to assemble a small personal group of advisors to help her consider the many professional service requests she received. This group was one of the most beneficial things she did to navigate her career. It consisted of three senior women of color, at different ranks, from different organizations, and with different experiences, who all cared about her success, knew what mattered to her, and knew what it would take to succeed. Their advice came from years of experience, and they kept her focused on securing the right NPTs for her career.

"No" advisory councils can include senior people from inside or from outside your organization. In choosing who to include in yours, consider the pros and cons of each. Insiders understand what work your organization considers promotable and how to best navigate the idiosyncrasies of the system. But, as more senior members of your organization, they have influence over how you are viewed within the firm, and sharing your vulnerabilities with them could negatively impact their opinion of you when you're being considered for a new project or role. While you don't run the same risk with outsiders (a pro), they have less insight into the politics and norms within your company (a con).

This speaks to an additional benefit of a club—because the power dynamic is equal, it is easier to be forthcoming about your weaknesses and share what might appear as deficiencies. Your club members, whom you've chosen carefully, will not have a direct impact on your career. They're a sounding board, not a launching platform. A club is a two-way street where peers gain equally from advice, feedback, and ideas. Organizing an advisory council like Camille's or finding a mentor both have great advantages for you, but more limited benefits for the advisors beyond the fulfillment of helping someone else.

In truth, any of the above ideas will help you balance your workload. We think a club, supported by this book, can help you the most, and we'd encourage you to start one. It isn't hard, but if you want advice based on our experience, we've included a do-it-yourself guide in the appendix.

As you consider the type of support that best fits your needs, think about your personality, time limits, and networks. Do you function better with a group? Can you identify the right people to participate? Will working with just one advisor fit more neatly into your schedule? Be sure that your club or advisor is willing to put in the time needed to help you (and each other)—you want consistency throughout the process.

Now it's time for you to create your own ideal portfolio of work and optimal set of non-promotable tasks using the exercises below. Doing so will help make room for the work that your organization values the most. Once you have identified how much time you should spend on NPTs and which NPTs you want, you'll be ready to have an initial discussion with your supervisor, as we described above. Getting the right set of NPTs is, honestly, one of the most important steps you can do not only for yourself, but also for your organization. As you'll see in the next chapter, your organization benefits when you allocate your work time in the best possible way.

EXERCISE 5: OPTIMIZING YOUR WORK PORTFOLIO

After completing the exercises from Chapters 2, 3, and 5, you should have a comprehensive list of your NPTs in terms of promotability, time spent, and how you ended up with them. The exercise in Chapter 6 illuminated whether you are suffering from work/work imbalance or work overload. This set of exercises will help you identify how much time you want to spend on NPTs and how to choose which are right for you, as well as which NPTs are worth keeping and which aren't. The answers are not one-size-fits-all. They depend on who you are, what type of organization you work for, and what your aspirations are. What we want for ourselves and what we enjoy can determine how happy we are with the work we do.

EXERCISE 5.1: Compare Time You Spend on NPTs with Your Organization's Expectations and Your Colleagues' NPT Hours

Step 1. How Much Time Do You Spend on NPTs?

Look back to Exercise 1.4 in Chapter 2, where you assessed your tasks for promotability. Transfer over the tasks that you rated low in promotability and the time spent and insert that information here. Take a second look at the tasks you rated as moderately promotable and include them as well if you think they might be more non-promotable than you first thought. How much time are you spending on NPTs per week?

Task (NPTs only)	Hours/week
Total NPT Hours per Week	

Step 2. Assess Your Peers' NPT Hours

1. Look at colleagues who hold positions similar to yours (both men and women, if possible). How much time are they spending on NPTs?
2. Who is spending the least amount of time on NPTs? The most?

Step 3. Assess Organizational Expectations

1. Does your organization have formal expectations for time spent on NPTs? If so, what are they? If not, are there implicit guidelines?
2. If your organization has not outlined the expectations for time spent on NPTs, what do you think the upper and lower bound for NPT hours might be? Who can you ask without worrying about sending a bad signal?

Step 4. Compare Your Hours to Expectations and Peers

1. Where do you land in comparison to expectations? To your peers? Are you higher or lower than average? By a lot or a little?

Name	Weekly	
	Actual Hours	Expected Hours
Me		
Peer 1		
Peer 2		
Peer 3		

2. You should now be able to judge the NPT hours that are reasonable for your position. Is a couple of hours a week enough? A day? A couple of days? Should you change the number of hours you spend to better conform to your peers?

EXERCISE 5.2: What Is the Right Number of NPT Hours for You?

You've identified what your organization expects and how much time you and your peers currently spend on NPTs. Your next task is to figure out how many hours you *want* to spend.

Step 1. Do you show any signs of carrying too heavy a load of NPTs? Do you have work/work imbalance? Are you suffering from work overload? Check your answers to Exercise 4 in Chapter 6.

Step 2. If you were to decrease the number of NPT hours you spend per week, what would you do instead? Would this change be good for you, your career, and/or your family? Could you do a better job on your other tasks or take on more or new promotable tasks? Could you reduce the hours you spend trying to catch up in the evening? Spend more time with friends and family? Read a book for pleasure? Develop a new hobby?

Step 3. Considering your answers to Exercise 5.1 above, how many hours should you spend on NPTs per week? (This number should reflect what the organization expects, what your peers are doing, and what you aspire to.)

EXERCISE 5.3: Determining Which NPTs Are Right for You

Step 1. Look at your list of NPTs from Exercise 5.1. Think carefully about the tasks on your list and rate them from 1 through 3, according to the following descriptions:

- "1" is a task that you definitely want to do.
- "2" is a task that you don't mind doing but would be just as happy for someone else to take on.
- "3" is a task that you would be relieved to hand off.

In rating your tasks, consider the attributes we discussed in the chapter:

- Does this task fulfill you?
- Does the task leverage your expertise?

Task (NPTs only)	Hours Spent	Rating 1-3

- Is there a good return on the time you spend?
- Does the task give you a mental break?
- Does the task fit with your current assignments?

Once you've rated the tasks, identify all the 1s and the 3s. The 1s are keepers, and the 3s can be targeted to go to someone else.

Step 2. Now, think of the NPTs that your colleagues do that you would rate as a "1," a task you would definitely like to do. Would you prefer these tasks to some of your current NPTs? If so, add them to your list.

Step 3. Take your rated list of tasks (for now, the 1s and the 2s), along with those tasks you'd like to pick up from your colleagues. Assess the total time commitment. Is it consistent with your number of NPT hours from Exercise 5.2 above? How would you change the list to make it match the goal you set for hours spent? Which NPTs would you get rid of? Finalize this list so that the tasks match the time you wish to allocate. This is your optimal set of NPTs, the tasks you should strive for as your current assignments change and as you respond to incoming requests and opportunities.

CHAPTER 9

Organizations Benefit When Employees Share Non-Promotable Work

Up to this point, we have focused on the inequitable allocation of NPTs from a woman's perspective—how and why women are burdened, and what you, as a woman, can do to improve your situation. However, the inequitable allocation of non-promotable tasks is not just a problem for individual women, it's also a problem for your organization, and in this chapter we explain why. *Improving the management of NPTs doesn't only help women; it helps organizations meet key business objectives.*

Most employers haven't considered how the distribution of NPTs impacts their employees' ability to contribute to the organization, nor have they realized that it affects the quality of employees they can attract and retain. Employees are an organization's most important asset, and how they allocate their time across tasks is perhaps *the* most important business decision, so getting it right has real consequences for the organization's health and prosperity. In this chapter, we show how changing the allocation and reward structure of non-promotable work can advance five key business objectives that drive productivity and profits:

1. Utilizing the workforce most efficiently
2. Creating a culture where everyone pitches in
3. Promoting an engaged and satisfied workforce
4. Retaining valuable employees
5. Attracting the best talent

We will demonstrate how current policies and practices associated with unrewarded work interfere with meeting these objectives, and we will present research to back up these bold claims. But first, we'll share a disturbing case study of what happened in one organization, where its mismanagement of non-promotable work harmed both its employees and the financial health of the organization.

Teresa, an aeronautical engineer, began her career at Winthrop Air in the operations planning group. Teresa was quickly identified as a "high potential" employee, and her (mostly) male coworkers saw her as a team player and respected her for her abilities and hard work. After a stellar twelve-year track record, she was promoted to assistant VP of operations. When the CEO learned that she was successfully mentoring junior female employees, he tasked her with starting a company-wide mentoring program. Teresa committed herself to the work, sometimes at the expense of her other duties. She developed and delivered a training program for potential mentors, identified candidates for mentoring, designed a system for pairing mentors with mentees, and did periodic check-ins with everyone involved to ensure the quality of mentorship was high. These programs paid off—mentors, mentees, and their supervisors were happy with the program, and retention levels of those involved increased. The CEO praised her for her innovative leadership and contributions to the company.

For Teresa, working on the mentorship program was exciting at first, but three years in, the nature of the work had changed. Teresa had completed the creative and challenging components of launching the initiative—including designing the training for mentors—and now the tasks had become far more routine and logistical, replete with mind-numbing details like scheduling mentor luncheons. The work didn't require a graduate degree in engineering or management, and Teresa knew she wasn't using her time in the best way, but she had no additional help or anyone to hand the program off to. She met with her CEO and proposed names of staff who could take over the day-to-day operation of the program and asked that he appoint one of them so she could return to her work on engineering systems. He said he'd think about who would be a good fit, but several reminders later, he hadn't done anything about it. Teresa kept waiting and waiting for him to act, all the while working away on the mentoring program.

Clear proof of Teresa's career getting off track came when her direct supervisor, Rosaria, who had successfully served as VP of operations, suddenly left for a CEO position at another airline. Years earlier, everyone considered Teresa to be her natural successor, but now, Teresa was spending less time on the high-profile department work, mostly because of the mentoring program. When it came time to select the next VP of operations, the CEO chose Henry, a talented senior industrial engineer. Henry was well respected and had spent a number of years designing processes for efficient aircraft maintenance, which created tremendous cost savings for the company. While Henry provided clever technical solutions, he had limited leadership and managerial experience.

Why did the CEO promote Henry instead of Teresa? While management saw Teresa as a valuable leader, she had spent a large portion of her time (at the request of the CEO!) on an initiative that impacted the bottom line indirectly, rather than directly, as Henry's work had. While Teresa's program mattered greatly to the company, its effect was difficult to track, and she was no longer utilizing the specialized skill set she had been hired for. The work she had been doing was *non-promotable*. When selecting Rosaria's replacement, the CEO chose the person he thought made the greatest contribution to the company's bottom line.

Throughout the chapter, we will use Teresa's story to demonstrate the negative consequences of mismanaging non-promotable work. We will show how saddling Teresa with NPTs had wide-ranging effects on Winthrop Air: allocating resources inefficiently, harming the company culture, creating a dissatisfied and disengaged workforce, increasing turnover, and reducing the company's ability to attract the best talent. While we won't ignore the effect the CEO's decision had on Teresa herself, we want to point out the negative impact this had on the company as a whole. We think that once organizations see the damage, they'll want to follow our suggestions to improve the allocation of non-promotable work and avoid the fate that befell Winthrop Air.

Improve the Management of NPTs to Utilize Your Workforce Most Effectively

Using people's time well drives organizational success, which means that organizations lose money and productivity when the assignment of tasks—including NPTs—is not strategic. Teresa was passionate about mentoring, but managing the logistical details of the program was a poor use of her time. While she was the right person to provide vision and direction for the program, the logistics could have been handled by anyone else who had the appropriate skills and job responsibilities—they didn't require an expert in operations. Teresa's time was better spent on her core responsibilities, and it would have been better for both her and the organization to put her on the work that leveraged her specialized skills.

Supervisors can avoid these potential pitfalls and assign NPTs to the right people by paying attention to how employees perform the task and how else their time could be used. Assessing and comparing the performance of relevant employees will help identify who is best suited for the task. As an example, suppose Shandra and James are both in sales and spend their time recruiting new clients (highly promotable work). You need one of them to work on a new sales tracking database with the IT department (non-promotable work), which requires basic skills that both Shandra and James possess. Both can do it and would do it well. Who should you ask? Shandra always steps up, so it's easy to say, "Let's get Shandra on it." Before doing that, you need to think about the downside of assigning this task to Shandra, because it will take Shandra away from recruiting new clients, which helps the company meet its revenue goals. If Shandra is better at recruiting clients than James (let's say in this instance, she is), then the organization loses out by "getting Shandra on it." The firm loses more value—new clients that bring in revenue—when Shandra does the non-promotable task than when James does it. The likelihood of allocating the NPT incorrectly is even higher if Shandra is *also* better than James at the database task. While tempting to get Shandra on it because she is better at it, this simple rationale is misguided. To make the correct assignment, the manager needs to assess how valuable the work is on both tasks and how much better Shandra is at each of them. With client recruitment being the more valuable task, Shandra should only be assigned to the database task if she is *much* better on the database task than James. In particular, her advantage over James on the database task would have to be substantially larger than her advantage over James on sales.

In the example above, the organization knows the relative skills of its employees and can assign the NPT accordingly. But how do organizations learn who is good at what? A straightforward approach is to observe the tasks new employees excel at and struggle with, but an unequal distribution of NPTs throws a monkey wrench into our ability to do so. If we give more NPTs to new female recruits than to males, we make it difficult to infer who is better at what. To identify the relative skills of a new set of recruits, we need to assign them *similar* work and give them *similar* opportunities to demonstrate talent. When we don't, we have a hard time identifying their individual abilities, and we risk assigning work in a way that won't use their skills to the fullest.

Building optimal work portfolios for each employee so that a business can meet its objectives won't happen unless managers make work assignments thoughtfully. Instead, they tend to allocate NPTs reactively, by considering how to hand off a task quickly, rather than how to have it completed effectively. That's certainly what happened at Winthrop Air, where supervisors regularly asked for volunteers when tasks arose. Asking for volunteers is just one of many common mistakes made in assigning work. Others include asking the person most likely to say yes, or assigning it to the person who seems "right" for the job and delivers A+ work on everything. Any of these increases the likelihood that a woman ends up with the NPT. That is not how work ought to be assigned, nor does it produce the best results for employees or the company. Ideally, organizations should consider the entirety of work to be performed and ensure that all employees have equal opportunity to demonstrate their skill and talent, and thus reach their potential at work.

We know that someone reading this book will say, "But wait, women are better than men at doing NPTs, so shouldn't that factor into assignments?" Ask yourself *how much better* and whether the alternative use of their time justifies the assignment. Keep in mind that while women might be adept at NPTs because they've handled these tasks for years and "practice makes perfect," they are likely to accomplish even more if they aren't bogged down by this unrewarded work and can spend more time on promotable work. Given the chance, men also will develop expertise in NPTs, but since we haven't given them that chance (yet), women carry the load.

There is dramatic historical evidence of the cost associated with US companies failing to use their human resources most effectively. White men accounted for 94 percent of people in highly skilled occupations in 1960, and it is inconceivable that, in all of those jobs, white men were more qualified than everyone else. While women and people of color were hurt by their inability to secure jobs for which they were well-qualified, organizations and society in general were hurt as well because of the failure to utilize their talent.

In fact, research has estimated how much productivity was gained by reducing discrimination and improving the allocation of talent. In the United States, between 1960 and 2010, output per worker grew enormously, and as much as 40 percent of that growth occurred because organizations improved how they allocated people to jobs. (Other factors, technology chief among them, account for the other 60 percent of growth in productivity.)

Maximizing productivity and profits means efficiently utilizing your human assets. To do that, assign new employees similar portfolios of work so that you can learn about their skills. Once you've identified each employee's skills, then assign tasks by considering the value of the work, performance on the task, alternative use of their time, and how this compares to other employees. When you do, you'll be using your organization's resources to its fullest advantage.

Improve the Management of NPTs to Create a Culture Where Everyone Pitches In

After Teresa lost the promotion, her enthusiasm for the mentoring program languished. She realized that the time she dedicated to it took time away from more promotable work and interfered with her advancement. Her other colleagues realized this as well, especially the women. They noticed that Teresa's work on the mentoring program didn't seem to matter to the company. They began to realize that the problem was bigger than just Teresa—they all spent much more time than the men on work that didn't help them advance. When supervisors had asked for volunteers, the women had stepped up. They had helped colleagues with their work, served on company-wide committees and task forces, pitched in to solve problems, and organized the social activities. After Teresa's experience, they stopped doing this work bit by bit and started to protect their time to focus on promotable tasks. But the non-promotable work still needed to be done, so who would do it now?

When an organizational culture evolves from one where everyone pitches in to an individualistic one, as it did at Winthrop Air where everyone was out for themselves, important activities may be delayed or left undone. Lise remembers one particular morning early in her career, when she arrived at work a few hours later than most of her colleagues. They were busy at their desks, like any other day, but this wasn't like any other day. The reception area furniture—couches, tables, chairs—was missing! The space was empty. Lise knew there were no plans for construction or painting, so she was perplexed. How had the department's furniture vanished?

She checked in with her colleagues. Each of them had noticed that the furniture was gone, but none of them had called about it because it wasn't *their* job. A dozen people had a chance to act, hours had passed, and no one had done a thing. Lise took it upon herself, and her first phone call revealed that someone had misread a work order. The movers were supposed to take furniture from the fifth floor, but instead took it from Lise's department on the fourth floor. By then it was too late; a truck was en route to the storage facility with some of the furniture, but worse, much of it had already been discarded. Because no one owned the problem and acted right away, the department had to buy new furniture.

In situations like Lise's, where people avoid doing non-promotable tasks that arise, costs quickly mount up. Organizations need employees to step up and take responsibility, even if the task is outside their job description (like making a call about missing furniture). In a study of over 3,500 business units, researchers found that higher levels of employee engagement in these unrewarded everyday activities were associated with higher productivity and efficiency.

Cultivating a culture where everyone pitches in and does what needs to be done benefits both employees and the organization. Making sure that NPTs are assigned fairly means that employees will be willing to step up. That's good citizenship, and it results in a healthy employee environment and an equally healthy bottom line.

Improve the Management of NPTs to Create a More Engaged and Satisfied Workforce

When Teresa was passed up for promotion, the women felt betrayed. The CEO had assigned her to work on the mentoring program and overlooked her contributions by not promoting her to a position for which she had been trained and was ready. The women talked in small groups about how it wasn't just Teresa's work that was being discredited, but how the work they performed and thought mattered was going unnoticed as well. Their mood was sour, and their frustrations became viral; before long, the entire workforce was affected, not just the women. Why bother working hard if the company was going to ignore their efforts? Why agree to help other people if it never showed up on their performance evaluations? The company was no longer a fun, positive, and supportive environment where everyone pitched in to get the job done. People started looking out for themselves, and job satisfaction fell.

Dissatisfied employees can become disengaged, which affects organizational performance and the bottom line. Disengagement costs US companies up to $550 billion per year. Research consistently shows that when employees perceive their organization's procedures to be unfair or unjust, they are more likely to become detached from their jobs. In a meta-analysis of over 450 studies (that surveyed 2.7 million employees across 112,000 business units in 96 countries), Gallup reports a striking relationship between employee engagement and economic outcomes: the top-quartile business units on the measure of employee engagement outperform bottom-quartile business units by 10 percent in customer loyalty, 18 percent in sales productivity, and 23 percent in profitability. If you need more convincing, a meta-analysis combining the results of over three hundred studies involving more than fifty-four thousand people revealed a robust positive correlation between job satisfaction and job performance. Making sure your employees are engaged and happy yields better business results.

The ill effects of overloading women with NPTs compound the problem of disengagement. When women do more NPTs, they struggle to perform the same amount of promotable work as men. The women's workload—and stress level—increase because they simply cannot match the men's output on promotable tasks. Then, as the women commiserate about how overloaded and stressed they are, a new culture forms from their shared experience—it becomes part of the reality of the organization. Eventually, the aggregation of individuals' stress takes a toll on the organization as a whole.

Stress, as we've seen, is detrimental to individuals, but it also affects organizations through lower productivity, and more accidents, absenteeism, and employee turnover. The World Health Organization has called stress the "health epidemic of the 21st century," and some estimates suggest that it costs American businesses up to $300 billion a year.

How can your organization reduce this stress? Make sure that your employees have a balance of promotable and non-promotable work that helps them reach their potential and feel fulfilled by and engaged in their jobs. Satisfied employees are more motivated, more likely to internalize the organization's goals and values, put forth extra effort, and remain with the organization. Studies across the globe find that satisfied and engaged workers create higher customer loyalty, productivity, quality of performance, and safety, and lower employee turnover and absenteeism.

Improve the Management of NPTs to Retain Valuable Employees

When the company chose Henry to become the new VP, Teresa was crushed, and before long, she left for a VP position at another regional airline. By overtaxing Teresa with non-promotable tasks, the company ultimately lost one of its most valued employees. Unrewarded at Winthrop Air, she looked for greener pastures.

This is not uncommon. A 2019 report by the Work Institute indicates that the top reason people voluntarily leave their organization is to pursue better opportunities for career growth and advancement. Another survey of almost four thousand employed women from over seventy countries looked at why women specifically leave their jobs. Both studies agree on the major reasons women leave: the work is not meaningful or interesting, the opportunities for career progression are limited, and the rewards for skills and talents are unsatisfactory. These all tie in with the promotability of work: carrying a large load of non-promotable work causes women to leave because their assignments are routine and not impactful, reduces their career opportunities, or results in limited rewards—the characteristics of NPTs we described in Chapter 2. A 2021 McKinsey report concurs; women, more than men, are emerging as stronger leaders by engaging in extra work to support their teams and by contributing to diversity, equity, and inclusion initiatives. Because this critical work is often unrewarded, the report concludes that "Companies risk losing the very leaders they need right now . . ."

An inequitable distribution of NPTs can also result in the loss of valuable talent if women see it as a sign of broader gender disparities. A study of women in the construction industry found that those who perceived higher levels of gender inequity in their workplace were more likely to consider quitting their jobs.

Voluntary turnover should concern all organizations—it's very expensive. An estimated forty-one million people in the United States voluntarily quit their jobs in 2018, and during the COVID-19 epidemic, women quit in record numbers. The Society for Human Resource Management estimates that each departure costs about a third of that worker's annual earnings, but other estimates are even higher. We would add that organizations striving to improve gender diversity and inclusiveness make it much harder to do so if they are losing women who are burdened with NPTs.

It doesn't have to be this way. Think about your employees—is there someone like Teresa whose skills are not well utilized on her assignments? Are there employees who are weighed down with non-promotable work because they volunteered, helped others, or were assigned this work? You can—and should—take steps to fix this and retain your valuable employees.

Improve the Management of NPTs to Attract the Best Talent

The culture for female employees imploded when Teresa left for a VP position at another regional airline. The company had spent more than a decade establishing its reputation as a great place for women, and that collapsed, virtually overnight. As turnover increased, the word spread, and the company struggled to attract new female talent.

When deciding whether to accept a job offer, two-thirds of both men and women explore whether the organization has positive role models who are like them. This is *especially* true for women in male-dominated fields and women of color. Without female role models, women will not see themselves as the type of person who can advance in the organization.

Companies have increased their focus on recruiting female talent and are spending significant amounts of money to do so. The best way to recruit women is to be known as a great place for women to work. A simple internet search of the "best workplaces for women" shows countless articles and surveys that rank companies on this metric. Companies that don't make the cut have a harder time hiring women employees because, just as employees leave organizations where they can't advance, they judge new ones on that basis as well. Changing how you allocate and reward NPTs will create opportunities for women to succeed, and this, in turn, will help you attract the best female talent.

Let's turn back to Winthrop Air. Their mismanagement of NPTs meant that women, and one prominent woman in particular, were encumbered with work that management didn't recognize as critical to the company's success. If Winthrop Air had better managed the allocation of NPTs, Teresa might have remained and become the new VP of operations, and the company would likely have seen greater productivity and profits. The other women in the firm would have had the opportunity to handle more of the promotable work, thus making their own contributions to the bottom line. Additionally, Winthrop Air would have benefited from an improved company culture, strong employee satisfaction, reduced turnover because of an effective mentorship program, and robust hiring of the most qualified candidates.

How could they have achieved those gains? What should they have done differently? Fortunately, we have answers. The next two chapters will focus on how women like Teresa and her colleagues can kick-start change and how organizations can better manage non-promotable work.

CHAPTER 10

How to Seed Change in Your Organization

The management at Winthrop Air got it wrong. They should have provided employees equal opportunities for success and allocated work to best utilize the talents of their workforce. Instead, they disproportionately shouldered women with non-promotable work and in doing so harmed morale and the bottom line. They ignored the crucial fact that fixing NPTs isn't just good for women, it's also good for business. The moral of their story is simple: companies need to change the way they manage non-promotable work. Had the women at Winthrop Air been aware of the perils of NPTs, they might have helped their employer see it needed to address the problem. Changing an organization—whether Winthrop Air or your own—needs to start somewhere, and individual employees, like you, can spur management to act. While this may sound daunting, you can be optimistic about the possibility of change, and you can be an agent of that change.

How can you get the ball rolling? Start seeding change within your organization by educating people about the problem and showing them how to solve it. Your goal is for your organization to embrace your ideas and create processes that improve how it allocates and rewards NPTs. While your individual efforts will be non-promotable in the short run, over time they will pay off as NPTs become more equitably distributed. This chapter looks at the bottom-up process that you and your allies can undertake to ready your organization for change. But please know that this isn't only up to you. The next chapter looks at what your institution can do to fix the problem to secure lasting improvement in how employees spend their time at work.

When we think of organizational change, we usually envision a top-down process in which leaders set a new course that others follow. But change doesn't have to start at the top; you can be instrumental in activating a change initiative from any level, and there are a number of reasons to be optimistic that when it comes to NPTs you will succeed in readying your organization and jump-starting the process.

First, understand that organizational practices gradually evolve; they're not set in stone, and can change when there are growing and persistent demands from employees or management. We are not always conscious of the norms that guide our behavior, and we rarely question them; we may assume that if "this is how we do it," then it must be the best way. Practices and norms arise because we need a way to coordinate our behavior, not because the practice we adopt is the best one (like Brenda always taking notes at a meeting). As you begin to question the practices of assigning NPTs to women and suggest new ones that are better and/or fairer, you pave the way for new norms, and these improvements prepare the organization for broader change. We think of these as small, but important, wins.

Second, know that change is easier when an existing practice conflicts with the organization's mission. As we saw in the previous chapter, women carrying the brunt of NPTs is at odds with organizational goals of optimally utilizing the workforce, retaining and attracting talent, creating a culture where everyone pitches in, and keeping the workforce engaged and satisfied. This gulf between the company's mission and its practice is an important part of the message for change. Had employees at Winthrop Air recognized how the mismanagement of NPTs was harming the company, they could have made a persuasive case that motivated the need for change.

Third, there is a "eureka" moment when leaders recognize the inequitable allocation of NPTs and its downstream effect on the organization's diversity challenges. Research in both psychology and economics find that eureka-like solutions lead to faster and more sustainable change, because once you see the right answer, it suddenly becomes obvious and can't be unseen. Organizations struggling with the advancement and retention of women are quick to see that a discrepancy in work assignments hinders the success of these efforts. They recognize that non-promotable work suppresses women's compensation and advancement and that providing equal opportunity hinges on changing how people spend their time at work.

Many of the strategies we share with you are grounded in *issue selling*—that is, how to take an idea and make it concrete, focus attention on it, demonstrate its viability, and reduce the perceived risk of implementing it. We base other strategies on our own successes. When we started on the journey of discovering NPTs, our institutions were unaware of the detrimental consequences, but as we shared what we learned, they came to recognize the problem and began the process of changing.

Organizational change can start like a grassroots movement—by people passionate for improvement sowing seeds of resistance. The bottom-up change process entails three steps: create awareness, identify your allies, and work with those allies to build momentum for change.

Create Awareness

Lise arrived early to set up for a lunchtime research talk she was giving at another university about non-promotable tasks. During her presentation, she put this image on the screen.

In the photo, Kirstjen Nielsen, then United States secretary of homeland security, is leaving a meeting regarding former president Trump's border wall. Lise noted that Nielsen was the key figure at the meeting—being head of the department of homeland security, the third-largest department in the US government, this was her meeting and her policy agenda—but despite that, she was carry-

Credit: Sarah Silbiger/*The New York Times*/Redux

ing a box of coffee from the meeting. The expectation that women handle these unrewarded tasks is so ingrained that her colleagues likely didn't notice, and she may not have either. The incongruity of the scene might even have escaped the newspaper publishing the photo. We are so accustomed to women stepping up to the task that we don't notice it when they do.

The mostly male audience recognized the absurdity of the image. Then, Lise shared with them that one of their colleagues, a female junior professor, had arrived early to set up their lunch. Only then did they realize the problem was in their house too. All around us, all the time, women perform unrewarded work and we fail to notice.

That is how Lise began the process of raising awareness. She used some basic strategies that you can employ to get colleagues to listen, understand, and be willing to address the issue of NPTs. Present the issue in relatable terms, tie the issue to important organizational goals, and be persistent.

Present the Issue in Relatable Terms

Introduce the *promotability of work* in conversations with colleagues and management, with a goal of making it part of your organization's vocabulary. Help your coworkers see how promotable and non-promotable tasks propel or prevent people's success in your organization. When you talk about NPTs, use language that your coworkers understand, value, and can relate to. How does your organization communicate ideas—through data, stories, research? Do they use logic or emotional appeals to make arguments? Where do people typically exchange ideas (e.g., meetings, the "water cooler," social gatherings, instant messaging platforms, chat rooms)? Introduce your ideas in a way that conforms to the norms of your organization. Don't describe the issues around NPTs (or their solutions) as particularly radical—research suggests that change agents find more success when they describe new ideas conservatively and introduce them slowly. Introduce the concept of promotable and non-promotable work and let people share their stories. Facts and figures help to identify the problem and demonstrate its scale, but stories communicate the toll NPTs can take in a way that charts and graphs cannot. The more your colleagues engage in discussions, the more the language becomes embedded in your organization. The seminar audience got it when Lise displayed the photo of Kirstjen Nielsen and then related it to the female faculty member who set up their lunch. While the language of NPTs was new, it helped them see what they hadn't noticed before—the dead-end work that women were doing. Non-promotable tasks became part of their language, and it was an easy seed to plant.

To avoid potential pushback, start defining and discussing NPTs *before* framing the issue in terms of distribution of work and inequity. Your colleagues—male and female—will relate to the idea of promotability of tasks. Use definitions and examples from this book when discussing work with colleagues and relate it to current work assignments at your office. If a coworker lands a high-profile client or assignment, congratulate them on scoring a highly promotable task; if another complains about getting dragged onto another low-profile committee, sympathize by noting that the assignment is low in promotability. Help managers and coworkers understand what affects the promotability of a task using characteristics described in Chapter 2 (the task's visibility, impact on organizational currency, need for specialized skills, or opportunity to develop skills or build relationships).

Had they known about NPTs, employees at Winthrop Air could have used these strategies to slowly introduce the idea of the promotability of work, particularly to the female employees who were dragged down by NPTs. There was a lunch-and-learn program in place (organized by a woman), which would have been a natural forum to introduce the idea. There they could have defined promotable work and engaged their colleagues in deciphering the promotability of various tasks in the organization. Imagine the stimulating discussions they could have had where opinions varied and employees debated what mattered to the company (and themselves). By making the promotability of work part of your organization's vocabulary, you will develop a collective awareness of the types of assignments that matter most for advancement. This will help managers and employees identify NPTs and question how they are distributed.

Tie the Issue to Important Organizational Goals

Once your colleagues and managers understand which tasks are low in promotability, help them see how the allocation of NPTs may be interfering with organizational goals. In doing so, consider: What are the organization's goals? What are the critical strategic issues for top management? What concerns exist in the organization (e.g., stress or turnover)? You might not know what keeps your leadership awake at night, but you can glean some relevant information from documents you've already used in Chapter 2's exercises, like the strategic plan and mission statement, and what messages are emphasized in company-wide meetings, on the intranet, and in corporate email. Use these to frame your discussion of NPTs.

For example, you could help your manager see that the current inequity in allocating NPTs makes it difficult to identify talent because those overburdened with them don't have as much opportunity to demonstrate skills on promotable work. Or that there might be a mismatch of task and employee that results in lost revenue and costs to the organization. Help them see that when a supervisor asks for volunteers, the task is unlikely to go to the person who can most afford to take the time. Worse still, the process creates inequity for women, especially women of color—consequences that are often at odds with an organization's values and goals for equal opportunity. Lise gave talks on this very topic throughout her university, raising awareness and demonstrating how NPT allocation negatively affected the organization's goals. She introduced research on the disparity of NPT workloads for men and women and described how it affects both women and their organizations. If your organization values data like hers does, then introduce our research on how women end up with more NPTs not because they enjoy it, but because we expect them to. You can reference this book or other works we've published on the topic.

Be Persistent

Through the process of seeding change, you'll likely encounter snags along the way, resistance you didn't expect, or apathy from some quarters. But don't give up. Keep talking with as many people as you can to build awareness. If opportunities to discuss your ideas in formal settings aren't possible, share information at a happy hour or lunch. If remote work makes this harder to do, you'll need to be proactive—add the topic to an agenda, bring it up when discussing new business, or schedule a virtual workshop. If one communication channel doesn't work, try another. Enlist others who can help you spread the word.

Identify and Mobilize Your Allies

We can't overstate the importance of allies who can create powerful coalitions for change. The women at Winthrop Air had many allies, though they didn't realize it. To start, they were allies to one another—they were all overburdened, they were part of affinity groups, and they could tap into broad company-wide networks. Some of the women were supervisors or managers themselves, who could enact some of the ideas the group generated. They could have built a strong coalition to address the NPT issue at Winthrop Air.

There are many potential allies in your organization. They might be established groups, which provide strength in numbers, or colleagues who wield influence with others. Make a list of the potential partners in your organization. We have some suggestions, but first, think about the groups and coworkers who might be supportive of changes to NPTs. Who do NPTs affect most? Who has the power to promote the issue—either informally or formally? Which groups can help advocate for change? As you read through our suggested allies, add to your list.

Colleagues Who Carry Excessive Loads of NPTs

You're probably not the only one overloaded with NPTs. Who in your department is doing a disproportionate share of NPTs? Are there colleagues at your level or below who are similarly overburdened? These are natural allies. Understanding the damage too much dead-end work does to them professionally and personally can convince them to work with you. Look also to overburdened colleagues at higher levels for other (very influential) allies. Successful managers sometimes pitch in to take on work that someone else should handle, and so they also understand the challenges of NPTs. Turn to them, as Lise did. In her conversations with a top-level manager, she secured an important partner who immediately grasped the concept of NPTs. This connection facilitated the many talks she gave throughout the organization and gave her the platform and endorsement to communicate the need for change.

Colleagues Who Get It

Some of your coworkers may catch on right away when you talk about the promotability of work. They may not have an NPT overload problem, but they are able to identify with the problem of overwork and the stress and burnout that result. They may incur a cost from changing the practices of allocating NPTs, but still want to serve as allies. Some of these colleagues will be women who have somehow succeeded in keeping a manageable NPT load, and others will be men.

Do you remember Linda's story about her colleague George who said he would have refused to serve on the review board? When he realized that his saying no meant Linda had to say yes, he was remorseful. He told her that he didn't want to make women pick up the slack for him; that's not the kind of person he is. And he put those words into action. George began coordinating the recruitment of new faculty and screening potential PhD students—NPTs that took time but were critical to the success of their department. He also stepped up his contributions to departmental camaraderie by hosting events at his house (and no, his wife did not bear the burden). Many men are like him—they see themselves as women's allies; they believe in equality in the workplace and at home. Given some education on the problem, we believe they will step up and help.

Men with female partners often see them struggling to keep up with an excessive load of unrewarded work. Time and again, we have had male audience members ask for copies of our research to share with their partners or daughters. Research shows that men with daughters tend to support public policies that address gender equity and are more open to nontraditional gender roles than men without daughters. Men who seek equity for the women in their lives can be powerful allies.

Existing Affinity Groups

Members of affinity groups at your organization can also be natural partners and women's affinity groups are an especially effective group to engage. They quickly understand the impact of NPTs on women's advancement and are anxious to be a part of the conversation. BIPOC affinity groups are also important allies as their members often are doubly taxed, not only by diversity initiatives, but also by discriminatory expectations that they take one for the team.

Once you've identified your affinity group allies, you can create awareness about NPTs by attending their meetings. Members of these groups cross units and divisions and give you a wide reach to trigger broader organizational discussions. This, in turn, builds allies across the entire organization who can create awareness in their own departments. That's what Lise did—as she met with affinity groups throughout the university, word of her message spread, people understood the concepts she presented, and small changes began. You might think about venues in your own organization. If your organization has book clubs, you might propose this book as one of the upcoming reads. Or maybe you could bring in outside speakers to discuss non-promotable tasks. Gradually, the language of NPTs will spread throughout the organization, making it ripe for change.

Your Supervisor or Other Management

In Chapter 8, we encouraged you to talk with your supervisor about how best to spend your time at work and which tasks were most likely to impact your career growth. We cautioned that if your supervisor was not ready for the conversation, to hold off. But if you have a supervisor you can engage, you may have identified your strongest ally. Supervisors can offer support to changes you propose, they may take it upon themselves to change the way they allocate work, and they are in the ideal position to communicate demonstrated success to other departments and upper management. There may be an upside for your supervisor as well. Management might recognize their leadership in the promotable realm of deploying resources more effectively, creating equity, and improving the workplace culture for their division. More on this in the next chapter.

Informal Leaders

Are there people on your team who don't hold formal leadership positions but nonetheless are particularly influential? Or colleagues who are held in high esteem by their peers—whose ideas are often adopted in meetings? These informal leaders can become your allies as well. Every organization has a formal hierarchy and an informal one, often referred to as a social network. Social networks are powerful tools for organizational change, and understanding who in the network has influence is imperative.

People are influential when they are closely connected to many people or when they bridge disconnected subgroups within their network. You will have more success in changing organizational practices if you can bring individuals like these on board, or at least make sure they don't object.

You've laid the groundwork for change by creating awareness and identifying your allies. Now it's time to roll up your sleeves and take some direct action, which involves nudging your organization for broader changes, but also instituting small, nonthreatening ones.

Take Action

Your work on seeding change will be a gradual process of discrete steps, concrete actions, and small wins. Work with your allies to build momentum and eventually capitalize on those wins. This measured process will make change more palatable. Small demonstrations will provide evidence that changing NPT allocations can improve the bottom line, morale, and opportunities for all.

Consider when to act. Change is a continual process, so you'll need to be ready to move when an opening presents itself. Be opportunistic: know when people are ready to hear what you have to say and when it might be better to hold off. If NPTs are on people's minds, they are more likely to consider how to address their unequal distribution.

Interrupt the Status Quo

You diagnosed how your organization typically assigns NPTs in Exercise 3.2, and that information will help you disrupt how such decisions are made. For example, if your organization typically recruits volunteers for NPTs, then the next time this happens, casually suggest, "Hey, why don't we just draw names from a hat? That would be easier!" Lise suggested this as an alternative to asking for a volunteer to write the promotion committee's report. If the task is small, your proposal will seem so reasonable that it would be hard for anyone to object. If a volunteer is acceptable for the work, then the assignment isn't critical, and a random draw should be fine as well. If someone does object, then be ready to counter. Explain that the task is an NPT and no one is eager to take it on, so perhaps it is better to share the burden equally. In Lise's case, drawing names from a hat replaced the practice of asking for a volunteer. Because the solution was so obviously fair, it stuck. If drawing names doesn't fit within the norms of your organization, you could try something else, like: "Instead of relying on volunteers, how about trying to find another way to assign work since we know that some people are more likely to volunteer than others?"

If your colleagues say that they are "just too overwhelmed and busy now," you can suggest taking turns and that you will take the first turn, if everyone will sign up now for the next ones. Research suggests you might get a good reaction to this idea of turn taking. People tend to put too much weight on avoiding unpleasant tasks (as NPTs sometimes are!) today and happily delay and procrastinate things they dread until later. The relief of not having to do a non-promotable task today may very well get your colleagues to agree to taking turns in the future.

Engage in Coordinated Stealth Initiatives

You'll be more successful if you obtain backup for your plan ahead of time. Let's say you want people to take turns doing a particular task. If you chat with Ali in advance and she is on board, she can then support your idea and even take it a step further. At the department meeting, if you ask people to take turns, she can add, "Sign me up for the second slot. How about you, Blake? Do you want to go after that?"

These coordinated initiatives have traction, and they can be very effective. Women in the Obama White House strategized about how to get their voices heard in meetings—a problem most of us know all too well. With careful and purposeful planning, they devised a solution, called *amplification*, that was simple yet effective. Women would repeat key points made by others, mentioning by name the woman who had originally made the suggestion. In recounting the success of this strategy, *Washington Post* reporter Juliet Eilperin noted, "This forced the men in the room to recognize the contribution—and denied them the chance to claim the idea as their own." And it worked. President Obama became more aware and began calling more on women and junior aides.

The beauty of their approach was that although it was well coordinated, it *seemed* spontaneous and natural, and the women remained persistent and disciplined in carrying it out. That kind of stealth initiative can help as you seed changes for NPTs.

Use Any Power You Have

If you have a managerial role, use your power for good and do things differently. This is what Laurie did when she enlisted her colleague's help in rethinking how they allocated work. Laurie and Mike were both senior associate deans at the business school in the early years of our club. Jointly responsible for assigning faculty to school governance committees, Laurie asked Mike to help address the distribution of NPTs. Mike cared about equity and Laurie wanted to know if her theory that women were bearing the burden of committee work was correct. Since data is the way the business school communicates ideas and results, she and Mike set up a spreadsheet to track the number of committees each faculty member served on. Laurie was right: women were significantly overrepresented among faculty carrying heavy committee loads—27 percent of women as compared to 12 percent of men sat on more than two standing governance committees within the school. And it was no better at the bottom end of the distribution. Twenty-four percent of male faculty had no committee assignments, but only 9 percent of women were absolved from serving. It was easy to see that women were bearing a disproportionate burden compared to their male colleagues, so Laurie and Mike moved people around to even the load. Now, many years later, the current senior associate deans still use that spreadsheet to distribute assignments equally.

Laurie was pleased with the changes within the business school, but she wanted to impact her university more broadly, and she knew she needed to reach top management. She emailed a research article documenting the imbalance of service loads for male versus female faculty to the university's vice provost for faculty, who she suspected would be responsive to the issue. In her email, she also described how she made committee assignments in her school that balanced NPT loads across all faculty. The problem and Laurie's solution resonated with the vice provost, effectively planting a seed, which led to meetings among all the deans to consider university-wide approaches. Having your supervisor, or other superiors, as an ally can dramatically further your efforts.

Speak Out

You might feel a bit of relief when some other woman is assigned to the holiday party committee, but this is setting a bad precedent, and you need to act. You need to speak out, to interfere, when you see allocations of NPTs that hinder equal opportunity for your co-workers to demonstrate their talent. When you see something that needs to be fixed, draw inspiration from John Lewis's quote: "Get in good trouble, necessary trouble . . ."

When Peter "volunteers" Rachel to run the annual fundraiser again; when Tennesha is brought in to choose the food served at a meeting because she is a good cook; or when Brenda is the go-to scribe for the next meeting—*speak out*! If they hold a lower rank than you, consider it your duty to protect them. Say that you "would like to ensure she has the time to devote to her PTs right now, so let's find someone else" or note that "it would be good to have backup on all tasks, so it would be ideal if everyone takes turns and gets experience." You can do the same with your peers, suggesting mechanisms like taking turns to share the load.

Once everyone understands the concept of the promotability of work, speaking out against unfair distributions of tasks is much easier. A university's school-wide committee met for the first time, and the science departments (which are heavily male) had designated only women as representatives. The women spoke up about the poor composition of the committee. The chair adjourned the meeting, dismantled the committee, and required the departments to submit members who better represented the makeup of the faculty. Be like these women and speak out right away. Recognize that this is a learning (or unlearning) process and that the appointments were likely well-intentioned, if wrong. Nudge your colleagues to change by noting that these types of assignments create excessive NPT loads for women. Question women's overrepresentation on a particular NPT assignment; see if it can be changed to allow them time for their PTs.

Mentor Early Career Colleagues

Maybe some of your junior colleagues don't have a good grasp of what matters for promotion and you see them taking on an excessive NPT load. Reach out and mentor them regarding what tasks are more central to their success. Better yet, talk with their mentors and suggest that it's time to have a conversation on what matters for promotion. If you see Francesca spending all her time on the summer intern program, meet with her or her mentor, or even address it with her supervisor (if you are in a position to do so). If Francesca is relieved of the unrewarded task, she'll spend more time on the work that matters. Tell her! Make sure that new hires, who are always eager to please, get guidance on which tasks they should avoid for now or warn them about not taking on too much at first.

Create an NPT Innovation Team

One route for seeding change and organizing your allies is to start a team within the company focused on advocating for change. This

NPT innovation team is very different from a No Club; the latter is a personal group to support you as you navigate NPTs and work/work imbalance—a journey that is highly individual and sometimes emotional and one that requires confidential sharing of information. An NPT innovation team, on the other hand, is strategic and action-oriented, with a professional focus on organizational change. Members can share experiences and best practices and lobby for improvements. To keep your personal struggles separate from your professional aims, keep the focus of the NPT innovation team on organizational fixes, and use your No Club for personal growth, support, and camaraderie. Your current—or future—boss could be on your innovation team, but probably should not be a member of your club.

Your innovation team can prioritize where change is needed most and where you can improve work assignments. Also consider changing organizational practices that supposedly "help" women, but instead harm them (referred to as *benevolent sexism*; see Chapter 5). We discussed how some organizations assign women to special teams or projects to train them for leadership positions. If men do not have to participate in these activities to become leaders, then why should women? This practice diverts women from the promotable work that actually matters to achieve leadership positions.

The women at Winthrop Air really could have used an innovation team. The root of their problem was how the company allocated NPTs—either directly by supervisors (who disproportionately asked women) or by seeking volunteers (who were disproportionately women). An innovation team could have strategized alternatives for sharing non-promotable tasks and held discussions throughout the organization, as Lise did.

Hopefully, your efforts to create awareness, build allies, and take action have made your organization ripe for change. You've started the initiative; now your organization and its leaders need to take the next step to broaden it so that everyone benefits and the organization thrives. Our next chapter describes the steps your organization can take to ensure that the NPTs are appropriately distributed and rewarded and that the changes are lasting.

CHAPTER 11

Managing Non-Promotable Work to Advance Women and Organizations

At last! We have shown that organizations can improve their bottom line and employee morale by better managing non-promotable work—now we demonstrate how to do that. Mismanagement of NPTs is not something that women can or should fix by themselves. Instead, the only real and lasting solution is to change organizational practices and policies for allocating and rewarding work.

This chapter lays out solutions that are straightforward and generally easy to implement. We have seen them work in a wide range of organizations, and we are confident that they will bring progress to yours. We'll also share how to handle potential pitfalls and hidden pockets of resistance.

If you are wondering whether this chapter is relevant to you, we assure you it is. If you are a senior manager, you'll be able to take the ideas presented here and lead the charge. If you're in middle management, you can implement many of the recommendations in your department or team. If you hold no supervisory role, you can nudge your boss or other organizational leaders to implement the changes you think would make a difference.

So yes, we are talking to *you*.

Change initiatives come in all sizes. They can be small scale, occurring within a department or division, or they can be large-scale, addressing deeply rooted policies and practices that affect the entire organization. Large or small—effective change processes include a basic set of four phases.

Phase 1: Diagnose the Problem and Set Objectives

Phase 2: Select, Design, and Develop Solutions

Phase 3: Communicate the Change Vision

Phase 4: Institutionalize the Change

We use these four phases to present our solutions for developing and implementing lasting improvements in how NPTs are managed.

Phase 1. Diagnose the Problem and Set Objectives

As the saying goes, "What does not get measured cannot be fixed." You need to measure the allocation of NPTs to improve it. Take a close look at who is doing what in your organization. Are employees performing tasks appropriate for their expertise, or have they outgrown them? Are some carrying a load of NPTs that is very different from that of their peers or others in the organization? Is there a gender divide? Are women of color particularly affected? Is changing work allocations warranted and feasible? What does a successful reallocation look like?

We use two methods to diagnose whether an organization has a problem with the distribution of non-promotable work. The first is *task-oriented*, where you identify NPTs and record which subset of employees are assigned to each. The second is *employee-oriented*, and uses existing (or gathers new) data on how employees spend their time to assess the number of hours spent on work that is high or low in promotability. One advantage of the second method is its ability to fully quantify differences in NPT loads across employees, which can irrefutably demonstrate the need for change. Presented with the facts, employees and managers cannot dismiss the initiative as being unfounded or built on mere anecdotes. To help you undertake the process, we provide tools for each of these approaches in the exercises at the end of this chapter.

We worked with a professional services firm that had detailed data on billable and non-billable time, and they used the employee-oriented approach to diagnose whether NPTs were equitably and optimally allocated. The firm categorized work assignments by promotability and then coded how employees spent their time. The results showed a gender gap in who performed NPTs and proved that women's excessive load of NPTs wasn't just a potential problem, but a real one. This finding generated organization-wide support for a change initiative, and by repeating the analysis later on, they could monitor success and guide subsequent modifications.

Whichever approach you undertake, you need employee engagement to gather the necessary data. You want everyone to understand that an inequitable distribution of NPTs is a problem, that there are workable solutions that are fair and profitable, and that everyone has a role to play in developing and implementing them.

Start by educating employees about the promotability of tasks and its effect on both them and the organization. To aid your communication, you may want to distribute articles (and this book!). We recommend developing a communication plan that includes written information, in-person meetings, and presentations. State the organization's motivation for focusing on NPTs so employees understand why their participation is important. Articulate how tackling this issue can help the organization optimally utilize the workforce, retain and attract talent, create a culture where everyone pitches in, and keep the workforce engaged and satisfied. Communicate that the goal is for no single group to take on an excessive load of NPTs. "Equity in NPTs" does not mean that everyone carries an identical load, but rather that work is distributed to provide equal opportunities for people to demonstrate skill and contribute to the organization. Each person's load will vary by department and by the employee's rank, skill, and experience. Note that the problem may be systemic and one that could continue undetected. Share that this problem is present in most organizations, that you want to determine whether it is in yours as well, and that if it is, no one person is to blame.

Once you have assessed the current assignment of work and magnitude of the problem, then evaluate existing practices to identify which are driving the unequal distribution of NPTs. Are managers disproportionally asking women to do non-promotable tasks, or do they rely on volunteers, who tend to be women? Once you understand what contributes to the problem, it will be easier to choose your best options for improvement from the suggestions we provide below.

You may be excited to share your findings with your employees and believe that demonstrating the extent of the problem will get the ball rolling. We caution you against doing so prematurely. An organization we worked with presented their results, (which revealed very large gender differences in who spent the most time on NPTs), without a clear vision for the future or a plan for addressing the issues. They thought that creating awareness of the problem was a good first step, but it wasn't enough. People wanted to know how it would be addressed. The women were outraged, the men were caught off guard, and the leadership didn't know what to do next. The women effectively went "on strike" and refused to do any more NPTs. There were hurt feelings on all sides and a great deal of disruption. Eventually, the organization's leadership regrouped, created a plan, and implemented some of the solutions we outline in this chapter, but they would have saved *a lot* of trouble if they'd had a plan at the outset.

To start, we recommend assembling a steering committee to help you make sense of your data, set direction, and identify effective solutions, challenges, and pockets of resistance. The committee's membership should span the organization. Include employees who are likely to benefit from the change initiative, and, yes, this is the time to ask women and underrepresented minorities to serve (and when you do, we ask you to relieve them of other NPTs in return). You also want to include employees who may be less favorably inclined toward your efforts to help you anticipate concerns and potential resistance up-front. Your steering committee can provide valuable input, communicate with their constituents, and oversee your progress. They should set direction by articulating what the organization wants to achieve, defining objectives and goals. Ask yourself, "What does success look like?" Ask others the same question. Your organization's success could include the following objectives:

- Provide equal opportunity to demonstrate success (the PTs)
- Ensure that NPT distribution is not influenced by demographic characteristics (e.g., gender, race, age, ethnicity, sexual orientation)
- Be transparent about the distribution of NPTs across people

Phase 2: Select, Design, and Develop Solutions

Deciding which new practices and policies to implement will depend on your organization and its specific challenges with NPTs. We offer many possible solutions, recognizing that not all will work for every organization. To decide which are right for you, consider your organization's readiness and current situation. Small or relatively flat organizations will approach the problem differently from large and layered ones, the latter of which need more coordination between departments. You might try an experimental approach to see what changes are effective. An organization we worked with introduced small pilot programs in separate geographic locales, which enabled them to identify what worked best, the resources needed, and how easily the changes could be implemented. The pilot locations felt special for being on the leading edge of organizational best practices, and their success secured the buy-in of other units.

We list our solutions by ease of implementation, starting with the simplest, which do not require coordinated organizational efforts and can be introduced in individual departments. Then we present efforts that are best implemented uniformly throughout the organization. These require greater levels of both executive and HR involvement, and so create a bit more complexity. We refer to the first as *department-specific initiatives* and the second as *organization-wide initiatives*. Look through the options and consider which could be effective components of your change initiative.

Department-Specific Initiatives

To change allocations of work, we need to change both *how* we distribute work and to *whom* we distribute it. Rather than using the same approaches for assigning work (like giving it to the first person who springs to mind), we suggest the following alternatives.

Random assignment. Stop asking for volunteers, and instead randomly assign the work. If you are willing to ask for volunteers, then *who* performs the work isn't critical, and random assignments ensure that everyone has the same chance at being chosen. You could draw names out of a hat, draw straws, or generate a program that selects eligible employees at random, with the stipulation that those who most recently performed the task are exempt from the draw. Everyone can see that the approach is fair, so it's difficult to put up resistance.

Taking turns. Institute turn-taking among those suitable for the task and keep track of who did it most recently. A standing meeting can have a new note taker each week—and the rotation isn't hard to track. Remember Dorothea from Chapter 3, who worked for a government agency training enforcement officials? The men in her group were almost always the presenters, and the women, the scribes. The women were just as qualified to present. Rotating these roles, with each person taking on both, would have shared the workload and produced a strong bench of trainers, all of whom had unique contributions to make.

Assign NPTs strategically, based on the skill sets of your employees. When allocating one-off or large-scale non-promotable tasks, it might matter who is assigned. Asking for a volunteer so you can dodge the decision of whom to ask could be a costly mistake.

As we saw in Chapter 9, when deciding whom to assign to NPTs, a manager needs to consider the alternate use of the employee's time. Recall the example of the two salespeople, Shandra and James, where selling was a PT, and their manager needed one of them to work on a new sales tracking database (an NPT). While they could do an equally good job on the database task, Shandra was much better at sales than James. Even though Shandra would probably volunteer to work on the database, it would be a mistake to let her do it. The firm would be better off keeping Shandra fully in sales and diverting some of James's time to developing the database. Who is best at the promotable task that will help your company hit its metrics? Prioritize that, instead of trying to quickly off-load that pesky NPT.

You might wonder how you can assign work strategically if you don't know your employees' relative skill sets, as is the case with new employees. As noted in Chapter 9, these assignments are straightforward. To determine who, among new employees, is good at what, equally distribute work so you can see how each employee performs various tasks (promotable and non-promotable). Assigning similar portfolios of work to new hires at comparable levels provides equal opportunities for them to demonstrate skill and makes it possible for you to evaluate their talents, and to assign subsequent work strategically.

Develop a list of people who can do NPTs. In Chapter 6, we shared the story of Gerri, who had gotten stuck giving company-wide presentations. Gerri always did a great job, and so the requests kept coming. However, assigning Gerri to presentations wasn't just bad for Gerri, it was also bad for the company, because her greater value-added was on PTs, for which she no longer had time. If your first instinct is to ask the tried-and-true person, like Gerri, stop yourself. Develop a list of people to rotate through the job, especially jobs that come up often. Prioritize suitable men who don't have a lot of NPTs. Rather than asking the person who will say yes, consider the skills needed and the lost output from diverting the wrong person's time. Then use this to identify a slate of employees who could do as good (or close to as good) a job as Gerri.

Train new people to do NPTs. What can a manager do if no one is as good as Gerri? Gerri, or women more generally, may be better at the task today because they have done it in the past, but you can change that. Use employees who have experience performing the NPT to train others. In the short run, this is an NPT for the trainer, but it will be beneficial in the long run by enlarging the pool of qualified candidates, improving the distribution of work, and increasing the skill set of your organization.

Use mentors and sponsors and be ready to intervene. Break the NPT cycle by interceding as soon as an employee comes on board. Use existing mentor programs to guide new employees toward the right mix of NPTs and PTs. Properly guided mentees will know that a successful portfolio of work contains both NPTs and PTs, but will also know what work matters most for career advancement and be able to direct their efforts toward that. This approach also educates mentors, who can monitor and modify their own behavior to more equitably assign NPTs.

An organization we spoke with struggled with considerable differences in the work portfolios of junior men and women at the time of promotion. Relative to men, the women's portfolios were light on revenue-generating work. To address this, mentors advised women against taking on specific low-revenue or low-reward clients, pushed them toward clients with greater growth potential, and gave them clarity on what tasks to avoid or pursue when they attended department meetings. As a result, the mentees were well prepared for meetings and felt empowered. They stopped volunteering for less advantageous assignments, provided compelling arguments to block unwanted requests, and most important, could demonstrate their readiness to handle high-profile clients.

Sometimes, good advice just isn't enough, and advocacy and sponsorship are needed. That's what ultimately got Gerri out of her predicament of never-ending presentations. Gerri's manager, Ayana, became aware of the large amount of unrewarded work Gerri performed, and together, they cataloged her current NPTs and put a limit on the time she could spend on them. While Ayana didn't assign Gerri more NPTs, other people kept coming to her for help. Gerri said Ayana ultimately put a stop to it:

There was one point when I was about to get promoted, where I was really trying to focus on one last area of growth, and one of my VPs comes to me and says, "Gerri, we need a presentation for this big meeting to almost everyone in the company. It's two days from now." Ayana comes storming over to my desk: "I heard the VP asked you to take on the presentation—he shouldn't have asked you. Enough! In a 500-plus organization, you can't be the only one who knows how to do PowerPoint! I will put an end to this."

And she did. Ayana advocated for Gerri and got the VP to back off. She educated him about the situation, which changed his behavior. Direct supervisors are better informed of how their employees spend their time, and if given the latitude to manage assignments, they can protect and take action on behalf of their employees.

Reassign and redistribute NPTs to boost employee success. A more complex step is for supervisors to systematically take stock of who handles various work tasks and, where needed, redistribute the work. Even without a full picture of someone's use of time, you can still move forward. Have a conversation with an employee you suspect is overburdened so you can understand her workload, and then assess and reassign some of her excessive NPTs. That is how Gerri ultimately secured her promotion:

> I was put up for promotion twice, and the first time, it didn't go through because I didn't demonstrate the strategy piece. My manager, Ayana, most likely had been in the situation before, and she farmed out a bunch of stuff [that I had previously been doing] to my team and my focus for the next six months was building a strategy for the business. That was the thing that eventually got me there.

Even without formal data and tracking, Gerri's manager could see that non-promotable work was derailing her promotion. By redistributing her NPTs, she gave Gerri more time to focus on the business strategy—a promotable task. She protected her from future assignments and kept her focused. There's an additional upside to encouraging this behavior: Gerri was grateful for her manager's coaching and adopted the same approach when she later managed her own team.

The solutions listed above can be implemented on a small scale, in specific departments and units, and may serve as evidence to secure buy-in and change more broadly. Their success can serve as a catalyst for bigger change and may even get you noticed for your innovative leadership. The key to scaling the solution and getting broader execution is to document your process and track the effectiveness of your changes.

Organization-Wide Initiatives

What distinguishes this set of solutions from those above is that they require more uniform and coordinated implementation throughout the organization. These changes typically take more time and require management and/or HR support, but they are likely to result in lasting improvement.

Enforce standards for doing NPTs. Whether an individual takes on an NPT is often guided by a set of norms, and we have shown that these norms differ for men and women. To address this, you can require that employees take on a minimum number of NPTs. Harvard University's Kennedy School of Government took this approach. After reading our research, their leadership developed a point system and required faculty to conduct a minimum amount of non-promotable work:

> . . . a faculty member receives points for teaching and administrative tasks such as, for example, committee work. Faculty have substantial flexibility in how they want to meet these obligations. Some might end up teaching more than the minimal requirement, and others might spend more time on search, appointments, or IRB [Institutional Review Board] committees. A full-time faculty member should contribute 100 points (with a margin of error of 10 percent plus or minus); over-contributors receive extra compensation, and under-contributors need to adjust either their time status or their pay.

A benefit of the point system is that it brings attention to inequities. That was how the Kennedy School discovered that one Black female professor mentored an exceedingly large number of BIPOC women on campus. It also uncovered that the school had created an unfair burden on women by having at least one woman on every administrative committee and thereby requiring each female to serve on more committees than each male faculty member had to.

Notice that the system does not change the reward for or promotability of the work, it is still non-promotable. But by setting a minimum requirement, the Kennedy School made NPTs more visible and secured a wider set of employees to share the load. The initiative could have gone a step further and included a maximum load of NPTs. Setting a cap would ensure that individual employees wouldn't be overburdened and would provide an additional lever in equalizing the load. When setting the requirement, remember that rank and qualification affect not only what tasks are promotable, but also the amount of time employees should spend on non-promotable work. You do not want a VP handling the same number of NPTs as an assistant, but instead, want VPs to carry loads comparable to one another. Organizations should ideally set minimum and maximum NPT loads by level of the position.

Relative skill sets factor in as well. If employees have a minimum requirement of NPTs, and they have flexibility in what they take on, then they will seek out the ones they are best suited for. This ensures that the work is assigned to those who either enjoy the specific task or have skills that match it.

Provide incentives for doing NPTs. There is little reward for doing NPTs—they won't advance your career or fatten your wallet. But what if organizations changed that? What if they used incentives to entice more people to take them on?

Many years ago, Brenda worked as an administrator at a small college. The head of the school's fundraising efforts called and asked her if she'd "do him a favor" and write a grant proposal to fund student scholarships. The proposal had nothing to do with her department or her job, and it was an unfamiliar topic for her. The only reason he picked her was because he knew she had written proposals in the past. Since it would take time away from her regular job at a busy time of year, she said no and gave him the names of a few others to ask. He called her a few days later and asked again. This time, he said it came with an extra payment. That made it much easier for her to say yes—the extra money was very welcome at that point and so she was willing to do the extra work on weekends. If the head of fund-raising had widely circulated his request, and its accompanying payment, he probably would have had more people willing to take on the task, perhaps even some from the appropriate departments!

Incentivizing NPTs shows that the task is valued and deserving of attention. It helps compensate for the time taken away from an employee's PTs, and makes more people willing to do the work. We are *not* suggesting that women should just be paid more to handle their overload of NPTs—that merely perpetuates the current distribution problem. Rather, by compensating NPTs, it helps solve the problem of a lack of volunteers and encourages a wider set of employees to take on work that serves the organization but won't advance their careers. The ultimate goal is to change the distribution of these tasks, and attractive, clearly communicated incentives are one mechanism for doing that.

Perhaps you can provide an extra day off to the person who organizes the golf tournament or a onetime payment to the person who handles the search committee. Maybe a gift card to the person who headed the renovation committee. Paying for conference attendance, training programs, coaching or other professional development opportunities are great ways to encourage employees to do NPTs *and* upskill the organization. Be sure the rewards are the right ones for your employees—find out what they value and allow them to choose among options, if possible.

Avoid cultural taxation. Organizations want diverse membership on task forces and committees, and, to ensure that multiple perspectives are heard, they often look to representation from minority groups, whether women or people of color. That's what the Kennedy School did when they required representation on administrative committees that exceeded the representation on faculty. Because these assignments are usually non-promotable, this places a disproportionate burden or *cultural tax* on employees who are numerical minorities in your workforce. We are not advocating for *proportional* representation across the board—quite the contrary; there are times when diverse representation is essential, but management needs to assess *when* and *why*. There are tasks where representation by women or people of color is important, for example, when dealing with issues that are especially relevant to them, where they have unique insights or experiences, or that are mission critical. But, believe it or not, you don't need to be a woman to help choose a food vendor for the cafeteria, plan a staff appreciation day, or refurbish the employee lounge. Before you say, "We need more women on this committee," ask yourself, "Why?" Make sure you have a good answer. Figure out where representation is needed and assign people accordingly.

Cultural taxation will result if you have overrepresentation on some tasks and don't allow corresponding underrepresentation on others to balance the load, and it can cause your diversity, equity, and inclusion (DEI) efforts to backfire. Instead, consider taking women and people of color off other NPT assignments where their presence is less critical, but be careful not to remove them from activities that might afford them status or access to senior leadership. Limiting their NPTs to DEI-related activities could impede their ability to contribute to other strategic initiatives that align with their expertise.

Eliminate NPTs that aren't worth it. You might find some surprises when you review tasks that employees undertake. You may encounter some that are just, well, a waste of time. One organization started a new product team a decade earlier. Each department appointed a representative, and the committee's goal was to vet new products and provide perspectives on their viability from all functional areas. The team met monthly, but the work was perfunctory. Over time, it grew increasingly difficult to get anyone to serve because the committee work had become an NPT—it was not contributing to the effectiveness of new product launches. If your department requires similar NPTs, now may be the time to examine whether they deliver on their goals. If the answer is no, then it's time to disband the group and have employees devote that time to other work that matters.

Or say that in a task review with your administrative assistant, Pam, you find that she spends a couple hours each week watering and tending to the plants for your department. She's an important administrative assistant, and her time is needed on other tasks. Where is her time better spent? If other departments also have employees tending to their department's plants, then it may be wise—and more cost-effective—to outsource the activity. Resources are lost when employees handle jobs far below their pay grade and level of expertise.

Redesign jobs so that NPTs for one role become PTs for another. An organization gets the most out of its workforce when it effectively leverages employee skill sets. For that to happen, NPTs need to be reassigned if they were originally given to the wrong person, or when an employee outgrows them. Makayla had been with an insurance company for six years. She joined as a junior underwriter, and two successful promotions had advanced her to supervisor. One of her early assignments was to update a monthly report on applicant bankruptcies. It was tedious and did not require her underwriter skills, but it had helped her get acquainted with the division's procedures and risk programs. Six years later, she was still running the report, but she had long ago outgrown the task. She suggested to her boss that the task be reassigned, and this time, not to another junior underwriter, who wouldn't grow or advance from the task, but to an administrative coordinator who did the department's data entry. Her boss agreed. The coordinator's position was the right one for the task, and it gave him an opportunity to work with Makayla's group of underwriters, providing him more visibility, and a potential reward for good performance. Redesigning the coordinator's job was a win-win.

Provide feedback on work/work balance as part of the performance evaluation process. Increase an employee's awareness of how her time is distributed across promotable and non-promotable work by discussing it during her performance evaluations. Institute a new procedure to include this topic in each evaluation meeting to highlight the importance of hitting the right work/work balance and to allow the employee and supervisor to make changes that benefit the employee and organization.

Change the way performance is evaluated. NPTs have a negligible impact on performance evaluations—otherwise they would be promotable! Managers need to outline what is promotable and what is not, but that rarely happens. Instead, employees rely on cues, often subtle ones, and may mistakenly think that something matters because they were asked to do it. It's in the organization's and employees' interest to distinguish between promotable and non-promotable work. Use performance evaluations as an opportunity to discuss and potentially reconsider what is promotable.

Linda was invited to speak at an organization about our work on NPTs, and the timing was fortuitous, as the company was redesigning their performance evaluation system. Linda's visit prompted them to look more closely at what they defined as *promotable*. The company's leadership realized that helping others was critical to the organization, but not reflected in evaluations. They understood that helping others encompassed a host of activities, all of which benefited the company. They began tracking it: during the year, employees submitted "notes of appreciation" to be placed in the files of other employees that had provided them with valuable help. There was no downside to your evaluation for receiving help, and there was an upside for providing it as employees with more appreciations in their file had higher performance evaluations. And these higher evaluations translated into improved overall assessments and compensation. Through this policy, the company turned NPTs into PTs.

Organizations need to consider carefully what to assess and reward. Changing evaluation criteria can be beneficial in the long run, but it is a complex process that will entail coordination from HR and involve leaders and managers across the organization. That doesn't mean it shouldn't be undertaken—it is an important step toward equalizing opportunities and work—but it requires planning, monitoring, and adjustment to get the incentives right.

Phase 3: Communicate the Change Vision

It is time to communicate your vision for change throughout the organization. In preparing your change vision for NPTs, there are two compelling arguments: the *business case* and the *fairness case*. Both can be included in an NPT vision statement, perhaps one like this:

To support our values of equity and effective workforce utilization, we will ensure that all employees have equal opportunity to demonstrate skill and potential. We will provide employees of similar ability, rank, and role with comparable work assignments. We all share responsibility for the change, and managers and employees will collectively work to equalize NPT workloads among peers.

Your goal should be to reach as many people in your organization as possible and bring them on board. Update your initial communication plan with organization-specific data and information on your change initiative so employees understand why changing NPT practices is worth everyone's effort.

A firm we worked with developed an information campaign to communicate their plan. They had used a task-oriented approach to diagnose the problem: first assessing the promotability of work assignments and then speaking with employees in different roles to determine how work was distributed. The results were clear—change was, in fact, warranted. They developed a slide deck presenting the core content of their messaging, which was grounded in the research on NPTs and provided concrete examples of how NPTs played out in their organization. They defined task promotability in the context of their work and the cost of unequal NPT distribution to employees and the organization. Most important, they articulated how everyday practices such as asking for volunteers can unintentionally create work/work imbalance for some employees (mostly women).

The firm distributed this information throughout the organization, which made the concepts and current challenges concrete. They included recommendations to change the allocation of NPTs, like rotating tasks, and they had supervisors meet with their employees to discuss achieving the right balance of work. You can do the same. Communicate your challenges, present your organization's commitment to change, and share new practices and policies to implement. This will put everyone on the same page, so they value and work toward the same goals.

Everyone needs to be engaged and committed for new organizational practices to stick. For your initiative to succeed, you need to rely on your allies as well as others who might resist the change. The most likely opposition is from those who benefit from the status quo, like managers and employees with light NPT loads. Try to engage them and address their concerns up front. Managers might be wary of the disruption that changes will bring or worry that new processes will encroach on their autonomy and limit their ability to protect certain staff from extra work. They may be uncertain about the upside of change. Consult with them for feedback throughout the process. Remind them that even though the transition may be disruptive, the changes will benefit everyone in the long run through improvements in resource allocation, organizational culture, employee retention, and productivity. Employees with lighter NPT loads may feel threatened by changes that could limit their access to promotable tasks. It's possible, however, to win them over. They might be surprised to learn that they haven't been doing their share, feel contrite about burdening their colleagues, and view the initiative as needed progress. We have seen previous NPT freeloaders agree that the current state is inequitable and needs to change. Help them keep an open mind by appealing to their better selves—they can right a past wrong, where others suffered from the inequitable treatment.

Phase 4: Institutionalize the Change

You've made important initial changes to your organization's policies and practices. Now you need to embed them in ongoing operations, continue to assess them for their effectiveness, and, when needed, make improvements.

Monitor the New Practices

After all the effort you've put in, you don't want things to slip back to the way they were. We know, and so do you, that the reasons women end up doing NPTs will not magically disappear. So keep a sharp eye on the practices you've enacted to maintain your progress. The exercises at the end of this chapter will help you assess current work assignments and provide you with tools for monitoring.

When NPTs are redistributed, a task might fall through the cracks. Allow for failure, use it to learn, and make adjustments to ensure continued improvement. When recommending new policies, encourage managers and employees to also develop and try other, potentially better, approaches. If those experiments don't work as intended, let them keep developing new approaches. Create an environment that allows for documented trial and error. You will learn what does and does not work in your organization, and in time, your initiative will have taken shape and reflect a series of best practices.

Assess Progress Toward Goals

Translate your objectives for change into goals that you can measure progress toward. The goals you set need to be SMART (specific, measurable, achievable, relevant, time-bound). For example, you can specify when practices have to be adopted and reported on, or based on the data you collected, you can set minimum and maximum targets for the number of hours employees at different levels should spend on NPTs and specify the date by which you want this achieved. Put in place the data collection efforts that you need to measure progress toward goals and commit to specific timelines for communicating status reports, which could take the form of *performance scorecards*.

Institutionalize What Works

Make fixing NPTs across the organization a priority, and hold managers accountable. Develop reporting requirements for supervisors to describe their NPT initiatives and improvements. Share creative solutions throughout the firm to encourage widespread adoption. Improving NPT policies and practices should be a high priority for supervisors, where superior performance and improvement is rewarded with a raise or bonus.

Especially during the early days, make sure that NPTs remain top of mind. Just like you, your organization needs reminders. Research in behavioral science shows that text reminders for vaccinations decrease missed appointments, reminders to parents about school attendance reduce absenteeism for young children, and reminders to take prescriptions increase compliance with medication regimes. Anything you can use to call attention to new procedures—a newsletter, announcements, emails—will help remind and encourage employees to do things the new way and will signal that your organization is serious about change. Use these channels throughout your process to communicate the latest developments and learnings to make implementation easier for everyone.

As you change your organization's work allocations, even small steps will go a long way in improving organizational and employee well-being. When everyone recognizes the challenges associated with women spending more time on NPTs, they will modify their behavior, and new initiatives will organically arise. When you re-distribute and monitor NPTs, you broaden the set of employees handling non-promotable work. The result will be a fairer and more efficient allocation of work, equal opportunities for all employees, and a measurable impact on your organization's productivity and profitability. The improvements we recommend are straightforward and achievable, and we hope you will lead the charge. We've helped plenty of organizations better manage their non-promotable work to achieve their potential, and we know you can do it too.

EXERCISE 6: EVALUATE THE DISTRIBUTION OF PTs AND NPTs ACROSS EMPLOYEES

There are two methods to assess how NPTs are distributed in your organization. The first, a task-oriented process, is a coarser assessment, but easier to complete. The second, an employee-oriented process, is more granular and the data collection effort is more in-volved.

Exercise 6.1: Task-Oriented Process for Understanding NPT Distribution

Consider this a big-picture diagnosis in which you identify your or-ganization's NPTs and who does them. A simple spreadsheet will help you track and assess the information.

Step 1. List the NPTs in your unit or division. Think of the most obvious and jot them down, like taking notes or organizing parties. Refer to The No Club's Top Ten NPTs from Chapter 2 for ideas, such as training employees and helping others with their work. Expand your list by considering tasks that are not visible, don't require specialized skills, or are not tightly tied to the currency of the organization but still need to be done (see Chapter 2 and especially Exercise 1.4 for guidance). Look for tasks that are no one's formal job responsibility, that are done by volunteers, that no one wants to do, or that people take turns doing or have to be asked to do.

Step 2. Meet with others who are in the know (your colleagues, fellow managers), share your list, and see if they have additions. Ask them to put their own lists together and to share them with you. Refine your list to include all the NPTs that surface in these discussions.

Step 3. Cluster tasks that are similar to one another to make them easier to think about.

Step 4. Now list names next to the tasks. Focus on those who do the task most often rather than those who do it only now and then.

Step 5. Estimate the number of hours you think each person spends on the task based on your estimate of how time-consuming the tasks are and how much that person does.

Step 6. Now, with information on the jobs, employees, and time spent on NPTs, look at how tasks are distributed. Are there differences among employees with similar roles and qualifications? Are there common themes in who is doing this work? Are more NPTs distributed to one gender than the other, relative to each gender's representation? What about race? Are more NPTs distributed to women of color?

Non-Promotable Tasks	How time consuming? (H/M/L)	Who most often performs these tasks?	Weekly Time Estimate
Task Category A - task 1 - task 2			
Task Category B - task 1 - task 2			
Task Category C - task 1 - task 2			

Exercise 6.2: Employee-Oriented Process for Understanding NPT Distribution

Organizations that can gather data on how employees spend their time will easily see how NPTs are distributed across the entire organization. This more complex process requires time and resources. In an ideal scenario, your organization will create a database to gather, track, and report time use. Many organizations already use these systems for billing or other accounting purposes.

Step 1. To start, management needs to assess the organization's currency by completing Exercise 1.1, to determine the promotability of all tasks.

Step 2. Ask each of your employees to complete Exercises 1.2 and 1.3 from Chapter 2.

Step 3. Combine the lists of tasks and rate them in terms of promotability, considering their visibility, reliance on specialized skills, and alignment with the currency of the organization (identified in Step 1).

Step 4. Analyze the data:
- How much time are individual employees in job x spending on NPTs? On PTs?
- Is there variation in NPT and PT hours by grade level or rank?
- Is there variation in NPT and PT hours by gender? How much time are women spending on NPTs? Men? Are there racial disparities? Do women of color spend more time on NPTs?

CHAPTER 12

What We've Learned

Women's excessive load of non-promotable work is the anchor that has been holding them back. Our pioneering finding that this burden results from a collective expectation that women will do this work provides critical insight on how to free them from this anchor. We wrote this book because we're determined to fix this problem. We remember how overwhelmed we felt when we showed up for our first No Club meeting, and now we see our female colleagues, friends, and you struggling similarly. We've all been there—unsure how to improve our situation, and often wondering if we're the problem ourselves, but now we know better! We've shared what we've learned with you in the hopes that you will find relief, resources, and inspiration to make change happen. We're on the cusp of something that can help all of us, and we're excited to be part of that movement.

We started the book with our club, and it seems fitting to end with the progress we've made. For the last twelve years, as of this writing, we have been living with, thinking about, researching, and trying to change the landscape of non-promotable tasks for our-

selves, other women, organizations—and now you. We've shared
our struggles and our successes, and now we'll leave you with a coda
of our personal gains, along with a few thoughts from each of us.

Our differences in occupations, career stages, and preferences
led us to separate destinations from our journey. Brenda retired.
Laurie moved into an interim role in university leadership, then
back to her faculty role. Lise's research received widespread recognition, and along with that came a job offer from an Ivy League
institution. Linda began putting our work into practice with a global
firm in addition to her role at Carnegie Mellon. These career and life
stages made each of us think deeply about how NPTs played a role in
our choices and actions. We offer our insights to show what's possible for you and provide a caution that the journey really doesn't
end—we are still learning.

To start, we can now see when NPTs are hurtling toward us. We
know how to spot them and when we're being asked to do them. We
each have gotten better at evaluating these requests and deciding
which to accept. But to be completely truthful, we sometimes still
say yes when we want to say no, for all the reasons we've outlined
in this book. We have yet to fully shake loose from the demons of
disappointing others, wanting to be a team player, or needing to be
liked or respected for our work ethic. We are better at protecting our
own time and continuously rebalancing our work portfolios, but we
haven't solved the problem—yet. As we pointed out, that's because
none of us can do it alone. We need organizations to recognize their
obligation to identify and best use employee talent and to strategically manage NPTs to fulfill that obligation. Until this happens, we
just won't make the progress needed to provide employees with equal
opportunities, and they, along with their organizations, will continue
to suffer. So we reemphasize the idea that *organizations need to fully*

embrace responsibility for correcting the current imbalance of NPTs. That is our primary lesson. This is not a fix-the-women problem.

Despite changes in our organizations and our improvement in balancing our workloads, we still very much need, and want, our club. It provides us with focus when we are wavering and support when we need it most. In Chapter 1, we told the story of MJ Tocci, who was the fifth member of the club. Our club changed when we lost her, and we needed one another to grieve her loss. But rather than faltering, we doubled down on our efforts. We knew we had to honor her memory by continuing to examine the issue of NPTs. We've raised our glasses to her on many occasions and apologized to her for making the same damn mistake again—and again. We can still sense her frustration with us when we mess up, her cheers as we get better at managing our NPTs, and her pride in how we have helped organizations to change. She would be thrilled to see that we succeeded in our quest to help other women.

Our progress accelerated when we moved from changing ourselves through our club to conducting research to change our organizations, and then, ultimately, to working with other women and their organizations. Our club migrated from being only a sounding board for us personally to a platform to consider how to improve NPT allocations more broadly. We feel great satisfaction in seeing the term *non-promotable tasks* catch on. Employees overloaded with unrewarded work immediately recognize the term, and being able to name it helps them comprehend and respond to the challenges they face. Through the lens of NPTs, companies are able to see a path to enhancing their productivity and profitability. We hope our book will spread this understanding even more broadly; we've seen how powerful it has been for the lives of women we've mentored and the organizations we have worked with.

Little did we know that our first meeting on a dreary February day would take us on such a transformative journey. We each learned so much through our club meetings, our research, and the process of writing this book. As we close the book, we thought you'd like to know how it's worked out for us. Here are our stories.

Brenda retired several years ago, so she had limited opportunities to put our ideas into practice in her organization. As she thought about her new status, she wondered whether decisions about how to spend time would arise for a no-longer-working woman, and as it turns out, they do. Although retired from her day job, she still gets requests to participate in professional activities, and now she considers the value of her time as a factor in her decisions. What is she willing to give up this precious commodity for? She understands the tasks she really likes and agrees to do those. She said yes to mentoring young faculty (it was fulfilling), but no to teaching a class (a set schedule wouldn't work for her anymore). She said yes to writing this book (a labor of love and homage to MJ). Choosing the tasks that were right for her brought her joy, and she is grateful for The No Club's help in identifying what those tasks were. In looking back, she's considered what she would do differently. She would have stopped saying "happy to" to so many tasks that she could easily do, but didn't need or want. She'd have been more confident about asking her colleague to pick up his share of course scheduling and other tasks, and she wouldn't have felt guilty, or worried that he'd be upset or think badly of her. Most important, she would have saved "happy to" for the things that really *did* make her happy and matter to her career, and thankfully, there were many of those.

Brenda also learned about thankless work on the home front. We haven't spent much time talking about tasks outside of work, but Brenda suddenly saw them up close and discovered so many! She was the one who bought birthday gifts and cards for family members. She kept the family calendar. Her husband hates answering the phone, and since he is the only human without a cell phone, they have a landline, which Brenda must answer because he won't. She lets him know (with great frequency) that this is a thankless job. He smiles and shrugs. She knows this won't change, and she's okay with that—he also does thankless tasks (they have two dogs). Their balance is pretty even, but that isn't the case for everyone. Most often, women handle thankless tasks at home after addressing NPTs at work. If you are one of those women, then you might consider how you and your partner can more equitably share the work.

Brenda's lessons were few but important: save "happy to" for when it counts. Learn what you love. For example, if mentoring others matters to you, as it does to Brenda, then find opportunities to do that—even though it's an NPT (remember, you have to do some). Limit *both* your loads of non-promotable tasks at work and thankless tasks on the home front.

Laurie served for a year and a half as the interim provost (i.e., chief academic officer) for Carnegie Mellon and then returned to a traditional faculty role. Having served in leadership and administrative positions for over ten years, the return was abrupt. Tasks that were part of her job as a senior associate dean and provost were no longer in her portfolio. She was no longer leading strategic initiatives, heading a team, and making consequential decisions. Instead, she had returned to conducting research and teaching students in the classroom. Work that she had enjoyed doing—and was good at—but that tapped a very different skill set than she had been using for the last ten years.

Using the lens of the promotability of work helped Laurie navigate this transition. She had to reanalyze what was promotable and not promotable, which as a professor again meant focusing on research and teaching. She soon realized that tasks that were promotable for one career path were not promotable for the other, and she needed to choose wisely. And if she wanted to reinvigorate her research (and write this book!), she needed to revise her ideal NPT portfolio to ensure her assignments were well aligned with her revised objectives.

She tried to be even more intentional regarding the NPTs she said yes to so she could have a manageable load. She chose NPTs that she cared about and where she had expertise to contribute, and said yes to activities that helped maintain her visibility in the profession. She tried not to commit to more than one large university-level initiative at a time. Laurie took on committee work that focused on diversity, spearheaded an effort to incorporate teamwork into the curriculum through classroom and experiential learning, and mentored and sponsored junior faculty. All those tasks mattered to her and played to her strengths.

Earlier in the book, we described Laurie as intuitively knowing what to steer toward. Her lesson was to turn that intuition into conscious choice. Now she knowingly agrees to the tasks that are right for her and declines those that are not.

Lise had a winding path. Her years of overcommitment and work overload were hard to change. Her battle with hypertension was the inciting event in her effort to pare down her workload. It helped her understand that she couldn't just work harder to keep up with all her yeses, so she needed to focus on what mattered most, and the club ensured she didn't lose her way. She stepped down as chair of her department and began saying no to the NPTs that others could do, but stepped up her commitment to her family and to the NPTs she cared about. She had spent her career examining obstacles to women's advancement, and while the obstacles were plentiful, the solutions were few. Lise realized that NPTs were different: their impact on women's success was first order and the solutions straightforward. She replaced her existing NPTs with extensive mentoring and countless talks to bring NPT awareness to her own institution, to organizations, and to individual women.

Lise learned on a personal level the answer to a problem she had been contemplating for over a decade. Her work on gender differences in competition had prompted diversity officers of leading companies in New York to ask for her guidance on how to encourage their best female employees to join the C-suite. The companies were troubled because these women, who were highly successful and valued, had climbed the corporate ladder and, at the last rung, opted not to go any further. Seen through the lens of NPTs, the decision made sense. Having handled excessive PT and NPT workloads, these women reached a point where further advancement wasn't all they wanted in life.

Lise ultimately faced a related decision. Over time, her research had gained substantial traction and recognition. She had become an important and visible scholar in her field, which led to a number of job offers, including the most recent one from an Ivy League university. She had dreamed of this job, and if she accepted it, it would virtually guarantee significant professional success: more visibility, higher compensation, access to people and organizations that would help further her research. But it also meant starting over: establishing new research relationships, raising funds, taking on more administrative duties and new committee assignments (NPTs) to gain visibility with her new colleagues.

She was torn. While she was happy and had been very productive at the University of Pittsburgh, the new opportunity was fantastic. But she knew that the move meant longer hours and more time away from family, which she very much wanted to avoid. As she agonized over the decision (and she did), she had clarity about what mattered to her. She loved using her mind and doing research, and she wanted more, not less, time to continue her work on non-promotable tasks and the impact they have on women's lives and organizations. Her professional life was key to her happiness, but so was her family. She cherished the relationships she had with friends, her home in Pittsburgh, time to travel overseas to see her family in Denmark, and her ability to be with her husband and children—to be present. Her life, the life that mattered to her, was more than her career. So she declined the offer. For her, it was the right decision. She doesn't rule out the possibility of accepting an offer later, but for now, this is where she wants and needs to be.

Lise's lesson was to reassess and rebalance her life. She is at the stage in her career where she can make this choice (and she recognizes that it would have been harder to do so earlier in her career). Her choice may not be one you would make, but her lessons about prioritizing what matters are worth pondering. So we ask, what matters most to you and how can you achieve that?

Linda has always worked to put research into practice—to take important insight from academia and make it accessible to individuals and organizations. She wrote a seminal book on women and negotiation to help women close the pay gap that exists between them and men. She founded an executive education institute to teach negotiation to women. She created a research center—PROGRESS—that examines issues related to, fittingly, women's and girls' progress. She even worked with the Girl Scouts to create a negotiation badge. Her focus on uncovering roadblocks to women's success also led her to look at issues like hiring protocols, the promotion process, and mentorship and sponsorship. In her work, she has shown how organizational practices have (unknowingly) impeded women's progress.

You'll recall that Linda went through a period of time where she questioned her work and her value as a researcher. Our work on NPTs showed her that she was still a productive and insightful scholar, and it gave her a new and exciting research focus. Even better, she was able to take our solutions and show that they can make a difference in the real world. She's spent the past two years consulting with a large firm's global task force to break down the barriers to women's success, and a centerpiece of that activity was non-promotable work. The firm has raised awareness of the gender divide in who does NPTs and, more important, has instituted numerous system-wide interventions to allocate NPTs more equitably. In a long career filled with interesting work, this was Linda's most rewarding experience. She now understands that this is the work she wants to do: to use our research to improve women's prospects and organizations' success. Not by fixing women but by fixing organizations. To do that, she's been slowly shifting her tasks at the university to make the time for this work that really matters to her. She's gained clarity on both her value and her direction. Now she says no so that she can say yes.

We wouldn't have learned any of this if we hadn't met in that restaurant over a decade ago to talk about how we couldn't say no. Nor would we have learned so much about other women's struggles with NPTs. We wouldn't have found our passion for setting this problem right and developing solutions for women and their organizations, solutions that are easy to implement. Non-promotable work is the critical barrier to women's advancement, and now, more than ever, this is the time to address it. Not only is it a persistent problem, it is worsening as organizations increasingly rely on remote work. So we're making NPTs a clarion call for you and your organization. It is time to put a stop to women's dead-end work.

Imagine how great you'll feel when you can walk into a meeting with the confidence that you won't be the note taker yet again, that this time it will be Ron's job. Sharing this load means that your career can take the shape you want it to and your organization can reap the benefits of *all* of your talents and efforts. It's not hard; it just takes will. You can do it, and so can your organization.

We're rooting for you, and we'll keep wishing for your success. We hope that you will have a shorter journey than we did, that you recognize NPTs more easily, that you balance your work portfolio more quickly, and that your organization takes to heart its obligation to systematically address the problem. We hope your club brings you wisdom and joy, support and friendship. Most of all, we hope that the lessons in this book will help you move your career, and your life, in the direction you want. And last, we hope that you will join us in doing the hard, meaningful work to move our organizations toward greater gender equity, to a future where NPTs are distributed fairly so that women and their organizations—finally—reach their potential.

How to Start a No Club

We're excited that you're thinking about starting a club, and if you're looking for guidance, we believe our experience will help. As a recap, our club began more than ten years ago with five members, the fifth being our dear departed friend MJ Tocci. We had different jobs, worked for different organizations (but mostly in the same industry), and had different interests and talents. We met in person at a local restaurant where we could drink $10 bottles of wine as we explored our difficulties with saying no, ultimately improving how we spent our time at work. Over the years, our club discussed and planned ways to change our institutions' organizational practices— to improve not only our lives but also those of our colleagues. To this day we turn to one another for guidance. Our No Club was the path to reducing our excessive load of NPTs and bringing the problem to light for others. We talked about the club—a lot—and other women asked for advice on starting clubs too. Since then, we've helped several clubs come into existence, each with its own character. To provide you with different perspectives for starting your own club, we also share how these other clubs function and what their experiences have been like.

In 2015, Linda was speaking about our work at a conference. Katherine Milkman, a behavioral scientist in attendance, pounced on the idea of the club and formed one with two of her colleagues, Dolly Chugh and Modupe Akinola, both of whom were in New York (Katy was in Philadelphia). They met virtually, long before the days of COVID-19-necessitated Zoom meetings. Some of their club experiences mirrored ours. Like us, Dolly felt that their club helped her decide what to say no to, how to say no, and what to ask for *before* saying yes. Interestingly, while our club still meets and our members rely on one another, Dolly feels that her club taught her to operate more independently: "I now rarely even ask the No Club because I feel like I know what they would say and that trained me to ask better questions of myself and others before responding." Katy echoed Dolly's comment: "Helping my colleagues decide when it's right for them to say no has boosted my confidence that I can judge for myself when it's right to say no, so I lean on the club less and less with each passing year." Within our own club, we think we also are better at knowing when to say no, but we have developed such a tight bond that we can't imagine not meeting or looking for advice from one another. For us, the club is a standing entity; for Katy's group, the club had its greatest value early on.

While we met in a restaurant and Katy's club met over Zoom, a third club in Berkeley, California, convened at their homes. The members have very different jobs, from web designer to nurse to project manager and professor. They knew one another, vaguely, through their children's school, but their club created a strong bond. All women with young children, they felt the pressures of both their professional and personal lives and were committed to doing right by both. They navigated a huge range of issues: how to say yes to the important tasks at work, how and when to say no to family, friends, and the many requests they got to volunteer in the community, at their children's schools, or even with their kids' friends. The language of guilt dominated their early meetings, but their later meetings reflected the language of women coming into their own space—they were confident about saying no and regaining control of their very full lives. Their club met less frequently than ours did, perhaps once every few months, because that's all their schedules allowed.

Camille, the epidemiologist from Chapter 8, had two groups: her "no" advisory council, composed of three senior women who advised her on important career issues, and a club , where she could focus on more personal and individual struggles. Her club's members all worked in the same organization and all had children at home, which mattered to them because they, like the Berkeley club, needed help from others who understood the challenges they faced. They noted a benefit to working for the same employer: they could speak with a collective voice. Early in the COVID-19 pandemic, when they were all working from home and managing their kids' schooling, they spoke to leadership about the problems they encountered trying to meet unreasonable expectations at work. They realized that speaking as a group allowed them to better represent a broader set of women, and that added strength to their arguments and protected each of them from being the lone voice in the wilderness. They were persuasive; their male boss saw their challenges, and he worked with them to calibrate the organization's expectations. Together, they put nonessential tasks on the back burner and made deadlines more flexible to let them and other caregivers cope with additional pressures due to COVID-19.

There really are no rules for forming the perfect club; each takes on the character and needs of its members. And, of course, your club doesn't need to be perfect—a good club will be very helpful as well—although we suspect that, like us, you will end up with a club that you think is pretty fantastic. There are a few things we learned that we'll pass on for your consideration: to be purposeful, focused, and above all, supportive. At your first meetings, it's good to reach common ground on why you're all there, and defining your purpose is a great starting point.

Purpose

The purpose of a No Club is to help you make better decisions about how to spend your time at work. The club helps you do this by:

- assessing the promotability of tasks you're asked to do or might volunteer for
- making sure you are saying yes and no to the right things
- holding you accountable for your choices
- making you aware of the implicit no that comes with every yes
- giving advice about how to say no to NPTs at the right time and in the best way
- helping you to change your organization

Club Members

1. Keep the group small—no more than five or six women. This keeps everyone engaged. No one gets lost on the periphery.
2. Invite others with whom you have things in common, but not too many things. Find the balance that allows for comfort and diversity of experience. People do not need to know everyone else in the group (each of us

was friends with Linda but not one another), but you do need to be comfortable with one another. At the same time, working in similar industries makes it easier to relate, while having variety in workplaces adds fresh perspectives.

3. Aim for diversity—try to find women of different races, ages, jobs, and organizational ranks. Our club had a range of ages, and MJ and Brenda had different jobs from the others, which led to some great perspectives.

4. Should you include men? You could, but including men can make it more difficult to focus on the specific issues that women face and the solutions that work best for us. We chose not to have men in our club, though several asked! We said no, which thankfully we had some practice doing.

Club Meetings

1. Timing: NPT requests are frequent and breaking old habits is hard, so meet regularly (every three to four weeks) to discuss challenges and solutions and provide support. We scheduled our meetings months in advance to fit them into everyone's calendar. In contrast, Camille's club functioned like a flash mob because planning didn't work for them. They agreed that when a member reached out, the rest would drop everything (including their kids) and say to their partners, "We're going out!"

2. Location: The conversations can get personal and emotional, so meet face-to-face or via videoconferencing

to make it easier to connect. We liked meeting in person and think that's best, so we met at a restaurant that was convenient for all of us. Camille's club did the same thing. Katy's club had members in different cities, so they used phone calls and video chats. The California club met in one another's homes. In our experience, alcohol helps.

3. Retreats: We've had several club retreats where we squirrel ourselves away in a remote location for a couple of days. We cook, play cards, go for long walks, and have intense (and fun) conversations. If you can do this relatively early on in your club tenure, it can jump-start your bonding experience.

Club Norms

1. Trust is necessary for people to be willing to share. Keep conversations confidential.
2. Hold one another accountable for your actions, but don't judge.
3. Recognize that everyone has different vulnerabilities and reasons for saying yes—some are personal; some are situational. Respect those differences and tailor suggestions with them in mind.
4. Celebrate successes, no matter how small. Laugh if you will, but we started a tradition of awarding a tiara to the person who had the most success in saying no that month. Likewise, we awarded a dunce cap to the person who had fallen into old, bad habits. We all wore both hats.

5. Be on call for one another. Respond to SOS emails as soon as you can. If you have an idea, offer it; if you don't, say so, but be supportive.

6. Only cancel a meeting for a dire emergency. Otherwise, figure out how to get there. Work "emergencies" are not an excuse.

Best Practices

1. Take some time at your first meeting to get to know one another, including personal facts and your work environments. Spend time sharing information and context.

2. Share your professional and personal goals with the club. They'll change over time, so be sure to keep everyone up to date. Ask for feedback on your ideal portfolio of NPTs and keep the club updated as it changes over time.

3. At every meeting, everyone takes a turn discussing recent requests and challenges in managing existing NPT assignments. Share successes, failures, and ongoing struggles.

   - Tell your story. Provide enough detail to paint a picture of the situation surrounding new requests and your existing load of NPTs. Include who was involved, what you were asked to do, where it occurred (e.g., was it public?), why you were asked, how promotable the task is, how aligned it is with your ideal portfolio, your implicit no, how you are planning to or did respond, how you will or do feel about your response, and why this is a hard choice (if it is) for you.

- Do you feel good about how you responded?
    - Success = glad you said yes; glad you said no.
    - Needs Improvement = mad, disappointed you said yes; wish you would have said no differently.
- When discussing challenges in managing your current NPT load, provide details on your overall load and how it compares with your ideal NPT portfolio. Discuss the assignments you would like to change. Give insight on how such changes might or might not be achieved. Present details on people involved in the decision to help align your portfolio of NPTs with your goals. Discuss the consequences to you and to your organization. Ask the club for advice and ideas on what you'd like to do. Solicit their input before you talk with your supervisor to be sure you present a compelling case for change.

4. Be open to feedback.
    - Does the club see things the way you do? Are you being too hard on yourself? Do you have a blind spot regarding what is and is not an NPT?
    - For a decision you made: What would the club suggest you could or should have done differently? What worked well that you would like to repeat?
    - For a pending decision: Does the club think you should say no? How would they recommend you best communicate your no to mitigate any negative repercussions? If the club thinks you should say yes, be sure to discuss your implicit no and whether you can offload assignments in return for agreeing to a new request.

- For a challenge in managing your load of NPTs: Does the club have creative ideas for how you can lighten your load? Are there tasks that belong to someone else, that are promotable for others? Can you swap assignments to get work that is more compatible with your other assignments?

5. Listen. *Really* listen. Stay focused on the story you're hearing. Ask questions to help your clubmate figure out what's going on. Avoid the temptation of saying, "I know how you feel," and augmenting the story by sharing something similar that happened to you. While it's natural to respond to another's story by sharing your own, it shifts the focus away from the original story and the person telling it.

6. Finally, we'd encourage you to enjoy the time you spend together. It's increasingly rare to find a group of people invested in your success, and the club provided that for us. Along with solid professional advice, we have developed deep, lifelong friendships, and we hope your club does the same for you.

Glossary of Terms

Backlash: A punishing reaction for violating a norm of behavior. For example, women are expected to help and may be punished for declining requests for help.

Benevolent sexism: A positive orientation of protection and affection toward women. It is a patronizing form of sexism that paints women in a positive light to perpetuate their subordinate status to men.

Coordination game: Used in game theory to characterize a situation where players are better off if they coordinate their behavior by choosing the same or corresponding strategies. For example, two people who meet at an intersection are better off if they coordinate their actions, with the driver on the left yielding to the driver on the right.

Cultural taxation: The extra unrewarded work that results from assigning members of a minority group to serve as representatives of their minority group. While the aim is to hear voices from underrepresented groups, there is a negative outcome as the affected individuals are "taxed" by having to engage in more unrewarded work than their colleagues do.

Emotional labor: The effort exerted to regulate or manage one's own emotional expressions to satisfy expectations of one's professional work role.

Faculty senate: An official organization in an academic institution that participates in the shared governance of the institution by considering and making recommendations concerning educational policies and other matters of institution-wide concern. It is typically a non-promotable task.

Game of chicken: Used in game theory to characterize a situation of conflict between players. The classic example of this game is when two drivers are headed toward a single-lane bridge from opposite directions. The first to stop and yield the bridge to the other driver is the "chicken." We use this term to describe a situation where multiple people are asked to do an NPT and the first one to say yes is the chicken.

Gender congruence: The extent to which a person of a particular gender "fits" a job or situation. For example, it is gender congruent for a woman to offer to help (because women are expected to help), and it is gender incongruent for a woman to refuse to help (because it is unexpected).

Ideal portfolio of work: the set of promotable and non-promotable tasks that allows employees to be successful and reach their potential; the goal employees strive for when considering new requests and reallocating current assignments. It specifies both the appropriate division of time between promotable and non-promotable work, and the assignments that best help the employee succeed.

Implicit no: What an individual gives up by saying yes to something else. If I agree to serve on a committee that meets in the evenings, my implicit no might be the time I give up working out or being with my family. Economists refer to the value of what is given up as the *opportunity cost*.

Invisible work: Work that is unseen and unacknowledged.

Loose culture: Where social norms are flexible, informal, and allow for individual interpretation.

Median: The value or point at which half the data falls above and half falls below.

Non-promotable tasks: Tasks that matter to the organization but do not advance the career of the individual who completes them. Non-promotable tasks are not instrumental to increasing the organization's currency, are often not visible, and may not require specialized skills (many others can do them).

Norms: Expectations about how people will or should behave.

Optimal set of non-promotable tasks: Within the ideal portfolio of work, the set of non-promotable tasks employees strive for as they consider new requests and reallocate current assignments. It specifies the maximum amount of time to spend on non-promotable work and the assignments that would be best. To create this, employees select NPTs that are appropriate for the job, match their skill and experience level, meet the organization's expectations, are personally fulfilling, and allow appropriate time to focus on promotable work.

Organizational culture: The shared values and beliefs that create expectations for how people in the organization should behave.

Organizational currency: What an organization values most, e.g., profit, mission, customer satisfaction, growth. Promotable tasks are highly aligned with an organization's currency.

Promotability of a task (continuum): The more promotable a task, the more likely it is to advance the employee's career in terms of pay, performance evaluations, promotions, and status. Tasks low in promotability have little impact on career advancement, with the opposite holding true for tasks high in promotability.

Promotable tasks: Tasks that lead to career advancement. Promotable tasks are: closely aligned with organizational currency, visible, and often require specialized skills that can differentiate an employee from others. Tasks that prepare the employee for future promotable work are indirectly promotable.

Specialized skills: Abilities that are unique or that require specific training and talent.

Stereotype: A widely held, oversimplified belief about the characteristics or behavior of a person based upon that person's demographic group or aspect of identity.

Tenure: In academia, this refers to the granting of an academic appointment without limit in time and assures the appointee of continued employment.

Tight culture: Where social norms are well proscribed and defined, with little room for individual interpretation.

Work/life balance: The sweet spot where the division of time between our professional and personal lives makes us happiest.

Work overload: A too-heavy load of work. Employees with work overload spend excessive hours completing all their tasks, which causes work/life imbalance.

Work/work balance: The sweet spot where the division of time at work between *non-promotable* and *promotable* work allows an employee to be successful and reach their potential.

Work/work imbalance: When an employee's load of non-promotable work relative to promotable work exceeds that of their peers and harms their potential for advancement.

References

Acker, J. "Hierarchies, jobs, bodies: A theory of gendered organizations." *Gender and Society* 4, no. 2 (1990): 139–58.

Agovino, T. "To have and to hold: Amid one of the tightest labor markets in the past 50 years, employee retention is more critical than ever." *Society for Human Resource Management.* February 23, 2019. https://www.shrm.org/hr -today/news/all-things-work/pages/to-have-and-to-hold.aspx.

Albanesi, S., and J. Kim. "The gendered impact of the COVID-19 recession on the US labor market." NBER Working paper 28505, February 2021.

Alexandrova-Karamonova, A., I. Todorova, A. J. Montgomery, E. Panagopolou, et al. "Burnout and health behaviors in health professionals from seven European countries." *International Archives of Occupational and Environmental Health* 89, no. 7 (2016): 1059–75.

Andreoni, J., and L. Vesterlund. "Which is the fair sex: Gender differences in altruism." *Quarterly Journal of Economics* 116, no. 1 (2001): 293–312.

Antonio, A. L. "Faculty of color reconsidered: Reassessing contributions to scholarship." *Higher Education* 73, no. 5 (2003): 582–602.

Babcock, L., F. Flynn, and J. Zlatev. "Assigning non-promotable work." Unpublished working paper, 2015.

Babcock, L., M. Recalde, and L. Vesterlund. "Why women volunteer for tasks that don't lead to promotions." *Harvard Business Review*, July 16, 2018. https://hbr.org/2018/07/why-women-volunteer-for-tasks-that-dont-lead -to-promotions.

Babcock, L., M. Recalde, L. Vesterlund, and L. Weingart. "Gender differences in accepting and receiving requests for tasks with low promotability." *American Economic Review* 107, no. 3 (2017): 714–47.

Bacharach, S. B., P. Bamberger, and S. Conley. "Work-home conflict among nurses and engineers: Mediating the impact of role stress on burnout and satisfaction at work." *Journal of Organizational Behavior* 12, no. 1 (1991): 39–53.

Baez, B. "Race-related service and faculty of color: Conceptualizing critical agency in academe." *Higher Education* 39, no. 3 (2000): 363–91.

Battilana, J., and T. Cascario. "The network secrets of great change agents." *Harvard Business Review* (July–August 2013).

Bazerman, M., I. Bohnet, H. R. Bowles, and G. F. Loewenstein. "Linda Babcock: Go-getter and do-gooder." *Negotiation and Conflict Management Research* 11, no. 2 (2018): 130–45.

Bellas, M. L., and R. K. Toutkoushian. "Faculty time allocations and research productivity: Gender, race, and family effects." *Review of Higher Education* 22, no. 4 (1999): 367–90.

Benschop, Y., L. Halsema, and P. Schreurs. "The division of labour and inequalities between the sexes: An ideological dilemma." *Gender, Work, and Organization* 8, no. 1 (2001): 1–18.

Bianchi, S. M., J. P. Robinson, and M. A. Milkie. *Changing Rhythms of American Family Life.* New York: Russell Sage Foundation, 2006.

Bohnet, I. *What Works: Gender Equality by Design.* Cambridge, MA: Harvard University Press, 2016.

Boucher, C. "A qualitative study of the impact of emotional labour on health managers." *The Qualitative Report* 21, no. 11 (2016): 2148–60.

Braiker, H. B. *The Disease to Please: Curing the People-Pleasing Syndrome.* New York: McGraw-Hill, 2002.

Britton, D. M. "Gendered organizational logic: Policy and practice in men's and women's prisons." *Gender and Society* 11, no. 6 (1997): 796–818.

Bueher, R., D. Griffin, and J. Peetz. "The planning fallacy: Cognitive, motivation, and social origins." *Advances in Experimental Social Psychology* 23 (2010): 1–62.

Cech, E., B. Rubineau, S. S. Silbey, and C. Seron. "Professional role confidence and gendered persistence in engineering." *American Sociological Review* 76, no. 5 (2011): 641–66.

Chan, C. K., and M. Anteby. "Task segregation as a mechanism for within-job inequality: Women and men of the Transportation Security Administration." *Administrative Science Quarterly* 61, no. 2 (2015): 184–216.

Chugh, D. *The Person You Mean to Be: How Good People Fight Bias.* New York: Harper Business, 2018.

Colquitt, J. A., D. E. Conlon, M. J. Wesson, C. O. Porter, and K. Y. Ng. "Justice at the millennium: A meta-analytic review of 25 years of organizational justice research." *Journal of Applied Psychology* 86 (2001): 425–45.

Cooper, D., and J. Kagel. "A failure to communicate: An experimental investigation of the effects of advice on strategic play." *European Economic Review* 82, no. C (2016): 24–45.

Croson, R., and U. Gneezy. "Gender differences in preferences." *Journal of Economic Literature* 47, no. 2 (2009): 448–74.

Cross, R., and L. Prusak. "The people who make organizations go—or stop." *Harvard Business Review* (June 2002).

Crouter, A. C., M. F. Bumpus, M. R. Head, and S. M. McHale. "Implications of overwork and overload for the quality of men's family relationships." *Journal of Marriage and Family* 63, no. 2 (2001): 404–16.

Crouter, A. C., M. F. Bumpus, M. C. Maguire, and S. M. McHale. "Linking parents' work pressure and adolescents' well-being: Insights into dynamics in dual-earner families." *Developmental Psychology* 35, no. 6 (1999): 1453–61.

Daniels, A. K. "Invisible work." *Social Problems* 34, no. 5 (1987): 403–15.

De Pater, I., A. Van Vianen, and M. Bechtoldt. "Gender differences in job challenge: A matter of task allocation." *Gender, Work, and Organization* 17, no. 4 (2010): 433–53.

Dilmaghani, M. "Exploring the link between sexual orientation, work-life balance satisfaction and work-life segmentation." *International Journal of Manpower* 41, no. 6 (2019): 693–715.

Doran, G. T. "There's a S.M.A.R.T. way to write management's goals and objectives." *Management Review* 70, no. 11 (1981): 35–36.

Dotti Sani, G. M., and J. Treas. "Educational gradients in parents' child-care time across countries, 1965–2012." *Journal of Marriage and Family* 78, no. 4 (2016): 1083–96.

Dutton, J. E., S. J. Ashford, R. M. O'Neill, and K. A. Lawrence. "Moves that matter: Issue selling and organizational change." *Academy of Management Journal* 44, no. 4 (2001): 716–36.

Dutton, J. E., and A. Wrzesniewski. "What job crafting looks like." *Harvard Business Review*, March 12, 2020. https://hbr.org/2020/03/what-job-crafting-looks-like.

Eagly, A. H. *Sex Differences in Social Behavior: A Social Role Interpretation*. Hillsdale, NJ: Erlbaum, 1987.

Eagly, A. H., and S. J. Karau. "Role congruity theory of prejudice toward female leaders." *Psychological Review* 109, no. 3 (2002): 574–98.

Eagly, A. H., W. Wood, and L. Fishbaugh. "Sex differences in conformity: Surveillance by the group as a determinant of male nonconformity." *Journal of Personality and Social Psychology* 40, no. 2 (1981): 384–94.

Eckel, C. C., and P. J. Grossman. "Are men less selfish than women: Evidence from dictator experiments." *The Economic Journal* 108, no. 448 (1998): 726–35.

Eckel, C. C., and P. J. Grossman. "Differences in the economic decisions of men and women: Experimental evidence." In *Handbook of Experimental Economics Results, Vol. 1*, edited by C. Plott and V. Smith, 509–19. New York: Elsevier, 2008.

Fleister, C. "Women's work? Why female employees take on thankless tasks shunned by men . . . and how that hurts women's careers." American Economic Association. March 15, 2017. https://www.aeaweb.org/research /women-men-promotable-task-differences.

Fletcher, J. K. "Relational practice: A feminist reconstruction of work." *Journal of Management Inquiry* 7, no. 2 (1998): 163–86.

Flynn, F. J., and V. K. B. Lake. "If you need help just ask: Underestimating compliance with direct requests for help." *Journal of Personality and Social Psychology* 95, no. 1 (2008): 128–43.

Galambos, N. L., H. A. Sears, D. M. Almeida, and G. C. Kolaric. "Parents' work overload and problem behavior in young adolescents." *Journal of Research on Adolescence* 5, no. 2 (1995): 201–23.

Galanakis M., A. Stalikas, H. Kallia, C. Karagianni, and C. Karela. "Gender differences in experiencing occupational stress: The role of age, education and marital status." *Stress Health* 25 (2009): 397–404.

Gelfand, M. G. *Rule Makers, Rule Breakers: How Tight and Loose Cultures Wire Our World*. New York: Scribner, 2018.

Georgeac, O. "The business case backfires: Detrimental effects of organizations' instrumental diversity rhetoric for underrepresented group members' sense of belonging and performance." Doctoral dissertation, London Business School, 2020.

Gewin, V. "The time tax put on scientists of color." *Nature* 583. July 16, 2020. https://www.nature.com/articles/d41586-020-01920-6.

Gihleb, R., R. Landsman, and L. Vesterlund. "The effect of task assignment on compensation and negotiation." Working paper, University of Pittsburgh, 2021.

Glick, P., and S. T. Fiske. "The ambivalent sexism inventory: Differentiating hostile and benevolent sexism." *Journal of Personality and Social Psychology* 70, no. 3 (1996): 491–512.

Glueck, S., and E. Glueck. *Unraveling Juvenile Delinquency*. New York: Commonwealth Fund, 1950.

Glueck, S., and E. Glueck. *Delinquents and Nondelinquents in Perspective*. Cambridge, MA: Harvard University Press, 1968.

Gogoi, P. "Stuck-At-Home Moms: The Pandemic's Devastating Toll on Women," NPR, October 28, 2020. https://www.npr.org/2020/10/28/928253674 /stuck-at-home-moms-the-pandemics-devastating-toll-on-women.

Goldin, C. "A grand gender convergence: Its last chapter." *American Economic Review* 104, no. 4 (2014): 1091–119.

Goldin, C. *Career and Family: Women's Century-long Journey Toward Equity.* New Jersey: Princeton University Press, 2021.

Gompers, P. A., and S. Q. Wang. "And the children shall lead: Gender diversity and performance in venture capital." Working paper, *National Bureau of Economic Research.* May 2017.

Gorman, E. H. "Gender stereotypes, same-gender preferences, and organizational variation in the hiring of women: Evidence from law firms." *American Sociological Review* 70, no. 4 (2005): 702–28.

Greenhaus, J. H., and N. J. Beutell. "Sources of conflict between work and family roles." *Academy of Management Review* 10, no. 1 (1985): 76–88.

Guarino, C. M., and V. M. H. Borden. "Faculty service loads and gender: Are women taking care of the academic family?" *Research in Higher Education* 58, no. 4 (2017): 672–94.

Harter, J. K., F. L. Schmidt, S. Agrawal, A. Blue, S. K. Plowman, P. Josh, and J. Asplund. "The relationship between engagement at work and organizational outcomes." Gallup, 2020 Q12 Meta-Analysis: Tenth Edition, https://www.gallup.com/workplace/321725/gallup-q12-meta-analysis -report.aspx.

Heilman, M. E. "Sex bias in work settings: The lack of fit model." In *Research in Organization Behavior, Vol. 5*, edited by B. M. Staw and L. L. Cummings. Greenwich, CT: JAI Press, 1983, 269–98.

Heilman, M. E., and J. J. Chen. "Same behavior, different consequences: Reactions to men's and women's altruistic citizenship behavior." *Journal of Applied Psychology* 90, no. 3 (2005): 431–41.

Heilman, M. E., and M. C. Haynes. "No credit where credit is due: Attributional rationalization of women's success in male-female teams." *Journal of Applied Psychology* 90, no. 5 (2005): 905–16.

Hirshfeld, L. E., and T. D. Joseph. "'We need a woman, we need a black woman': Gender, race, and identity taxation in the academy." *Gender and Education* 24, no. 2 (2012): 213–27.

Hochschild, A. R. *The Managed Heart: Commercialization of Human Feeling.* Berkeley, CA: University of California Press, 1983.

Hsieh, C-T., E. Hurst, C. I. Jones, and P. J. Klenow. "The allocation of talent and U.S. economic growth." *Econometrica* 87, no. 5 (2019): 1439–74.

Jaroszewicz, A. "It does hurt to ask: Theory and evidence on informal help-seeking." Doctoral dissertation, Carnegie Mellon University, 2020.

Jex, S. M. *Stress and Job Performance: Theory, Research, and Implications for Managerial Practice*. Advanced Topics in Organization Behavior Series: Sage Publications Ltd., 1998.

Judge, T. A., C. J. Thoresen, J. E. Bono, and G. K. Patton. "The job satisfaction-job performance relationship: A qualitative and quantitative review." *Psychological Bulletin* 127, no. 3 (2001): 376–407.

Kahneman, D. *Thinking, Fast and Slow*. New York: Farrar, Straus and Giroux, 2011.

Kanter, R. M. *Men and Women of the Corporation*. New York: Basic Books, 1977.

Kaplan, R. S., and D. P. Norton. "The balanced scorecard—measures that drive performance," *Harvard Business Review* (January–February 1992).

Keck, S., and L. Babcock. "Who gets the benefit of the doubt? The impact of causal reasoning depth on how violations of gender stereotypes are evaluated." *Journal of Organizational Behavior* 39, no. 3 (2017): 276–91.

Kidder, D. L. "The influence of gender on the performance of organizational citizenship behaviors." *Journal of Management* 28, no. 5 (2002): 629–48.

Kimmel, S. E., A. B. Troxel, B. French, G. Loewenstein, et al. "A randomized trial of lottery-based incentives and reminders to improve warfarin adherence: The warfarin incentives (WIN2) trial." *Pharmacoepidemiol Drug Safety* 25, no. 11 (2016): 1219–27.

King, E. B., M. R. Hebl, J. M. George, and S. F. Matuski. "Understanding tokenism: Antecedents and consequences of a psychological climate of gender inequity." *Journal of Management* 36, no. 2 (2010): 482–510.

Kivimaki, M., M. Jokela, S. T. Nyberg, A. Singh-Manoux, et al. "Long working hours and risk of coronary heart disease and stroke: A systematic review and meta-analysis." *The Lancet* 386, no. 10005 (2015): 1739–46.

Kodz, J., S. Davis, D. Lain, M. Strebler, J. Rick, P. Bates, J. Cummings, and N. Meager. "Working long hours: A review of the evidence." Volume 1 – Main Report, Employment Relations Research Eseries, ERRS16, Department of Trade and Industry, 2003.

Kolb, D. M., and J. L. Porter. "'Office housework' gets in women's way." *Harvard Business Review*, April 16, 2015. https://hbr.org/2015/04/office-housework-gets-in-womens-way.

Laden, B. V., and L. S. Hagedorn. "Job satisfaction among faculty of color in academe: Individual survivors or institutional transformers?," *New Directions for Institutional Research 2000*, no. 105 (2000): 57–66.

Laibson, D. "Golden eggs and hyperbolic discounting." *Quarterly Journal of Economics* 112, no. 2 (1997): 443–77.

Lavner, J. A., and M. A. Clark. "Workload and marital satisfaction over time: Testing lagged spillover and crossover effects during the newlywed years." *Journal of Vocation Behavior* 101 (2017): 67–76.

Loewenstein, G., and J. Elster. *Choice Over Time*. New York: Russell Sage Foundation, 1992.

Loewenstein, G., and R. H. Thaler. "Anomalies: Intertemporal choice." *Journal of Economic Perspectives* 3, no. 4 (1989): 181–93.

Lu, S., K. M. Bartol, V. Venkataramani, and X. Zheng. "Pitching novel ideas to the boss: The interactive effects of employees' idea enactment and influence tactics on creativity assessment and implementation." *Academy of Management Journal* 62, no. 2 (2019): 579–606.

Lunstad-Holt, J., T. B. Smith, and J. B. Layton. "Social relationships and mortality risk: A meta-analytic review." *PLOS Medicine* 7, no. 7 (2010): 1–20.

Maruyama, S., and K. Morimoto. "Effects of long hours on lifestyle, stress and quality of life among intermediate Japanese managers." *Scandinavian Journal of Work Environment Health* 22 (1996): 353–59.

Mayor, E. "Gender roles and traits in stress and health." *Frontiers in Psychology* 6 (2015): 779.

McCrae, R. R., and A. Terracciano. "Universal features of personality traits from the observer's perspective: Data from 50 countries." *Journal of Personality and Social Psychology* 88, no. 3 (2005): 547–61.

McKinsey & Company, "Women in the Workplace," 2021, https://wiw-report.s3 .amazonaws.com/Women_in_the_Workplace_2021.pdf.

McKinsey & Company, "Achieving an inclusive US economic recovery," February 3, 2021, https://www.mckinsey.com/industries/public-and-social -sector/our-insights/achieving-an-inclusive-us-economic-recovery.

Milkman, K. L., M. S. Patel, L. Candhi, H. Graci, et al. "A mega-study of text-based nudges encouraging patients to get vaccinated at an upcoming doctor's appointment." *Proceedings of the National Academy of Sciences* 188, no. 20 (2021).

Misra, J., J. H. Lundquist, E. Holmes, and S. Agiomavritis. "The ivory ceiling of service work." *Academe Online*. January–February 2011. https://www.aaup .org/article/ivory-ceiling-service-work#.Ycn-9mjMI2w.

Misra, J., J. H. Lundquist, and A. Templer. "Gender, work time, and care responsibilities among faculty." *Sociological Forum* 27, no. 2 (2012): 300–323.

Mitchell, S. M., and V. L. Hesli. "Women don't ask? Women don't say no? Bargaining and service in the political science profession." *PS: Political Science & Politics* 46, no. 2 (2013): 355–69.

Moon, M. "Bottom-up instigated organizational change through constructionist conversation." *Journal of Knowledge Management Practices* 9, no. 4 (2008): 1–14.

Morgan Roberts, L., A. J. Mayo, R. J. Ely, and D. A. Thomas. "Beating the odds—Leadership lessons from senior African American women." *Harvard Business Review* (March–April 2018).

Moss-Racusin, C. A., J. F. Dovidio, V. L. Brescoll, M. J. Graham, and J. Handelsman. "Science faculty's subtle gender biases favor male students." *Proceedings of the National Academy of Sciences* 109, no. 41 (2012): 16464–79.

Mowday, R. T., L. W. Porter, and R. M. Steers. *Employee-organizational Linkages: The Psychology of Commitment, Absenteeism, and Turnover.* New York: Academic Press, 1982.

Netemeyer, R. G., J. S. Boles, and R. McMurrian. "Development and validation of work-family conflict and family-work conflict scales." *Journal of Applied Psychology* 81, no. 4 (1996): 400–410.

Niederle, M. "Gender." In *The Handbook of Experimental Economics, Vol. 2,* edited by J. H. Kagel and A. E. Roth, 481–562. Princeton, NJ: Princeton University Press, 2016.

Niederle, M., and L. Vesterlund. "Do women shy away from competition? Do men compete too much?" *Quarterly Journal of Economics* 122, no. 3 (2007): 1067–101.

Niederle, M., and L. Vesterlund. "Gender and competition." *Annual Review of Economics* 3, no. 1 (2011): 601–30.

Nock, S. L., and P. W. Kingston. "Time with children: The impact of couples' work-time commitments." *Social Forces* 67, no. 1 (1988): 59–85.

Olds, D. M., and S. P. Clark. "The effect of work hours on adverse events and errors in health care." *Journal of Safety Research* 41, no. 2 (2010): 153–62.

O'Reilly, C. A., D. F. Caldwell, J. A. Chatman, M. Lapiz, and W. Self. "How leadership matters: The effects of leaders' alignment on strategy implementation." *The Leadership Quarterly* 21, no. 1 (2010): 104–13.

Padilla, A. M. "Ethnic minority scholars, research, and mentoring: Current and future issues." *Educational Research* 23, no. 4 (1994): 24–27.

Pencavel, J. *Diminishing Returns at Work: The Consequences of Long Working Hours.* New York: Oxford University Press, 2018.

Podsakoff, N. P., S. W. Whiting, P. M. Podsakoff, and B. D. Blume. "Individual- and organizational-level consequences of organizational citizenship behaviors: A meta-analysis." *Journal of Applied Psychology* 94, no. 1 (2009): 122–41.

Porter, S. R. "A closer look at faculty service: What affects participation on committees?" *The Journal of Higher Education* 78, no. 5 (2007): 523–41.

Potts, M. K., M. A. Burnam, and K. B. Wells. "Gender differences in depression detection: A comparison of clinician diagnosis and standardized assessment." *Psychological Assessment* 3, no. 4 (1991): 609–15.

Pratt, M. G., K. W. Rockmann, and J. B. Kaufmann. "Constructing professional identity: The role of work and identity learning cycles in the customization of identity among medical residents." *Academy of Management Journal* 49, no. 2 (2006): 235–62.

Purvanova, R. K., and J. P. Muros. "Gender differences in burnout: A meta-analysis." *Journal of Vocational Behavior* 77, no. 2 (2010): 168–85.

Putnick, D. L., M. H. Bornstein, C. Hendricks, K. M. Painter, J. Suwalsky, and W. A. Collins. "Parenting stress, perceived parenting behaviors, and adolescent self-concept in European American families." *Journal of Family Psychology* 22, no. 5 (2008): 752–62.

PricewaterhouseCoopers. "Winning the fight for female talent." https://www.pwc.com/gx/en/about/diversity/iwd/iwd-female-talent-report-web.pdf. 2017.

Reid, E. "Embracing, passing, revealing, and the ideal worker image: How people navigate expected and experienced professional identities." *Organization Science* 26, no. 4 (2015): 997–1017.

Rhimes, S. *Year of Yes: How to Dance It Out, Stand in the Sun, and Be Your Own Person*. New York: Simon & Schuster, 2015.

Rogers, T., and A. Feller. "Reducing student absences at scale by targeting parents' misbeliefs." *Nature Human Behaviour* 2 (2018): 335–42.

Roth, L. M. *Selling Women Short: Gender and Money on Wall Street*. Princeton, NJ: Princeton University Press, 2006.

Sainsbury's Living Well Index, The. 2018. https://www.about.sainsburys.co.uk/~/media/Files/S/Sainsburys/living-well-index/sainsburys-living-well-index-may-2018.pdf.

Santee, R. T., and S. E. Jackson. "Identity implications of conformity: Sex differences in normative and attributional judgments." *Social Psychology Quarterly* 45, no. 2 (1982): 121–25.

Schelling, T. C. *The Strategy of Conflict*. Cambridge, MA: Harvard University Press, 1960.

Schmitt, D. P., A. Realo, M. Voracek, and J. Allik. "Why can't a man be more like a woman? Sex differences in Big Five personality traits across 55 cultures." *Journal of Personality and Social Psychology* 94, no. 1 (2008): 168–82.

Semmer, N. K., N. Jacobshagen, L. L. Meier, A. Elfering, T. A. Beehr, W. Kalin, and F. Tschan. "Illegitimate tasks as a source of work stress." *Work and Stress* 29, no. 1 (2015): 32–56.

Semmer, N. K., F. Tschan, L. L. Meier, S. Facchin, and N. Jacobshagen. "Illegitimate tasks and counterproductive work behavior." *Applied Psychology: An International Review* 59, no. 1 (2010): 70–96.

Shafer, E. F., and N. Malhotra. "The effect of a child's sex on support for traditional gender roles." *Social Forces* 90, no. 1 (2011): 209–22.

Skuratowicz, E., and L. W. Hunter. "Where do women's jobs come from? Job re-segregation in an American bank." *Work and Occupations* 31, no. 1 (2004): 73–110.

Society for Human Resource Management. "Employee job satisfaction and engagement: Optimizing organizational culture for success." Report, 2015, https://www.shrm.org/hr-today/trends-and-forecasting/research-and-surveys/pages/job-satisfaction-and-engagement-report-optimizing-organizational-culture-for-success.aspx.

Sonnentag, S., and M. Frese. "Stress in Organizations." In *Handbook of Psychology*, Volume 12, edited by W. C. Borman, D. R. Ilgen, and R. J. Klimoski, 453–91. Hoboken, NJ: Wiley, 2003.

Sorenson, S., and K. Garman. "How to tackle U.S. employees' stagnating engagement," Gallup, June 11, 2013. https://news.gallup.com/businessjournal/162953/tackle-employees-stagnating-engagement.aspx.

Sparks, K., B. Faragher, and C. L. Cooper. "Well-being and occupation health in the 21st century workplace." *Journal of Occupational and Organization Psychology* 74 (2001): 489–509.

Stouten, J., D. Rousseau, and D. De Cremer. "Successful organizational change: Integrating the management practice and scholarly literatures." *Academy of Management Annals* 12 (2018): 752–88.

Tewfik, B., T. Kundro, and P. Tetlock. "The help-decliner's dilemma: How to decline requests for help at work without hurting one's image." Unpublished working paper, 2018.

Thaler, R. H., and H. Shefrin. "An economic theory of self-control." *Journal of Political Economy* 89, no. 2 (1981): 392–406.

Tolich, M., and C. Briar. "Just checking it out: Exploring the significance of informal gender divisions amongst American supermarket employees." *Gender, Work, & Organization* 6, no. 3 (1999): 129–33.

Tulshyan, R. "Women of color asked to do more 'office housework.' Here's how they can say no." *Harvard Business Review*, April 6, 2018. https://hbr.org/2018/04/women-of-color-get-asked-to-do-more-office-housework-heres-how-they-can-say-no.

Turco, C. J. "Cultural foundations of tokenism: Evidence from the leveraged buyout industry." *American Sociological Review* 75, no. 6 (2010): 894–913.

Turner, C. S. V. "Women of color in academe: Living with multiple marginality." *Journal of Higher Education* 73, no. 1 (2002): 74–93.

Tuten, T. L., and R. A. August. "Work-family conflict: A study of lesbian mothers." *Women in Management Review* 21, no. 7 (2006): 578–97.

Ury, W. *The Power of a Positive No: How to Say No and Still Get to Yes.* New York: Bantam, 2007.

U.S. Bureau of Labor Statistics. Labor Force Statistics from the Current Population Survey, 2020. https://www.bls.gov/cps/cpsaat11.htm.

Vaillant, G. E., C. C. McArthur, and A. Bock. *Triumphs of Experience: The Men of the Harvard Grant Study.* Cambridge, MA: Belnap Press, 2012.

Vander Hulst, M. "Long workhours and health." *Scandinavian Journal of Work, Environment & Health* 29, no. 3 (2003): 171–88.

Warner, R. L., and B. S. Steel. "Child rearing as a mechanism for social change: The relationship of child gender to parents' commitment to gender equity." *Gender & Society* 13, no. 4 (1999): 503–17.

Washington, E. L. "Female socialization: How daughters affect their legislator fathers' voting on women's issues." *American Economic Review* 98, no. 1 (2008): 311–32.

Weeden, K. A., Y. Cha, and M. Bucca. "Long work hours, part-time work, and trends in the gender gap in pay, the motherhood wage penalty, and the fatherhood wage premium." *The Russell Sage Foundation Journal of the Social Sciences* 2, no. 4 (2016): 71–102.

Weirup, A., L. Babcock, and T. Cohen. "Gender differences in the response to requests to do non-promotable tasks." Unpublished manuscript, available from authors upon request. 2020.

Weirup, A., L. Babcock, L. Vesterlund, and L. Weingart. "How emotions affect the decision to do non-promotable tasks." Unpublished manuscript, available from authors upon request. 2017.

Wessel, A. "Does having a daughter make fathers more liberal?" Unpublished manuscript. 2020.

Wharton, A. S., and M. Blair-Loy. "Long work hours and family: A cross-national study of employees' concerns." *Journal of Family Issues* 27, no. 3 (2006): 415–36.

Williams, C. L. "The glass escalator: Hidden advantages for men in the 'female' professions." *Social Problems* 39, no. 3 (1992): 253–67.

Williams, J. C., and M. Multhaup. "For women and minorities to get ahead managers must assign work fairly." *Harvard Business Review*, March 5, 2018.

https://hbr.org/2018/03/for-women-and-minorities-to-get-ahead-manag ers-must-assign-work-fairly.

Williams, J. C., M. Multhaup, S. Li, and R. M. Korn. "You can't change what you can't see: Interrupting racial & gender bias in the legal profession." American Bar Association & Minority Corporate Counsel Association (2018). https://www.mcca.com/wp-content/uploads/2018/09/You-Cant-Change -What-You-Cant-See-Executive-Summary.pdf.

Williams, J. C., S. Li, R. Rincon, and P. Finn. *Climate control: Gender and racial bias in engineering?*, Center for Worklife Law & Society of Women Engineers (2016). https://worklifelaw.org/publications/Climate-Control -Gender-And-Racial-Bias-In-Engineering.pdf.

Williamson, T., C. R. Goodwin, and P. A. Ubel. "Minority tax reform—Avoiding overtaxing minorities when we need them the most." *The New England Journal of Medicine* 384, no. 20 (2021): 1877–79.

Wong, K., A. Chan, and S. C. Ngan. "The effect of long working hours and overtime on occupational health: A meta-analysis of evidence from 1998 to 2018." *International Journal of Environmental Research and Public Health* 16, no. 12 (2019): 2102.

Work Institute, The. 2019 Retention Report. https://info.workinstitute.com /hubfs/2019%20Retention%20Report/Work%20Institute%202019%20 Retention%20Report%20final-1.pdf.

World Health Organization. "Occupational health: Stress at the workplace." 2020. https://www.who.int/news-room/questions-and-answers/item/ccu pational-health-stress-at-the-workplace.

Notes

Chapter 1: The No Club

9 *"Often these situations which go on in a woman's career . . ."*: M. Pickett, "I Want What My Male Colleague Has and That Will Cost a Few Million Dollars," *New York Times*, April 18, 2019.

Chapter 2: What Are Non-Promotable Tasks?

18 *In a 2021 report, McKinsey & Company, in partnership with Lean In*: McKinsey & Company, "Women in the Workplace," 2021, https://wiw-report.s3.am azonaws.com/Women_in_the_Workplace_2021.pdf. Statistics that follow are from page 21 of the report.

19 *like this one from our zoo in Pittsburgh*: Pittsburgh Zoo & PPG Aquarium, "About the Zoo," accessed 5/3/2021, https://www.pittsburghzoo.org /about/.

20 *differentiate promotable tasks from non-promotable ones*: One note on our terminology. In their HBR article, Joan Williams and Marina Multhaup call tasks that lead to advancement "glamour work" instead of our term, "promotable tasks." While some promotable work may indeed be glamorous, we prefer the term we coined—"promotable work"—because of the word's alignment with career advancement and success. J. C. Williams and M. Multhaup, "For women and minorities to get ahead managers must assign work fairly," *Harvard Business Review*, March 5, 2018, https:// hbr.org/2018/03/for-women-and-minorities-to-get-ahead-managers-must -assign-work-fairly.

23 *which includes tasks such as getting coffee, planning parties, and taking notes*: R. M. Kanter, *Men and Women of the Corporation* (New York: Basic Books, 1977). The reference to office housework is on page 79.

Chapter 3: Women Are Burdened with Non-Promotable Tasks

41 *a survey of our faculty colleagues verified that they knew it too*: L. Babcock, M. Recalde, L. Vesterlund, and L. Weingart, "Gender differences in accepting and receiving requests for tasks with low promotability," *American Economic Review* 107, no. 3 (2017): 714–47.

42 *one that surveyed over five thousand faculty members across US universities*: C. M. Guarino and V. M. H. Borden, "Faculty service loads and gender: Are women taking care of the academic family?," *Research in Higher Education* 58, no. 4 (2017): 672–94.

42 *one that did an in-depth study of over three hundred faculty members at the University of Massachusetts at Amherst*: J. Misra, J. H. Lundquist, E. Holmes, and S. Agiomavritis, "The ivory ceiling of service work," *Academe Online*, January–February 2011, https://www.aaup.org/article/ivory-ceiling-service -work#.Ycn-9mjMI2w.

42 *another that surveyed fourteen hundred political science faculty members at US universities*: S. M. Mitchell and V. L. Hesli, "Women don't ask? Women don't say no? Bargaining and service in the political science profession," *PS: Political Science & Politics* 46, no. 2 (2013): 355–69.

42 *women's overrepresentation on faculty senate corresponded to them*: L. Babcock, M. Recalde, L. Vesterlund, and L. Weingart, "Gender differences in accepting and receiving requests for tasks with low promotability," *American Economic Review* 107, no. 3 (2017): 714–47.

42 *One study found that faculty of color spend three more hours per week*: J. Misra, J. H. Lundquist, and A. Templer, "Gender, work time, and care responsibilities among faculty," *Sociological Forum* 27, no. 2 (2012): 300–323.

43 *with Black and Latinx faculty spending more time on service activities relative to white faculty*: M. L. Bellas and R. K. Toutkoushian, "Faculty time allocations and research productivity: Gender, race, and family effects," *Review of Higher Education* 22, no. 4 (1999): 367–90. See also B. Baez, "Race-related service and faculty of color: Conceptualizing critical agency in academe," *Higher Education* 39, no. 3 (2000): 363–91; B. V. Laden and L. S. Hagedorn, "Job satisfaction among faculty of color in academe: Individual survivors or institutional transformers?," *New Directions for Institutional Research* 2000, no. 7 (2000): 57–66; C. S. V. Turner, "Women of color in academe: Living with multiple marginality," *Journal of Higher Education* 73, no. 1 (2002): 74–93.

43 *Women were "taxed" for their underrepresentation on the faculty*: The concept closely relates to that of cultural taxation. See A. M. Padilla, "Ethnic minority scholars, research, and mentoring: Current and future issues," *Educational Research* 23, no. 4 (1994): 24–27.

44 *male and female TSA workers spend their time differently*: C. K. Chan and M. Anteby, "Task segregation as a mechanism for within-job inequality:

Women and men of the Transportation Security Administration," *Administrative Science Quarterly* 61, no. 2 (2015): 184–216.

49 *females do more classroom work*: C. L. Williams, "The glass escalator: Hidden advantages for men in the 'female' professions," *Social Problems* 39, no. 3 (1992): 253–67.

49 *Female investment bankers work more often with clients in low-revenue-generating areas*: L. M. Roth, *Selling Women Short: Gender and Money on Wall Street* (Princeton, NJ: Princeton University Press, 2006).

49 *found that women were twenty percentage points more likely than men to report doing more administrative tasks than their colleagues*: J. C. Williams, M. Multhaup, S. Li, and R. Korn, "You can't change what you can't see: Interrupting racial and gender bias in the legal profession," Report for the American Bar Association's Commission on Women in the Profession and the Minority Corporate Counsel Association (2018), https://www.mcca.com/wp-content/uploads/2018/09/You -Cant-Change-What-You-Cant-See-Executive-Summary.pdf. Additional statistics from the report were received from a personal communication from the researchers at the Center for WorkLife Law at Hastings University.

49 *"Despite superior education credentials and being a lateral transfer from a far more prestigious firm . . .":* Ibid., 27.

49 *The Center for WorkLife Law's study of over three thousand engineers*: J. C. Williams, S. Li, R. Rincon, and P. Finn, *Climate control: Gender and racial bias in engineering?*, Center for WorkLife Law & Society of Women Engineers (2016), https://worklifelaw.org/publications/Climate-Control-Gen der-And-Racial-Bias-In-Engineering.pdf.

50 *"Just last year they hired a new female [engineer] . . .":* J. C. Williams and M. Multhaup, "For women and minorities to get ahead managers must assign work fairly," *Harvard Business Review*, March 5, 2018, https://hbr .org/2018/03/for-women-and-minorities-to-get-ahead-managers-must -assign-work-fairly.

50 *Female clerks were stuck in the checkout line*: M. Tolich and C. Briar, "Just checking it out: Exploring the significance of informal gender divisions amongst American supermarket employees," *Gender, Work, & Organization* 6, no. 3 (1999): 129–33.

51 *"If you squat to pee, you check before me":* Ibid., 131.

Chapter 4: Why Do Women Say Yes?

57 *While only 2.6 percent of male faculty members agreed to serve*: L. Babcock, M. Recalde, L. Vesterlund, and L. Weingart, "Gender differences in accepting and receiving requests for tasks with low promotability," *American Economic Review* 107, no. 3 (2017): 714–47.

58 *we conducted an experiment to determine whether women are more willing to perform non-promotable tasks*: Ibid.

62 *Deciding on their own to coordinate on a noticeable landmark and time*: T. C. Schelling, *The Strategy of Conflict* (Cambridge, MA: Harvard University Press, 1960).

63 *If altruism or risk aversion caused people to volunteer*: The literature on gender differences in preferences is substantive, and a number of the documented differences could contribute to women volunteering more. For example, women may be more likely than men to agree to requests to perform non-promotable tasks if they are more concerned for the welfare of others [e.g., C. C. Eckel and P. J. Grossman, "Are men less selfish than women: Evidence from dictator experiments," *The Economic Journal* 108, no. 448 (1998): 726–35; J. Andreoni and L. Vesterlund, "Which is the fair sex: Gender differences in altruism," *Quarterly Journal of Economics* 116, no. 1 (2001): 293–312] if they are more agreeable and have a greater desire to be liked by the requester [H. B. Braiker, *The Disease to Please: Curing the People-Pleasing Syndrome* (New York: McGraw-Hill, 2002)], if they have a greater desire to conform to a norm of accepting such requests [e.g., R. T. Santee and S. E. Jackson, "Identity implications of conformity: Sex differences in normative and attributional judgments," *Social Psychology Quarterly* 45, no. 2 (1982): 121–5; A. H. Eagly, W. Wood, and L. Fishbaugh, "Sex differences in conformity: Surveillance by the group as a determinant of male nonconformity," *Journal of Personality and Social Psychology* 40, no. 2 (1981): 384–94], if they are more risk averse [e.g., C. C. Eckel and P. J. Grossman, "Differences in the economic decisions of men and women: Experimental evidence," in *Handbook of Experimental Economics Results, Vol. 1*, eds. C. Plott and V. Smith (New York: Elsevier, 2008), 509–19] and more concerned about the consequences from declining the request [M. E. Heilman and J. J. Chen, "Same behavior, different consequences: Reactions to men's and women's altruistic citizenship behavior," *Journal of Applied Psychology* 90, no. 3 (2005): 431–41], or if they are less competitive [M. Niederle and L. Vesterlund, "Do women shy away from competition? Do men compete too much?," *Quarterly Journal of Economics* 122, no. 3 (2007): 1067–101; M. Niederle and L. Vesterlund, "Gender and competition," *Annual Review of Economics* 3, no. 1 (2011): 601–30]. See R. Croson and U. Gneezy, "Gender differences in preferences," *Journal of Economic Literature* 47, no. 2 (2009): 448–74 and M. Niederle, "Gender," in *The Handbook of Experimental Economics, Vol. 2*, eds. J. H. Kagel and A. E. Roth (Princeton, NJ: Princeton University Press, 2016), 481–562, for reviews on gender differences. As we will show, none of these gender differences explain the pattern of results we see in our experiments.

66 *A psychology study explored whether decisions to help or not help in work settings*:

M. E. Heilman and J. J. Chen, "Same behavior, different consequences: Reactions to men's and women's altruistic citizenship behavior," *Journal of Applied Psychology* 90, no. 3 (2005): 431–41.

68 *Women were more likely than men to say they felt anxious and guilty*: A. Weirup, L. Babcock, L. Vesterlund, and L. Weingart, "How emotions affect the decision to do non-promotable tasks." Unpublished manuscript, available from authors upon request, 2017.

68 *they described to participants four scenarios where a person needed help*: A. Weirup, L. Babcock, and T. Cohen, "Gender differences in the response to requests to do non-promotable tasks." Unpublished manuscript, available from authors upon request, 2020.

71 *we asked women and men why they would agree to do an NPT*: A. Weirup, L. Babcock, L. Vesterlund, and L. Weingart, "How emotions affect the decision to do non-promotable tasks." Unpublished manuscript, available from authors upon request, 2017.

71 *women are constrained by a* tight culture: M. G. Gelfand, *Rule Makers, Rule Breakers: How Tight and Loose Cultures Wire Our World* (New York: Scribner, 2018).

72 *Participants read a story about an employee who was asked to help a colleague*: M. E. Heilman and J. J. Chen, "Same behavior, different consequences: Reactions to men's and women's altruistic citizenship behavior," *Journal of Applied Psychology* 90, no. 3 (2015): 431–41.

73 *while those who were not expected to do the work, the men, were more likely than women to consider the rewards that would result from helping*: A. Weirup, L. Babcock, L. Vesterlund, and L. Weingart, "How emotions affect the decision to do non-promotable tasks." Unpublished manuscript, available from authors upon request, 2016.

73 *women, and men of color, were less likely than white men to say they can behave assertively or that they can show anger without pushback*: J. C. Williams, S. Li, R. Rincon, and P. Finn, *Climate control: Gender and racial bias in engineering?*, Center for WorkLife Law & Society of Women Engineers (2016); J. C. Williams, M. Multhaup, S. Li, and R. M. Korn, "You can't change what you can't see: Interrupting racial & gender bias in the legal profession," American Bar Association and Minority Corporate Counsel Association (2018).

74 *one leader reported being treated like the nanny and having to clean up after the male executives' hasty decisions*: L. Morgan Roberts, A. J. Mayo, R. J. Ely, and D. A. Thomas, "Beating the odds: Leadership lessons from senior African American women," *Harvard Business Review* (March–April 2018).

74 *faculty of color spend an average of three hours more on service than white faculty*: J. Misra, J. H. Lundquist, and A. Templer, "Gender, work time, and care responsibilities among faculty," *Sociological Forum* 27, no. 2 (2012): 300–323.

74 *the expectation for people of color to take on NPTs and their resultant larger service commitment is problematic*: A. L. Antonio, "Faculty of color reconsidered: Reassessing contributions to scholarship," *Higher Education* 73, no. 5 (2003): 582–602.

Chapter 5: Why Do Women Get Asked?

78 *We found very little research on how people allocate work tasks*: One study that explores how promotable assignments are made finds that managers are more likely to assign the promotable work to men, relative to women: I. De Pater, A. Van Vianen, and M. Bechtoldt, "Gender differences in job challenge: A matter of task allocation," *Gender, Work, and Organization* 17, no. 4 (2010): 433–53. Research that investigates workers' *perceptions* of the assignment of promotable work finds that for engineers and lawyers, people believe that men have access to more promotable assignments, relative to women: J. C. Williams, M. Multhaup, S. Li, and R. Korn, "You can't change what you can't see: Interrupting racial and gender bias in the legal profession," Report for the American Bar Association's Commission on Women in the Profession and the Minority Corporate Counsel Association, 2018; J. C. Williams, S. Li, R. Rincon, and P. Finn, *Climate control: Gender and racial bias in engineering?*, Center for WorkLife Law & Society of Women Engineers (2016), https://worklifelaw.org /publications/Climate-Control-Gender-And-Racial-Bias-In-Engineering.pdf.

78 *we still had three group members who had two minutes to find a volunteer to click the button*: L. Babcock, M. Recalde, L. Vesterlund, and L. Weingart, "Gender differences in accepting and receiving requests for tasks with low promotability," *American Economic Review* 107, no. 3 (2017): 714–47.

81 *For that reason, people may be more likely to ask them to do this work*: J. C. Williams, S. Li, R. Rincon, and P. Finn, *Climate control: Gender and racial bias in engineering?*, Center for WorkLife Law & Society of Women Engineers (2016), https://worklifelaw.org/publications/Climate-Control -Gender-And-Racial-Bias-In-Engineering.pdf.

81 *Other times, factors influence our decisions without our awareness*: D. Kahneman, *Thinking, Fast and Slow* (New York: Farrar, Straus and Giroux, 2011).

82 *Research shows that it is painful to ask and get "no" for an answer*: A. Jaroszewicz, "It does hurt to ask: Theory and evidence on informal help seeking." Doctoral dissertation, Carnegie Mellon University (2020); F. J. Flynn and V. K. B. Lake, "If you need help just ask: Underestimating compliance with direct requests for help," *Journal of Personality and Social Psychology* 95, no. 1 (2008): 128–43.

82 *Because the vast majority of carpenters—96.8 percent—are men*: Bureau of Labor Statistics, Labor Force Statistics from the Current Population Survey, accessed 2020, https://www.bls.gov/cps/cpsaat11.htm.

83 *This is called* gender congruence: A. H. Eagly and S. J. Karau, "Role congruity

theory of prejudice toward female leaders," *Psychological Review* 109, no. 3 (2002): 574–98; M. E. Heilman, "Sex bias in work settings: The lack of fit model," in *Research in Organization Behavior*, Vol. 5, B. M. Staw and L. L. Cummings, eds. (Greenwich, CT: JAI Press, 1983), 269–98.

83 *we expect women to be communal*: A. H. Eagly, *Sex Differences in Social Behavior: A Social Role Interpretation* (Hillsdale, NJ: Erlbaum, 1987).

83 *Because helping is more consistent with the female gender role*: D. L. Kidder, "The influence of gender on the performance of organizational citizenship behaviors," *Journal of Management* 28, no. 5 (2002): 629–48.

83 *stereotypes of women's abilities and status are congruent with characteristics of NPTs*: J. Acker, "Hierarchies, jobs, bodies: A theory of gendered organizations," *Gender and Society* 4, no. 2 (1990): 139–58; D. M. Britton, "Gendered organizational logic: Policy and practice in men's and women's prisons," *Gender and Society* 11, no. 6 (1997): 796–818; E. Skuratowicz and L. W. Hunter, "Where do women's jobs come from? Job resegregation in an American bank," *Work and Occupations* 31, no. 1 (2004): 73–110; E. H. Gorman, "Gender stereotypes, same-gender preferences, and organizational variation in the hiring of women: Evidence from law firms," *American Sociological Review* 70, no. 4 (2005): 702–28; C. J. Turco, "Cultural foundations of tokenism: Evidence from the leveraged buyout industry," *American Sociological Review* 75, no. 6 (2010): 894–913; E. Reid, "Embracing, passing, revealing, and the ideal worker image: How people navigate expected and experienced professional identities," *Organization Science* 26, no. 4 (2015): 997–1017; J. K. Fletcher, "Relational practice: A feminist reconstruction of work," *Journal of Management Inquiry* 7, no. 2 (1998): 163–86.

83 *Stereotyped perceptions of women being less skilled than men*: This is an extremely large and robust area of research. See, for example, M. E. Heilman and M. C. Haynes, "No credit where credit is due: Attributional rationalization of women's success in male-female teams," *Journal of Applied Psychology* 90, no. 5 (2005): 905–16; C. A. Moss-Racusin, J. F. Dovidio, V. L. Brescoll, M. J. Graham, and J. Handelsman, "Science faculty's subtle gender biases favor male students," *Proceedings of the National Academy of Sciences* 109, no. 41 (2012): 16464–79.

84 *they recruited people with full-time work experience to rate six hypothetical tasks on how* promotable *they are*: L. Babcock, F. Flynn, and J. Zlatev, "Assigning non-promotable work." Unpublished working paper, 2015.

85 *the NPTs were more congruent with women than they were with men*: For further evidence on the effect of gender congruency on task assignment, other research shows that men, more than women, evaluate their individual task assignments as challenging, and finds that these differences partially result from managers being more likely to assign challenging tasks to their male rather than to their female subordinates. I. De Pater, A. Van Vianen, and

M. Bechtoldt, "Gender differences in job challenge: A matter of task allocation," *Gender, Work, and Organization* 17, no. 4 (2010): 433–53.

85 *Remember the female supermarket clerks, who were more likely to be assigned to the checkout line day after day*: M. Tolich and C. Briar, "Just checking it out: Exploring the significance of informal gender divisions amongst American supermarket employees," *Gender, Work, & Organization* 6, no. 3 (1999): 129–33.

85 *"They don't give you a reason. It's like a parent who says 'because'"*: Ibid. Quote is on page 131.

85 *she says yes and she does a good job*: Personality research using surveys from more than seventeen thousand people from fifty-five cultures found that women rated themselves as more conscientious than did men, D. P. Schmitt, A. Realo, M. Voracek, and J. Allik, "Why can't a man be more like a woman? Sex differences in Big Five personality traits across 55 cultures," *Journal of Personality and Social Psychology* 94, no. 1 (2008): 168–82. Furthermore, research on twelve thousand people from fifty different cultures also finds that in general, people view women as being more conscientious than they view men: R. R. McCrae and A. Terracciano, "Universal features of personality traits from the observer's perspective: Data from 50 countries," *Journal of Personality and Social Psychology* 88, no. 3 (2005): 547–61.

87 *Professor Amado Padilla at Stanford termed this phenomenon cultural taxation*: A. M. Padilla, "Ethnic minority scholars, research, and mentoring: Current and future issues," *Educational Research* 23, no. 4 (1994): 24–27.

87 *with Black and Latinx faculty spending more time on service activities relative to white faculty*: M. L. Bellas and R. K. Toutkoushian, "Faculty time allocations and research productivity: Gender, race, and family effects," *Review of Higher Education* 22, no. 4 (1999): 367–90. See also B. Baez, "Race-related service and faculty of color: Conceptualizing critical agency in academe," *Higher Education* 39, no. 3 (2000): 363–91; B. V. Laden and L. S. Hagedorn, "Job satisfaction among faculty of color in academe: Individual survivors or institutional transformers?," *New Directions for Institutional Research* 2000, no. 105 (2000): 57–66; C. S. V. Turner, "Women of color in academe: Living with multiple marginality," *Journal of Higher Education* 73, no. 1 (2002): 74–93.

87 *"It gives you opportunities, at the same time, I think, you are expected to do a lot of things not expected of other faculty"*: C. S. V. Turner, "Women of color in academe: Living with multiple marginality," *Journal of Higher Education* 73, no. 1 (2002): 74–93. Quote is on page 82.

88 *"I say to you: I refuse"*: https://www.naacpldf.org/press-release/nikole-hannah-jones-issues-statement-on-decision-to-decline-tenure-offer-at-university-of-north-carolina-chapel-hill-and-to-accept-knight-chair-appointment-at-howard-university/.

88 *When people engage in it, their goal is to help women, but the actions taken end up*

harming them: P. Glick and S. T. Fiske, "The ambivalent sexism inventory: Differentiating hostile and benevolent sexism," *Journal of Personality and Social Psychology* 70, no. 3 (1996): 491–512.

90 *the only employees who successfully increased their pay through negotiation were those assigned to promotable work*: R. Gihleb, R. Landsman, and L. Vesterlund, "The effect of task assignment on compensation and negotiation." Working paper, University of Pittsburgh, 2021.

Chapter 6: The Cost of Non-Promotable Work

95 *women carry a larger load of non-promotable work than their male counterparts*: S. R. Porter, "A closer look at faculty service: What affects participation on committees?," *The Journal of Higher Education* 78, no. 5 (2007): 523–41; M. L. Bellas and R. K. Toutkoushian, "Faculty time allocations and research productivity: Gender, race, and family effects," *Review of Higher Education* 22, no. 4 (1999): 367–90; Y. Benschop, L. Halsema, and P. Schreurs, "The division of labour and inequalities between the sexes: An ideological dilemma," *Gender, Work, and Organization* 8, no. 1 (2001): 1–18; C. K. Chan and M. Anteby, "Task segregation as a mechanism for within-job inequality: Women and men of the Transportation Security Administration," *Administrative Science Quarterly* 61, no. 2 (2015): 184–216; M. Tolich and C. Briar, "Just checking it out: Exploring the significance of informal gender divisions amongst American supermarket employees," *Gender, Work, & Organization* 6, no. 3 (1999): 129–133.

96 *work/work imbalance if your load of non-promotable relative to promotable work exceeds that of your peers*: J. Misra, J. H. Lundquist, and A. Templer, "Gender, work time, and care responsibilities among faculty," *Sociological Forum* 12, no. 2 (2012): 300–323, coined the term "work/work balance." They use the term broadly to distinguish between multiple types of work, whereas we use the term more narrowly to describe the balance between non-promotable and promotable work.

100 *required to perform work that did not align with their own professional identities as surgeons*: M. G. Pratt, K. W. Rockmann, and J. B. Kaufmann, "Constructing professional identity: The role of work and identity learning cycles in the customization of identity among medical residents," *Academy of Management Journal* 49, no. 2 (2006): 235–62.

100 *female engineer interns were "too often relegated to 'female' roles of notetaker, organizer or manager"*: E. Cech, B. Rubineau, S. S. Silbey, and C. Seron, "Professional role confidence and gendered persistence in engineering," *American Sociological Review* 76, no. 5 (2011): 641–66. Interview is at: https://phys.org/news/2012-04-female-students-wary-workplace.html.

100 *Sociologist Arlie Hochschild calls this emotional labor*: A. R. Hochschild, *The

Managed Heart: Commercialization of Human Feeling (Berkeley, CA: University of California Press, 1983).

101 *they constantly interacted with customers and had to be pleasant on demand*: M. Tolich and C. Briar, "Just checking it out: Exploring the significance of informal gender divisions amongst American supermarket employees," *Gender, Work, & Organization* 6, no. 3 (1999): 129–33.

101 *the female TSA agents who did more pat-downs*: C. K. Chan and M. Anteby, "Task segregation as a mechanism for within-job inequality: Women and men of the Transportation Security Administration," *Administrative Science Quarterly* 61, no. 2 (2015): 184–216.

101 *females more than males engage in* surface acting: C. Boucher, "A qualitative study of the impact of emotional labour on health managers," *The Qualitative Report* 21, no. 11 (2016): 2148–60.

102 *where men had more opportunities to engage in promotable work than women did, women reported lower job satisfaction and greater job stress*: E. B. King, M. R. Hebl, J. M. George, and S. F. Matuski, "Understanding tokenism: Antecedents and consequences of a psychological climate of gender inequity," *Journal of Management* 36, no. 2 (2010): 482–510.

102 *reactions to task assignments that they saw as unreasonable*: N. K. Semmer, N. Jacobshagen, L. L. Meier, A. Elfering, T. A. Beehr, W. Kalin, and F. Tschan, "Illegitimate tasks as a source of work stress," *Work and Stress* 29, no. 1 (2015): 32–56; N. K. Semmer, F. Tschan, L. L. Meier, S. Facchin, and N. Jacobshagen, "Illegitimate tasks and counterproductive work behavior," *Applied Psychology: An International Review* 59, no. 1 (2010): 70–96.

105 *the* greedy professions, *require an enormous number of promotable work hours to advance*: C. C. Miller, "Women Did Everything Right. Then Work Got 'Greedy.'" *New York Times*, April 26, 2019, https://www.nytimes.com/2019/04/26/upshot/women-long-hours-greedy-professions.html; K. A. Weeden, Y. Cha, and M. Bucca, "Long work hours, part-time work, and trends in the gender gap in pay, the motherhood wage penalty, and the fatherhood wage premium," *The Russell Sage Foundation Journal of the Social Sciences* 2, no. 4 (2016): 71–102; C. Goldin, "A grand gender convergence: Its last chapter," *American Economic Review* 104, no. 4 (2014): 1091–119; C. Goldin, *Career and Family: Women's Century-long Journey Toward Equity* (Princeton, NJ: Princeton University Press, 2021).

105 *impact your personal life*: J. H. Greenhaus and N. J. Beutell, "Sources of conflict between work and family roles," *Academy of Management Review* 10, no. 1 (1985): 76–88; S. B. Bacharach, P. Bamberger, and S. Conley, "Work-home conflict among nurses and engineers: Mediating the impact of role stress on burnout and satisfaction at work," *Journal of Organizational Behavior* 12, no. 1 (1991): 39–53; R. G. Netemeyer, J. S. Boles, and R. McMurrian, "Development and validation of work-family conflict and

family-work conflict scales," *Journal of Applied Psychology* 81, no. 4 (1996): 400–410.

107 long hour *workers report that they often miss important events in their personal life*: J. Kodz, S. Davis, D. Lain, M. Strebler, J. Rick, P. Bates, J. Cummings, and N. Meager, "Working Long Hours: A Review of the Evidence," Volume 1 —Main Report, Employment Relations Research Eseries, ERRS16, Department of Trade and Industry (2003).

108 *Parents who work more hours tend to carve out quality time with their children*: S. M. Bianchi, J. P. Robinson, and M. A. Milkie, *Changing Rhythms of American Family Life* (New York: Russell Sage Foundation, 2006); G. M. Dotti Sani and J. Treas, "Educational gradients in parents' child-care time across countries, 1965–2012," *Journal of Marriage and Family* 78, no. 4 (2016): 1083–96; S. L. Nock and P. W. Kingston, "Time with children: The impact of couples' work-time commitments," *Social Forces* 67, no. 1 (1988): 59–85.

108 *affect the relationship you have with your children*: If work-related parental stress is left unaddressed, it increases the likelihood of parent-adolescent conflict and negatively affects child and adolescent well-being. N. L. Galambos, H. A. Sears, D. M. Almeida, and G. C. Kolaric, "Parents' work overload and problem behavior in young adolescents," *Journal of Research on Adolescence* 5, no. 2 (1995): 201–23; A. C. Crouter, M. F. Bumpus, M. R. Head, and S. M. McHale, "Implications of overwork and overload for the quality of men's family relationships," *Journal of Marriage and Family* 63, no. 2 (2001): 404–16; D. L. Putnick, M. H. Bornstein, C. Hendricks, K. M. Painter, J. Suwalsky, and W. A. Collins, "Parenting stress, perceived parenting behaviors, and adolescent self-concept in European American families," *Journal of Family Psychology* 22, no. 5 (2008): 752–62; A. C. Crouter, M. F. Bumpus, M. C. Maguire, and S. M. McHale, "Linking parents' work pressure and adolescents' well-being: Insights into dynamics in dual-earner families," *Developmental Psychology* 35, no. 6 (1999): 1453–61.

108 *negative impact on their domestic relationships*: J. Kodz, S. Davis, D. Lain, M. Strebler, J. Rick, P. Bates, J. Cummings, and N. Meager, "Working Long Hours: A Review of the Evidence," Volume 1—Main Report, Employment Relations Research Eseries, ERRS16, Department of Trade and Industry (2003); A. S. Wharton and M. Blair-Loy, "Long work hours and family: A cross-national study of employees' concerns," *Journal of Family Issues* 27, no. 3 (2006): 415–36.

108 *higher workloads at one point in time report lower marital satisfaction at a later point in time*: J. A. Lavner and M. A. Clark, "Workload and marital satisfaction over time: Testing lagged spillover and crossover effects during the newlywed years," *Journal of Vocation Behavior* 101 (2017): 67–76.

109 *Homosexual and heterosexual women give the same assessments of their work/ life balance*: M. Dilmaghani, "Exploring the link between sexual orientation,

work-life balance satisfaction and work-life segmentation," *International Journal of Manpower* 41, no. 6 (2019): 693–715.

109 *Work interfering with family is more pronounced among lesbian mothers who are not out at the office*: T. L. Tuten and R. A. August, "Work-family conflict: A study of lesbian mothers," *Women in Management Review* 21, no. 7 (2006): 578–97.

109 *People who work longer hours spend fewer hours socializing*: J. Kodz, S. Davis, D. Lain, M. Strebler, J. Rick, P. Bates, J. Cummings, and N. Meager, "Working Long Hours: A Review of the Evidence," Volume 1—Main Report, Employment Relations Research series, ERRS16, Department of Trade and Industry (2003).

109 *talk with their neighbors report being happier*: The Sainsbury Living Well Index, 2018. https://www.about.sainsburys.co.uk/~/media/Files/S/Sainsburys/living-well-index/sainsburys-living-well-index-may-2018.pdf.

110 *the effect of social isolation on mortality is comparable to that of smoking and alcohol consumption*: J. Lunstad-Holt, T. B. Smith, and J. B. Layton, "Social relationships and mortality risk: A meta-analytic review," *PLOS Medicine* 7, no. 7 (2010): 1–20.

110 *268 white young men from Harvard's classes of 1939–1944*: G. E. Vaillant, C. C. McArthur, and A. Bock, *Triumphs of Experience: The Men of the Harvard Grant Study* (Cambridge, MA: Belnap Press, 2012).

110 *456 economically disadvantaged white boys, ages 11–16*: S. Glueck and E. Glueck, *Unraveling Juvenile Delinquency* (New York: Commonwealth Fund, 1950); S. Glueck and E. Glueck, *Delinquents and Nondelinquents in Perspective* (Cambridge, MA: Harvard University Press, 1968).

112 *work overload will become too much, harming your health*: S. Sonnentag and M. Frese, "Stress in Organizations," in *Handbook of Psychology, Vol. 12*, eds. W. C. Borman, D. R. Ilgen, and R. J. Klimoski (Hoboken, NJ: Wiley, 2003), 453–91; S. M. Jex, *Stress and Job Performance: Theory, Research, and Implications for Managerial Practice* (Thousand Oaks, CA: Sage Publications Ltd., 1998); M. Kivimaki, M. Jokela, S. T. Nyberg, A. Singh-Manoux, et al., "Long working hours and risk of coronary heart disease and stroke: A systematic review and meta-analysis," *The Lancet* 386, no. 10005 (2015): 1739–46; M. Vander Hulst, "Long workhours and health," *Scandinavian Journal of Work, Environment & Health* 29, no. 3 (2003): 171–88.

112 *hypertension and cardiovascular problems are more likely for those who work long hours*: M. Kivimaki, M. Jokela, S. T. Nyberg, A. Singh-Manoux, et al., "Long working hours and risk of coronary heart disease and stroke: A systematic review and meta-analysis," *The Lancet* 386, no. 10005 (2015): 1739–46.

112 *poor and interrupted sleep, poor physical health*: For a recent meta-analytic study, see K. Wong, A. Chan, and S. C. Ngan, "The effect of long working

hours and overtime on occupational health: A meta-analysis of evidence from 1998 to 2018," *International Journal of Environmental Research and Public Health* 16, no. 12 (2019): 2102; see also K. Sparks, B. Faragher, and C. L. Cooper, "Well-being and occupation health in the 21st century workplace," *Journal of Occupational and Organization Psychology* 74 (2001): 489–509; S. Maruyama and K. Morimoto, "Effects of long hours on lifestyle, stress and quality of life among intermediate Japanese managers," *Scandinavian Journal of Work Environment & Health* 22 (1996): 353–9; A. Alexandrova-Karamonova, I. Todorova, A. J. Montgomery, E. Panagopolou, et al., "Burnout and health behaviors in health professionals from seven European countries," *International Archives of Occupational and Environmental Health* 89, no. 7 (2016): 1059–75; J. Kodz, S. Davis, D. Lain, M. Strebler, J. Rick, P. Bates, J. Cummings, and N. Meager, "Working Long Hours: A Review of the Evidence," Volume 1—Main Report, Employment Relations Research Eseries, ERRS16, Department of Trade and Industry (2003).

112 *"long hours working puts women under greater amounts of pressure"*: J. Kodz, S. Davis, D. Lain, M. Strebler, J. Rick, P. Bates, J. Cummings, and N. Meager, "Working Long Hours: A Review of the Evidence," Volume 1—Main Report, Employment Relations Research Eseries, ERRS16, Department of Trade and Industry (2003).

112 *Overwork also correlates with poor mental health*: S. Sonnentag and M. Frese, "Stress in Organizations," in *Handbook of Psychology, Vol. 12*, eds. W. C. Borman, D. R. Ilgen, and R. J. Klimoski (Hoboken, NJ: Wiley, 2003), 453–91.

112 *stress gap is confounded by physicians being more likely to provide such diagnoses to a female than a similar male patient*: R. Purvanova and J. Muros, "Gender differences in burnout: A meta-analysis," *Journal of Vocational Behavior* 77 (2010): 168–85. Trained clinicians and physicians when reading vignettes or seeing patients are more likely to diagnose female than male patients with depression or anxiety, e.g., M. K. Potts, M. A. Burnam, and K. B. Wells, "Gender differences in depression detection: A comparison of clinician diagnosis and standardized assessment," *Psychological Assessment* 3, no. 4 (1991): 609–15.

113 *men more than women experience burnout in the form of feeling* depersonalized: See the meta-analytic study: R. K. Purvanova and J. P. Muros, "Gender differences in burnout: A meta-analysis," *Journal of Vocational Behavior* 77, no. 2 (2010): 168–85.

113 *men and women being subjected to different stressors*: M. Galanakis, A. Stalikas, H. Kallia, C. Karagianni, and C. Karela, "Gender differences in experiencing occupational stress: The role of age, education and marital status," *Stress Health* 25 (2009): 397–404; E. Mayor, "Gender roles and traits in stress and health," *Frontiers in Psychology* 6 (2015): 779.

113 *working seventy hours a week get the same amount done as those putting in*

fifty-five hours: For evidence of diminishing returns to work, see D. M. Olds and S. P. Clark, "The effect of work hours on adverse events and errors in health care," *Journal of Safety Research* 41, no. 2 (2010): 153–62; J. Pencavel, *Diminishing Returns at Work: The Consequences of Long Working Hours* (New York: Oxford University Press, 2018).

Chapter 7: The No Club Playbook

123 *women were 60 percent more likely than men to write back*: L. Babcock, M. Recalde, L. Vesterlund, and L. Weingart, "Gender differences in accepting and receiving requests for tasks with low promotability," *American Economic Review* 107, no. 3 (2017): 714–47.

123 *underestimate how costly it will be to take on NPTs—both in terms of the time*: R. Buehler, D. Griffin, and J. Peetz, "The planning fallacy: Cognitive, motivation, and social origins," *Advances in Experimental Social Psychology* 23, no. 43 (2010): 1–62.

125 *In eleven months, your day is likely to look just like tomorrow*: G. Loewenstein and R. H. Thaler, "Anomalies: Intertemporal choice," *Journal of Economic Perspectives* 3, no. 4 (1989): 181–93.

126 *I had to learn how to not be the people pleaser*: S. Almond and C. Strayed, *Dear Sugars* (Radio Show), WBUR, July 15, 2017.

128 *The blogger Suzanne Gerber put it this way*: S. Gerber, February 29, 2012, https://www.nextavenue.org/why-even-strong-women-sometimes-have-hard-time-saying-no.

129 *Shonda Rhimes takes that a step further*: S. Rhimes, *Year of Yes: How to Dance It Out, Stand in the Sun and Be Your Own Person* (New York: Simon & Schuster, 2015), 222.

130 *To study this, researchers surveyed a group of employed college graduates*: B. Tewfik, T. Kundro, and P. Tetlock, "The help-decliner's dilemma: How to decline requests for help at work without hurting one's image." Unpublished working paper, 2018.

131 *He recommends responding with a* positive no: W. Ury, *The Power of a Positive No: How to Say No and Still Get to Yes* (New York: Bantam, 2007); W. Ury, "The power of a positive no," Oxford Leadership, https://www.oxfordleadership.com/wp-content/uploads/2016/08/oxford-leadership-article-the-power-of-a-positive-no.pdf.

133 *And those of us who don't have an assistant*: A. H. Petersen, "Against 'Feel Free to Take Some Time If You Need It,'" newsletter on Substack, April 21, 2021, https://annehelen.substack.com/p/against-feel-free-to-take-some-time.

133 *This will help the requester think critically*: R. Tulshyan, "Women of color get asked to do more 'office housework.' Here's how they can say no," *Harvard Business Review*, April 6, 2018, https://hbr.org/2018/04/women-of-color-get-asked-to-do-more-office-housework-heres-how-they-can-say-no.

138 *it is perfectly acceptable for men to say no to a request, while a woman who says no would face negative consequences:* M. E. Heilman and J. J. Chen, "Same behavior, different consequences: Reactions to men's and women's altruistic citizenship behavior," *Journal of Applied Psychology* 90, no. 3 (2015): 431–41; S. Keck and L. Babcock, "Who gets the benefit of the doubt? The impact of causal reasoning depth on how violations of gender stereotypes are evaluated," *Journal of Organizational Behavior* 39, no. 3 (2017): 276–91.

138 *And this is particularly true for women of color:* L. Morgan Roberts, A. J. Mayo, R. J. Ely, and D. A. Thomas, "Beating the odds: Leadership lessons from senior African American women," *Harvard Business Review* (March–April 2018).

140 *Instead of doing the entire NPT, you might negotiate doing a part of it:* D. M. Kolb and J. L. Porter, "'Office housework' gets in women's way," *Harvard Business Review*, April 16, 2015, https://hbr.org/2015/04/office-housework -gets-in-womens-way.

140 *When the person requesting a new NPT is your boss:* National Center for Faculty Development and Diversity, "The Art of Saying No," PowerPoint deck, https://www.facultydiversity.org/webinars/artofno21.

Chapter 8: Optimize Your Portfolio of Work

144 *there is a stronger expectation that women should do their share:* S. Keck and L. Babcock, "Who gets the benefit of the doubt? The impact of causal reasoning depth on how violations of gender stereotypes are evaluated," *Journal of Organizational Behavior* 39, no. 3 (2017): 276–91.

149 *Camille told us that her personal mission statement guided her decisions:* Personal mission statements are becoming quite popular: S. Vozza, "Personal mission statements of 5 famous CEOs (And why you should write one too)," *Fast Company*, February 25, 2014, https://www.fastcompany.com/3026791/per sonal-mission-statements-of-5-famous-ceos-and-why-you-should-write-one -too. Here is a guide for how to write one: "A step-by-step guide to creating a personal mission statement," Indeed.com, December 1, 2020, https://www .indeed.com/career-advice/career-development/personal-vision-statement.

Chapter 9: Organizations Benefit When Employees Share Non-Promotable Work

177 *research has estimated how much productivity was gained by reducing discrimination and improving the allocation of talent:* C-T. Hsieh, E. Hurst, C. I. Jones, and P. J. Klenow, "The allocation of talent and U.S. economic growth," *Econometrica* 87, no. 5 (2019): 1439–74.

179 *higher levels of employee engagement in these unrewarded everyday activities were associated with higher productivity and efficiency:* N. P. Podsakoff, S. W. Whiting, P. M. Podsakoff, and B. D. Blume, "Individual- and organizational-level

consequences of organizational citizenship behaviors: A meta-analysis," *Journal of Applied Psychology* 94, no. 1 (2009): 122–41.

180 *Disengagement costs US companies up to $550 billion per year*: S. Sorenson and K. Garman, "How to tackle U.S. employee's stagnating engagement," Gallup, June 11, 2013, https://news.gallup.com/businessjournal/162953/tackle-employees-stagnating-engagement.aspx.

180 *when employees perceive their organization's procedures to be unfair or unjust*: J. A. Colquitt, D. E. Conlon, M. J. Wesson, C. O. Porter, and K. Y. Ng, "Justice at the millennium: A meta-analytic review of 25 years of organizational justice research," *Journal of Applied Psychology* 86 (2001): 425–45; Society for Human Resource Management, "Employee job satisfaction and engagement: Optimizing organizational culture for success," 2015, https://www.shrm.org/hr-today/trends-and-forecasting/research-and-surveys/pages/job-satisfaction-and-engagement-report-optimizing-organizational-culture-for-success.aspx.

180 *the top-quartile business units on the measure of employee engagement outperform bottom-quartile business units*: J. K. Harter, F. L. Schmidt, S. Agrawal, A. Blue, S. K. Plowman, P. Josh, and J. Asplund, "The relationship between engagement at work and organizational outcomes," Gallup, 2020 Q12 Meta-Analysis: Tenth Edition, https://www.gallup.com/workplace/321725/gallup-q12-meta-analysis-report.aspx.

180 *revealed a robust positive correlation between job satisfaction and job performance*: T. A. Judge, C. J. Thoresen, J. E. Bono, and G. K. Patton, "The job satisfaction–job performance relationship: A qualitative and quantitative review," *Psychology Bulletin* 127, no. 3 (2001): 376–407.

181 *Stress, as we've seen, is detrimental to individuals, but it also affects organizations*: The American Institute of Stress, accessed July 2, 2020, https://www.stress.org/workplace-stress.

181 *The World Health Organization has called stress the "health epidemic of the 21st century"*: World Health Organization, "Occupational health: Stress at the workplace," 2020, https://www.who.int/news-room/questions-and-answers/item/ccupational-health-stress-at-the-workplace and https://www.who.int/occupational_health/topics/brunpres0307.pdf?ua=1.

181 *Satisfied employees are more motivated*: R. T. Mowday, L. W. Porter, and R. M. Steers, *Employee-organizational Linkages: The Psychology of Commitment, Absenteeism, and Turnover* (New York: Academic Press, 1982).

181 *satisfied and engaged workers create higher customer loyalty, productivity, quality of performance, and safety, and lower employee turnover and absenteeism*: J. K. Harter, F. L. Schmidt, S. Agrawal, A. Blue, S. K. Plowman, P. Josh, and J. Asplund, "The relationship between engagement at work and organizational outcomes," Gallup, 2020 Q12 Meta-Analysis: Tenth Edition, https://www.gallup.com/workplace/321725/gallup-q12-meta-analysis-report.aspx; T. A.

Judge, C. J. Thoresen, J. E. Bono, and G. K. Patton, "The job satisfaction–job performance relationship: A qualitative and quantitative review," *Psychology Bulletin* 127, no. 3 (2001): 376–407.

181 *the top reason people voluntarily leave their organization is to pursue better opportunities for career growth and advancement*: The Work Institute, 2019 Retention Report, https://info.workinstitute.com/hubfs/2019%20Retention%20Report/Work%20Institute%202019%20Retention%20Report%20final-1.pdf.

182 *why women specifically leave their jobs*: PricewaterhouseCoopers, "Winning the fight for female talent," 2017, https://www.pwc.com/gx/en/about/diversity/iwd/iwd-female-talent-report-web.pdf.

182 *A 2021 McKinsey report concurs*: McKinsey & Company, "Women in the Workplace," 2021, https://wiw-report.s3.amazonaws.com/Women_in_the_Workplace_2021.pdf. Quote is on page 5.

182 *those who perceived higher levels of gender inequity in their workplace were more likely to consider quitting their jobs*: E. B. King, M. R. Hebl, J. M. George, and S. F. Matuski, "Understanding tokenism: antecedents and consequences of a psychological climate of gender inequity," *Journal of Management* 36, no. 2 (2010): 482–510.

182 *An estimated forty-one million people in the United States voluntarily quit their jobs in 2018*: The Work Institute, 2019 Retention Report, https://info.workinstitute.com/hubfs/2019%20Retention%20Report/Work%20Institute%202019%20Retention%20Report%20final-1.pdf.

182 *during the COVID-19 epidemic, women quit in record numbers*: P. Gogoi, "Stuck-At-Home Moms: The Pandemic's Devastating Toll on Women," NPR, October 28, 2020, https://www.npr.org/2020/10/28/928253674/stuck-at-home-moms-the-pandemics-devastating-toll-on-women; McKinsey & Company, "Achieving an inclusive US economic recovery," February 3, 2021, https://www.mckinsey.com/industries/public-and-social-sector/our-insights/achieving-an-inclusive-us-economic-recovery; S. Albanesi and J. Kim, "The gendered impact of the COVID-19 recession on the US labor market," NBER Working paper 28505, February 2021.

182 *each departure costs about a third of that worker's annual earnings*: T. Avogino, "To have and to hold," Society for Human Resource Management Report, February 23, 2019, https://www.shrm.org/hr-today/news/all-things-work/pages/to-have-and-to-hold.aspx.

183 *two-thirds of both men and women explore whether the organization has positive role models who are like them*: PricewaterhouseCoopers, "Winning the fight for female talent," 2017, Available at https://www.pwc.com/gx/en/about/diversity/iwd/iwd-female-talent-report-web.pdf.

183 *Companies have increased their focus on recruiting female talent*: Ibid.

Chapter 10: How to Seed Change in Your Organization

187 *eureka-like solutions lead to faster and more sustainable change:* D. Cooper and J. Kagel, "A failure to communicate: An experimental investigation of the effects of advice on strategic play," *European Economic Review* 82, no. C (2016): 24–45.

187 *Many of the strategies we share with you are grounded in* issue selling: J. E. Dutton, S. J. Ashford, R. M. O'Neill, and K. A. Lawrence, "Moves that matter: Issue selling and organizational change," *Academy of Management Journal* 44, no. 4 (2001): 716–36. S. Lu, K. M. Bartol, V. Venkataramani, and X. Zheng, "Pitching novel ideas to the boss: The interactive effects of employees' idea enactment and influence tactics on creativity assessment and implementation," *Academy of Management Journal* 62, no. 2 (2019): 579–606.

190 *change agents find more success when they describe new ideas conservatively:* J. E. Dutton, S. J. Ashford, and K. A. Lawrence, "Moves that matter: Issue selling and organizational change," *Academy of Management Journal* 44, no. 4 (2001): 716–36.

191 *This will help managers and employees identify NPTs and question how they are distributed:* M. Moon, "Bottom-up instigated organizational change through constructionist conversation," *Journal of Knowledge Management Practices* 9, no. 4 (2008): 1–14.

192 *You can reference this book or other works we've published:* L. Babcock, M. Recalde, and L. Vesterlund, "Why women volunteer for tasks that don't lead to promotions," *Harvard Business Review*, July 16, 2018, https://hbr .org/2018/07/why-women-volunteer-for-tasks-that-dont-lead-to-promo tions; C. Fleisher, "Women's work? Why female employees take on thankless tasks shunned by men . . . and how that hurts women's careers," Research Highlights, American Economic Association, March 15, 2017, https://www.aeaweb.org/research/women-men-promotable-task-differ ences.

194 *Research shows that men with daughters:* E. L. Washington, "Female socialization: How daughters affect their legislator fathers' voting on women's issues," *American Economic Review* 98, no. 1 (2008): 311–32; R. L. Warner and B. S. Steel, "Child rearing as a mechanism for social change: The relationship of child gender to parents' commitment to gender equity," *Gender & Society* 13, no. 4 (1999): 503–17; E. F. Shafer and N. Malhotra, "The effect of a child's sex on support for traditional gender roles," *Social Forces* 90, no. 1 (2011): 209–22; A. Wessel, "Does having a daughter make fathers more liberal?," Unpublished manuscript, 2020; P. A. Gompers and S. Q. Wang, "And the children shall lead: Gender diversity and performance in venture capital," National Bureau of Economic Research, Working paper, May 2017.

195 *BIPOC affinity groups are also important allies:* V. Gewin, "The time tax put on scientists of color," *Nature* 583, July 16, 2020, https://www.nature.com /articles/d41586-020-01920-6; L. E. Hirshfeld and T. D. Joseph, "'We need a woman, we need a black woman': Gender, race, and identity taxation in the academy," *Gender and Education* 24, no. 2 (2012): 213–27.

196 *People are influential when they are closely connected to many people:* R. Cross and L. Prusak, "The people who make organizations go—or stop," *Harvard Business Review*, June 2002.

196 *bring individuals like these on board:* J. Battilana and T. Casciaro, "The network secrets of great change agents," *Harvard Business Review*, July–August 2013.

198 *People tend to put too much weight on avoiding unpleasant tasks:* G. Loewenstein and J. Elster, *Choice Over Time* (New York: Russell Sage Foundation, 1992); D. Laibson, "Golden eggs and hyperbolic discounting," *Quarterly Journal of Economics* 112, no. 2 (1997): 443–77; R. H. Thaler and H. Shefrin, "An economic theory of self-control," *Journal of Political Economy* 89, no. 2 (1981): 392–406.

198 *President Obama became more aware and began calling more on women:* J. Eilperin, "White house women want to be in the room where it happens," *Washington Post*, September 13, 2016, https://www.washingtonpost.com /news/powerpost/wp/2016/09/13/white-house-women-are-now-in-the -room-where-it-happens.

Chapter 11: Managing Non-Promotable Work to Advance Women and Organizations

206 *effective change processes include a basic set of four phases:* Hundreds of books and thousands of articles describe how to implement and manage change processes effectively, and they persuasively demonstrate that *how* change is implemented can be just as important as *what* change is implemented, see C. A. O'Reilly, D. F. Caldwell, J. A. Chatman, M. Lapiz, and W. Self, "How leadership matters: The effects of leaders' alignment on strategy implementation," *The Leadership Quarterly* 21, no. 1 (2010): 104–13. We can't, in just a few pages, do justice to what is known about change management, so we will briefly articulate some of the most important points as they apply to NPTs. Our discussion of phases one, three, and four draws heavily on the research from J. Stouten, D. Rousseau, and D. De Cremer, "Successful organizational change: Integrating the management practice and scholarly literatures," *Academy of Management Annals* 12 (2018): 752–88.

206 *"What does not get measured cannot be fixed":* Commonly attributed to management consultant Peter Drucker. See also I. Bohnet, *What Works: Gender Equality by Design* (Cambridge, MA: Harvard University Press, 2016).

207 *you may want to distribute articles*: Perhaps share L. Babcock, M. Recalde, and L. Vesterlund, "Why women volunteer for tasks that don't lead to promotions," *Harvard Business Review*, July 16, 2018, https://hbr.org/2018/07/why-women-volunteer-for-tasks-that-dont-lead-to-promotions, or R. Tulshyan, "The 'I Just Can't Say No' Club Women Need To Advance In Their Careers," *Forbes*, June 28, 2016, https://www.forbes.com/sites/ruchikatulshyan/2016/06/28/the-i-just-cant-say-no-club-women-need-to-advance-in-their-careers/?sh=bb35dff49173.

216 *their leadership developed a point system*: M. Bazerman, I. Bohnet, H. R. Bowles, and G. F. Loewenstein, "Linda Babcock: Go-getter and do-gooder," *Negotiation and Conflict Management Research* 11, no. 2 (2018): 130–45, quote is on page 141.

219 *taking women and people of color off other NPT assignments*: T. Williamson, C. R. Goodwin, and P. A. Ubel, "Minority tax reform—Avoiding overtaxing minorities when we need them the most," *The New England Journal of Medicine* 384, no. 20 (2021): 1877–79.

221 *Redesigning the coordinator's job*: For examples on how individuals can craft their jobs see J. E. Dutton and A. Wrzesniewski, "What job crafting looks like," *Harvard Business Review*, March 12, 2020, https://hbr.org/2020/03/what-job-crafting-looks-like.

222 *the* business case *and the* fairness case: O. Georgeac, "The business case backfires: Detrimental effects of organizations' instrumental diversity rhetoric for underrepresented group members' sense of belonging and performance," Doctoral dissertation, London Business School, 2020.

224 *they can right a past wrong*: D. Chugh, *The Person You Mean to Be: How Good People Fight Bias* (New York: Harper Business, 2018).

225 *The goals you set need to be SMART*: G. T. Doran, "There's a S.M.A.R.T. way to write management's goals and objectives," *Management Review* 70, no. 11 (1981): 35–36.

226 *which could take the form of* performance scorecards: R. S. Kaplan and D. P. Norton, "The balanced scorecard: Measures that drive performance," *Harvard Business Review* (January–February 1992).

226 *Research in behavioral science shows that text reminders*: K. L. Milkman, M. S. Patel, L. Gandhi, H. Graci, et al., "A mega-study of text-based nudges encouraging patients to get vaccinated at an upcoming doctor's appointment," *Proceedings of the National Academy of Sciences* 188, no. 20 (2021); T. Rogers and A. Feller, "Reducing student absences at scale by targeting parents' misbeliefs," *Nature Human Behaviour* 2 (2018): 335–42; S. E. Kimmel, A. B. Troxel, B. French, G. Loewenstein, et al., "A randomized trial of lottery-based incentives and reminders to improve warfarin adherence: The warfarin incentives (WIN2) trial," *Pharmacoepidemiol Drug Safety* 25, no. 11 (2016): 1219–27.

Acknowledgments

We are grateful to so many people for their help and support while writing this book.

MJ Tocci—our fifth No Club member—was our muse, and her legacy of helping women inspired us to write this book. We miss her. Profoundly.

Margo Beth Fleming, you understood our vision from the start and worked tirelessly to make this book all it could be. Your insight and humor, enthusiasm and encouragement made our job so much more fun.

Stephanie Frerich, our wonderful editor, took our manuscript and shaped it into the book that we hoped for. Your passion for changing the professional landscape for women kept us focused on writing a book that is both very personal and backed by research, while making clear that the challenges of non-promotable work need to be addressed by organizations. Our thanks, too, to the entire team at Simon & Schuster, who provided great ideas, strong support, and so much talent to this undertaking.

To the women who shared their stories with us, thank you for trusting us and allowing us to share your experiences. Your stories were critical in showing how pervasive and pernicious a problem non-promotable work is.

A huge debt of thanks to our universities, who provided support for our research and writing, and who listened and understood that changing the distribution of non-promotable work helps women and organizations reach their potential. Thank you for your willingness to change current practices to help equalize the opportunities offered to employees.

We are grateful to the National Science Foundation (SES-1330470), who provided resources instrumental in conducting our research.

Many thanks to our research partners, especially Maria Recalde and Amanda Weirup, who helped us lay the groundwork for the research in this book.

Our research assistants Felipe Augusto de Araujo, David Klinowski, Rachel Landsman, Ben Schenck, and Pun Winichakul seamlessly managed the research logistics for this project. We also thank David Danz, who always came to the rescue when we faced technical challenges in conducting our experiments.

We would not have understood the problem of NPTs without the organizations that worked with us—giving us access to data, trusting us with their problems, and working tirelessly to break down the barriers to women's advancement. You are trailblazers.

We are so appreciative of the more than one hundred institutions, organizations, and corporations that invited us to present our findings and provided us with insights on how the challenges of non-promotable work impacted them.

We gratefully acknowledge the scholars whose research laid the foundation for our own. We are lucky to have colleagues who inspired us and put up with our obsession about NPTs and just as lucky for the dear—and patient—friends who, for the past decade, encouraged our work and listened with interest and offered feedback as we continuously updated them on new studies and findings. We thank the Union Grill for providing our club with the perfect environment for connection and exploration.

Finally, we offer very personal and sincere thanks to those who offered the most critical support—our families.

Linda thanks her husband Mark for his encouragement and love and her daughter Ali for understanding when she broke her promise never to write another book.

Brenda is grateful to her family who cheered her on through this process: her husband, Bill, who makes her laugh every day and makes everything worthwhile; their children and their spouses: James, Rachelle, Beth, Joey, Joe, and Julie, who are truly the best kids ever; and their grandchildren: Brooke, Blake, Cole, Maddie, and Luna, who provide so much joy and energy and fun.

Lise thanks her magnificent husband, Daniel. His love, encouragement, and devotion to family were critical in making room for this book. She also thanks her beloved children, Laura and Jacob, who daily remind her of the wonders, love, and joy of life.

Laurie thanks her husband, Greg, for his love and support; her children, Rachel and Brett, for making the world a better place; and her mother, Bobbie, for encouraging her to be her own person and pursue her dreams.

Index

About the Authors

LINDA BABCOCK is the James M. Walton Professor of Economics at Carnegie Mellon University. She is the author of *Ask for It: How Women Can Use the Power of Negotiation to Get What They Really Want* and *Women Don't Ask: Negotiation and the Gender Divide*. A behavioral economist by training, Babcock focuses on understanding barriers to women's advancement in the workplace and developing evidence-based interventions to promote a level playing field. She is the founder and director of the Program for Research and Outreach on Gender Equity in Society (PROGRESS), which pursues positive social change for women and girls through education, partnerships, and research. Babcock's media appearances and mentions include *Good Morning America*, *ABC World News Tonight*, the *New York Times*, the *Washington Post*, the *Wall Street Journal*, *Glamour*, *Cosmopolitan*, *USA Today*, and more. She lives in Pittsburgh, Pennsylvania.

BRENDA PEYSER has held leadership positions in the corporate world and academia for over thirty years. Most recently, she was a Distinguished Service Professor of Professional Communications at Carnegie Mellon, where she also served as associate dean of the School of Public Policy and Management and was the founding executive director of Carnegie Mellon University Australia. Peyser has taught in the Carnegie Mellon Leadership and Negotiation Academy for Women and consulted with organizations to improve women's communication skills. Before coming to Carnegie Mellon, she worked for a major consulting firm and was a professional actress. She lives in Pittsburgh, Pennsylvania.

LISE VESTERLUND is the Andrew W. Mellon Professor of Economics at the University of Pittsburgh and directs the Pittsburgh Experimental Economics Laboratory (PEEL) and the Behavioral Economic Design Initiative (BEDI). She is a research associate with the National Bureau of Economic Research. Her highly influential work shows how gender differences in competition, confidence, and expectations contribute to the persistent gender gap in advancement. Published in the leading economics journals, her work has garnered interest from media, including the *New York Times*, NPR, the *Washington Post*, ABC, *The Economist*, *The Atlantic*, the *Guardian*, *Chicago Tribune*, and *Forbes*. Born and raised in Denmark, she now lives in Pittsburgh, Pennsylvania.

LAURIE R. WEINGART is the Richard M. and Margaret S. Cyert Professor of Organizational Behavior and Theory at Carnegie Mellon University and director of the Collaboration and Conflict Research Lab in the Tepper School of Business. She has served as CMU's interim provost and chief academic officer, as well as senior associate dean-education and director of the Accelerate Leadership Center in the business school. Weingart specializes in collaboration, conflict, and negotiation, with a focus on how differences across people both help and hinder effective problem solving and innovation. Her award-winning research has been covered by the *New York Times* and *Business Insider,* and published in top management and psychology journals. She lives in Pittsburgh, Pennsylvania.